SOCIAL STATISTICS WITHOUT TEARS

McGRAW-HILL BOOK COMPANY

New York St. Louis San Francisco Auckland Düsseldorf
Johannesburg Kuala Lumpur London Mexico Montreal New Delhi
Panama Paris São Paulo Singapore Sydney Tokyo Toronto

SOCIAL STATISTICS
WITHOUT TEARS

Allan G. Johnson, Ph.D.

Department of Sociology
Wesleyan University
Middletown, Connecticut

This book was set in Memphis Light by Progressive Typographers.
The editors were Lyle Linder and Michael Gardner;
the designer was Jo Jones;
the production supervisor was Dennis J. Conroy.
The drawings were done by ANCO Technical Services.
The cover illustration was done by Thomas Lulevitch.
R. R. Donnelley & Sons Company was printer and binder.

SOCIAL STATISTICS WITHOUT TEARS

1234567890   DODO   7832109876

Library of Congress Cataloging in Publication Data

Johnson, Allan G
    Social statistics without tears.

    Bibliography: p.
    Includes index.
    1. Social sciences — Statistical methods.
2. Statistics. I. Title.
HA29.J53   300'.1'82   76-8901
ISBN 0-07-032601-0

To Paul, Emily, and Carl

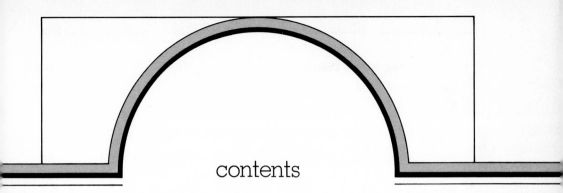

contents

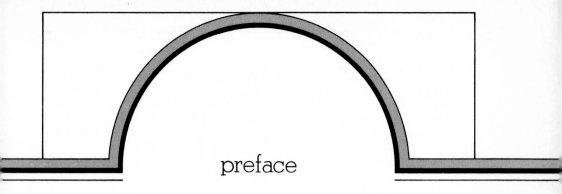

preface

My purpose in writing this book is to help you understand statistical language, techniques, and principles well enough to critically evaluate and learn from the literature that uses them. I'm not trying to make researchers of you; there are already many books designed for that. I am writing for those who may not consider themselves mathematically sophisticated (who may, in fact, hate math), who aren't necessarily preprofessionals but want to understand, who, as they skip over all the figures and tables, have an uneasy feeling that they really don't have any way of making up their own minds about the author's points and arguments.

To learn statistics, you'll need a willingness to think hard about what you read, to go back and try again if you don't feel right after the first go-around. However, I see my job as a teacher as translating information into terms that have meaning for you. If you don't understand, it's not necessarily because you aren't trying hard enough. The burden of proof is often unfairly placed on learners alone; I place it on myself as well.

In a classroom I can try different approaches if one doesn't work for you; in a book it's more difficult. In cases where I've experienced difficulty in students' understanding, I've deliberately explained concepts in more than one way.

Don't get the idea that this book makes statistics easy, and don't anticipate being an expert by the end of this book. I'm trying to cut away much of the formal mathematics that doesn't appreciably aid understanding but does inhibit many people. I've tried to humanize statistics, to make it less intimidating and more useful.

Be patient with yourself as you learn new words and new concepts. Acquire them at your own pace and try to learn them so that you can explain them in your own words to someone who doesn't already understand. Being able to give back an answer on an exam often represents only superficial learning. The deeper understanding comes when you can teach someone else.

I'm grateful to a number of people who've helped greatly in the preparation of this book. David Rynick, Stephen Garry, and Paula Eschenheimer, three good friends who read many portions of early drafts and gave valuable criticisms; anonymous reviewers from McGraw-Hill, Addison-Wesley, and Prentice-Hall whose thorough, thoughtful comments were most helpful; the people who taught statistics to me and greatly influenced my entry into the social sciences, James Davis, David Goldberg, and especially Edmund Meyers, who spent many long hours making detailed suggestions and giving me much encouragement; Phyllis Davis and Dorothy Sanstrom, who struggled through the typing of the many drafts patiently and expertly; and my students, whose desire to learn provided the reason for this work. Finally, I am grateful to the Literary Executor of the late Sir Ronald A. Fisher, F.R.S., to Dr. Frank Yates, F.R.S., and to Longman Group Ltd., London, for permission to reprint tables from their book *Statistical Tables for Biological, Agricultural and Medical Research*, 6th ed., 1974.

Allan G. Johnson

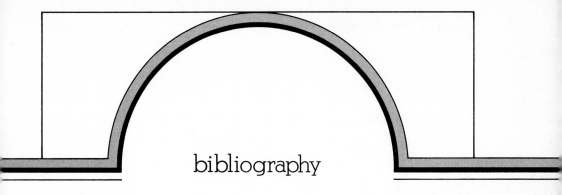

bibliography

There are a number of books you might want to refer to in the course of using this book, or to extend and deepen your understanding when you've finished. Although most will be cited within chapters of this book, I list some of them here.

General Statistics Texts

1 Blalock, Hubert M., Jr.: *Social Statistics*, 2d ed. New York: McGraw-Hill Book Company, 1972. This book is mathematically more sophisticated, covers a greater range of statistical problems and techniques, and is more appropriate for a first course in the training of researchers. You do not need calculus to understand it, although a good understanding of elementary algebra is assumed.
2 Hays, William L.: *Statistics for the Social Sciences*, 2d ed. New York: Holt, Rinehart and Winston, 1973. Among books written for social scientists, this is one of the most sophisticated general texts. It is heavy with mathematical derivations, but is comprehensive and well written. For those seeking to deepen their understanding of social science applications significantly, it's a must.
3 Loether, Herman J., and Donald G. McTavish: *Descriptive Statistics for Sociologists* and *Inferential Statistics for Sociologists*. Boston: Allyn and Bacon, 1974. A two-volume work, this is somewhat more sophisticated both mathematically and in terms of comprehensiveness. Anyone who wants to pursue statistics should consider this as a logical next step. The sections on graphic descriptions of data are particularly strong. They also make good use of substantive examples which form an effective link between statistical techniques and practical applications.
4 Two other statistics texts whose difficulty is in the middle range: Mueller, John H., Karl F. Schuessler, and Herbert L. Costner: *Statistical Reasoning in Sociology*, 2d ed. Boston: Houghton Mifflin Company, 1970; and Runyon, Richard P., and Audrey Haber: *Fundamentals of Behavioral Statistics*, 2d ed. Reading, Mass.: Addison-Wesley Publishing Company, 1971.

5 Zeisel, Hans: *Say It with Figures*, 5th ed. New York: Harper & Row, 1968. Especially strong in the problems associated with presenting and making sense of simple tables.
6 Tukey, John: *Exploratory Data Analysis*. Reading, Mass.: Addison-Wesley (forthcoming).

The Sociological Method

1 Cole, Stephen: *The Sociological Method*, 2d ed. Chicago: Markham Publishing Company, 1976. A particularly lucid and down-to-earth discussion of the empirical and theoretical tasks of sociology.
2 Hyman, Herbert H.: *Interviewing in Social Research*. Chicago: University of Chicago Press, 1975.

The Analysis of Relationships

1 Davis, James A.: *Elementary Survey Analysis*. Englewood Cliffs, N.J.: Prentice-Hall, 1971. This book may be difficult to understand at times, but it contains many valuable insights by one of the foremost practitioners of the art of data analysis.
2 Rosenberg, Morris: *The Logic of Survey Analysis*. New York: Basic Books, 1968. A classic description of the basic techniques used in analyzing relationships among more than two variables. It assumes the reader can make sense of simple cross tabulations and percentage distributions. No greater mathematical sophistication is assumed or required.

General Critical Works on the Use of Statistics

1 Huff, Darrell: *How to Lie with Statistics*. New York: W. W. Norton, 1954. The title says it all.
2 Reichmann, W. J.: *Use and Abuse of Statistics*. Baltimore: Penguin Books, 1961.
3 Lieberman, Bernhardt: *Contemporary Problems in Statistics*. New York: Oxford University Press, 1971. A collection of articles on special problems in the use of statistics, with an emphasis on measurement and inferential statistics. The articles on hypothesis tests are particularly worthwhile.

Readers Chock Full of Examples

1 Mosteller, Frederick, William H. Kruskal, Richard F. Link, Richard S. Pieters, and Gerald R. Rising: *Statistics by Example*, 4 vols. Reading, Mass.: Addison-Wesley, 1973. These four volumes, entitled "Exploring Data," "Weighing Chances," "Detecting Patterns," and "Finding Models," are full of examples of the applications of statistical techniques in many fields. They're great for browsing and need not be read from cover to cover.
2 By the same authors is *Statistics: A Guide to the Unknown*. San Francisco: Holden-Day, 1972. This is another set of applications of statistics in many fields. A most useful feature of this book is its three tables of contents, one general, one classified by the sources of data used in the example, and a third classified by the kinds of techniques used. A fascinating smorgasbord.
3 An excellent reader that treats a variety of methodological and statistical problems is Lazarsfeld, Paul F., and Morris Rosenberg (eds.): *The Language of Social Research*. New York: The Free Press, 1955.

SOCIAL STATISTICS WITHOUT TEARS

ONE

In Part One, we're going to describe the ways in which social scientists organize, summarize, analyze, and present data. We begin with the problem of measurement; what data do we gather? If we want to determine the length of an object, we can use a ruler; but if we want to measure an attitude, such as prejudice against women, the "rulers" are harder to find.

Once we've gathered information from a sample of individuals, we need to organize and summarize it intelligibly and efficiently. To do this, we may use such statistical tools as percentages, means, standard deviations, and graphs.

Finally, we'll turn our attention to the most

DESCRIPTION AND EXPLANATION

important area of social science, the differences between groups and the causes of such differences. Are upper-class people less prejudiced than lower-class people? Are men as smart as women? Why do women live longer than men? Why are lower-class high school graduates less likely to go on to college than upper-class graduates? Is it because they aren't as smart? Is it because they have less desire? Or is it because they're poor?

These are the kinds of questions that form the core of sociological research, and in the last three chapters of Part One, we'll see how statistics can help us describe and explain differences between groups.

1

introduction

If you're at all like me, you're interested in what's going on around you and find yourself increasingly reading articles and books that use statistics. Statistics deals with two problems. First, when researchers systematically gather information on a group of people or things, they face the problem of organizing all those individual observations in an intelligible way. They want to find the story the data tell, and they're concerned that the story tells something about the way things are. None of us want to be misled; we want the information to actually mean what we think it means. In short, we want facts gathered, organized, summarized, presented, and analyzed in ways that allow us to make intelligent decisions and learn about ourselves and the world we live in.

Second, because the groups of people or things of interest are often very large (sometimes infinite), researchers take samples. The second problem of statistics is to make decisions about the nature of a whole, using information on only a part. It's a process we all experience every day: we decide on going to one college or another even though we have only a limited sample of information on what various colleges offer. We face moving to a new job and a new home without knowing everything that might influence such a decision. We have attitudes on countless issues that affect us even though we know we have only limited information. To live, however, we have to make decisions, whether our information is "complete" or not: if we always waited to act until we thought we knew everything, we'd never do anything. The problem is to choose samples in such a way that we can be confident they accurately reflect the group we drew them from. Since we know there's always some chance of error, the task becomes that of accurately estimating the chance that our sample is representative of the larger group. In a world in which nothing is really certain, knowing the odds is a good position to be in. With statistics, we try to use samples to learn about the whole with precise estimates of the odds that the sample information is accurate. The task is the same one we all face daily; the differences are accuracy and a known chance of error.

In reading this book, keep in mind that learning statistics is partly a matter of learning a new language. You'll run into new terms, and it's important that you make them part of your active vocabulary. For example, one of the most common words is *data*. To some it sounds very scientific, and this may give it an undeserved air of mystery. *Data* is the plural of *datum*. A datum is simply a bit of information (for example, Joan is 29 years old, the field is 100 yards long, or Pete and Beth were divorced last year); data are bits of information (for example, the freshman class has 400 Protestants, 200 Catholics, and 125 Jews). Calling them "data" rather than "information" or "facts" doesn't make them any different, but "data" is the word used most often in the literature you're likely to find statistics in, so it's worth your while to get comfortable with it.

A *population* is a precisely defined group of anything (e.g., all American women who are currently married and living in the continental United States, or all 100-watt light bulbs produced by General Electric during October 1976). A *sample* is a group selected from a population. When we gather data on all members of a population, we have a *census*. How do we tell whether a group constitutes a population or a sample? If a group represents no group larger than itself, then it's a population. If, however, it does represent a larger group, then it's a sample and the larger group it represents is a population.

You'll also run into the terms *descriptive statistics* and *inferential statistics*. When we gather data on any group, whether it's a census or sample, and use them to describe how the group looks on a particular characteristic, then we're using descriptive statistics (e.g., half of all American families had incomes of $12,000 or more in 1973).[1] On the other hand, when we use the information contained in a sample to make statements about the entire population from which the sample was drawn, then we're using inferential (sometimes called *inductive*) statistics.

For example, let's say we're interested in how American registered voters feel about abortion-law reform. The population in this case con-

---

[1] U.S. Bureau of the Census, *Current Population Reports: Money Income in 1973 of Families and Persons in the United States*, ser. P-60, no. 93, July 1974.

sists of all American registered voters. If we went out and asked all of them for their opinions on the abortion question, we'd be taking a census. Every 10 years the U.S. Bureau of the Census does just this, although they usually don't gather data on opinions. If, on the other hand, we couldn't afford the astronomical cost of asking everyone, we could take a sample of American registered voters. Once we have data on the sample of people, we can do two things with them: we can confine ourselves to describing how the people in the sample feel (descriptive statistics), or we can use the sample information to estimate how the entire population feels about abortion (inferential — or inductive — statistics).

In 1971 I helped conduct a survey of married Mexican women living in Mexico City.[1] We were interested in a number of subjects, but my main interest was in attitudes toward women's roles. We were trying to measure how women felt about alternatives to marriage and child-bearing. One of the questions was: "Would you approve of a woman who decided she didn't want to get married and have children, because she wanted to do other things with her life?"

We drew a sample of 798 Mexican households, and our interviewers (all young Mexican women) went to the selected households and asked this question along with many others. The answers were recorded on a printed interview schedule.[2] Each type of response (*yes* and *no*) was assigned a number (1 and 0, called *codes*); the numbers were recorded on large sheets of paper ("code sheets") and then punched in Hollerith (IBM) cards. We have a Hollerith card for each woman, and on her card, in the column that corresponds to the question, there is a punch of 1 or 0, telling us what her response was. These cards can be "read" by a machine and the responses can thereby be quickly and accurately counted and sorted.

Now, to a consumer of this information, several questions occur here:

1 What does it *mean* when a woman says yes or no to the question the interviewer asks? How do you know her answer means what you think it means?

2 How do you physically handle 798 bits of information to somehow describe "how the women in the sample feel"?

3 To what degree do the answers given by 798 women represent those of all married women in a city of 7 million people?

4 Given the information you have about a *sample* of married Mexican women in Mexico City, what kinds of things can you say about the

---

[1] This was the Mexico City fertility study, directed by David Goldberg, a sociologist at the University of Michigan. See Allan G. Johnson, "Modernization and Social Change: Attitudes toward Women's Roles in Mexico City," unpublished Ph.D. dissertation, University of Michigan, Ann Arbor, Mich., 1972.

[2] A "schedule" refers to information gathered by an interviewer; a "questionnaire" is filled out by the respondent.

attitude of *all* married Mexican women in Mexico City? How precise can you be? What are the odds that you're right?

5 How do we explain the fact that some women approve and some women don't?

These are the kinds of questions that arise with all kinds of social research, whether the data are gathered by interviewers asking questions or by experimenters watching subjects. Whether you're looking at trends in local school enrollment, attitudes toward controversial issues, college-board scores, or the behavior of people in experimental situations, it's important that you know what kinds of critical questions to ask. For example: "How was the sample selected and how were the data gathered?" "What kinds of measures were used?" "Was information obtained from all members of the sample?" "Is the sample representative of the population?" "Do the data agree with the author's verbal descriptions and analysis?" "Can we use the sample information to make valid inferences about the population?" "How much error is involved and of what kind is it?" Having asked them, you then need to know enough to evaluate the answers intelligently.

Social life can be viewed as a serious game, and the task of the social scientist (the sociologist in particular) is to understand that game, how it works (a problem in social structure), the context in which it's played (a cultural problem), and its effects on the players, individually and collectively (an area that includes emotional and physical well-being, personality development, group relations, etc.). The game is a system of interaction that includes countless subsystems, each with its own rules and values it seeks to maximize.

The task of the social sciences can be broken down into a series of smaller tasks. The first is *description*. For example, while we're not concerned with the personality of one person in and of itself, we are interested in such questions as: "How does the possession of certain social characteristics (e.g., being a man, being a policeman, having four children, being divorced) affect personality?" "Do men and women tend to have different personality traits?" "How likely are Americans to exhibit pathological personality traits?" The answers to such questions are purely descriptive; they tell us how things *are*.

The second task is *explanation*. For example, men have much higher rates of coronary heart disease than women do. The explanatory question is, simply: "Why?"

If we return to the view of social life as a serious game, sex is a social status that distinguishes among the players. It is also a biological characteristic that makes distinctions that may transcend social life. In these terms, the problem of explaining sex differences boils down to this: (1) to what extent are such differences the result of biological factors, independent of social life? (2) to what extent are they due to the nature of social life and its differential effects on men and women? (3) to what extent does social life determine the individual's characteristics (such as personality) and, thereby, the way in which he[1] participates and his ability to meet individual needs within the structure and context of social life?

In studying this problem, the author[2] began with a *question:* "Does sex make a difference in heart-attack rates?" We then seek data that answer the question. The result (that men, at every age, have higher heart-attack rates) is called a *finding.* Our task is to explain this finding.

The search for such answers initially takes the form of fresh questions. For example, does the experience of chronic stress lead to heart attacks? Most findings suggest that it does. Are men more likely than women to experience chronic stress? At this point in time, we really don't know the answer to this last question.

When we logically put these questions together, we have a small theory:

1 Chronic stress increases the likelihood of a heart attack.

2 Men have higher heart-attack rates than women.

3 Men are more likely than women to experience chronic stress.

4 Therefore, the higher rates of heart attacks observed among men are in part due to differences in the experience of chronic stress.

The ultimate task of the social sciences is to formulate theories and then try to verify them. We verify them by gathering appropriate data (such as the stress experienced by men and women) and seeing how well the theory "fits" the data. If, for example, women experience *more* stress than men, the above theory will *not* be verified as it stands.

All the substantive problems discussed above lie within the province of description and explanation; we want to know how things are and how they work. If we gathered data from the entire male and female population of the United States, our research would never leave the realm of descriptive or explanatory statistics. When we draw samples of populations, however, we must contend with the facts that a sample is inherently less accurate than a census and that there are new sources of error that must be estimated and considered in the interpretation of our findings. With *inferential statistics,* we're trying to accomplish the same descriptive and explanatory tasks addressed above, using *sample data.* The *only* difference between inferential and descriptive statistics lies in the consideration of error inherent in the sampling process.

---

[1] Throughout this book, instead of saying "he or she" I'll use the generic term *he* in most cases. Unless the referent is clearly male, the reader should understand that the author is referring to either male or female.

[2] Allan G. Johnson, "Sex Differentials in Mortality and Morbidity: A Sociological Approach," unpublished manuscript.

This book is organized around the main tasks of the social sciences. Part One deals with descriptive statistics and begins with problems of measurement (how we measure "chronic stress," the quality of manufactured products, educational attainment, intelligence, or racism). This is the first problem encountered in the verification of any proposition. We'll then move to the organization, summarization, and presentation of data (percentages, means, standard deviations, etc.). Third, we'll talk about relationships between characteristics (e.g., the fact that men have higher rates of heart attack than women: there is a relationship between sex and coronary heart disease), with a particular emphasis on the many methods available for describing, clarifying, and explaining such findings.

Part Two of the book is devoted to inferential statistics; how can we address the same questions raised in Part One without taking a census?

If we're successful in the chapters to come, you'll be better prepared to protect yourself from the occasional abuses of statistics. More important, however, will be your increasing ability to consume intelligently the enormous amounts of high-quality data being made available today.

In this short introductory chapter I've tried to give you a feel for what's to come. If this book has a theme, it's that the work of empirical researchers closely parallels what all of us do in our daily lives, but with important differences such as precision, systematic observation, a known chance of error, and perhaps a higher degree of self-consciousness than most of us are used to.

A number of terms have come up already, such as *data* and *datum*, *population* and *sample*, *census*, and *inferential* and *descriptive statistics*. See whether you can explain in your own words what these words mean. Try to avoid pat definitions and concentrate on the full meaning of the ideas these words label. Think of some examples from your own experience.

Appendix A is a glossary of terms and symbols used in this book. I strongly recommend that you refer to it at the end of each chapter and for overall review purposes. You might find it helpful to read through it briefly now to give yourself an overview of the book.

2

measurement

In Chap. 1, we mentioned the sex differential in coronary heart disease and the possibility that chronic stress might explain some of the differences between men and women. Let's begin by looking at that problem from a measurement point of view.

There are three concepts involved in this problem. "Sex" is, at first glance, relatively straightforward. Theoretically, it's defined in terms of genetic characteristics: men have one X and one Y chromosome, women have two X chromosomes. A biologist could examine a sample of cells from a person and determine sex. There are, of course, exceptions: for example, some men have an extra Y chromosome.

We can also measure sex on the basis of secondary characteristics such as genital organs, breasts, body hair, etc., but even here there is room for ambiguity. The possession of male or female secondary characteristics is not a case of "either/or"; rather, it's a continuum. There are women with a great deal of body hair and men with very little. In more extreme cases, there are people with a combination of sex characteristics, "men" with female sex organs, for example.

In the conduct of social research, our first goal is to make distinctions between different kinds of people. We want a set of procedures that allows us to classify people or things on the basis of clear, unambiguous criteria. We start with a concept and try to devise a set of procedures that allows us to classify people with as little error as possible. This set of procedures is known as a *measurement instrument*, and the process of moving from a concept to a measurement instrument is known as *opera-*

tionalization. When sex is operationalized, it's called a *variable*, because it measures a characteristic that is not the same for all persons being observed.

If all members of a population or sample are alike on a variable (i.e., they all have the same score or fall within one category), then we call the characteristic a *constant* instead of a variable. If everyone in a population has the right to cast votes in an election, then suffrage is a constant. If, however, only landowners can vote, then the right to vote is a variable: some have it and some don't.

There are several ways we could operationalize sex. We could classify people according to their genetic composition. Most people would be clearly either male or female. Some, however, would have something other than an XX or XY chromosomal combination and we'd have to figure out what to do with them. We'd either create a third category (such as "in between") or make an assignment based on some other set of criteria. The important point is that any system of classification must unambiguously assign each person or thing to one and only one category of the classification scheme.

We could also simply ask people what sex they consider themselves to be. In our society the pressure is so great to be of one sex or the other[1] that virtually everyone would place himself in one of the two categories, "male" or "female."

Third, we could have an observer note the secondary sex characteristics (at least those that were visible) and make a determination. This is what happens when physicians write death certificates. If there are ambiguities, the physician must decide how to classify the deceased, since death certificates don't allow any response other than "male" or "female."

These three operationalizations represent three different conceptualizations of sex. The first defines sex in terms of genetic characteristics and ignores the fact that in spite of genetic characteristics some people have secondary characteristics of the sex opposite to their genetic configuration, and/or may for social purposes consider themselves to be of the opposite sex. The second operationalization sees sex as a social status, by looking at how people characterize themselves (which is, in turn, very much a product of how others characterize them). The third is a clinical measurement of sex, focusing exclusively on secondary sex characteristics. Thus, a person with male genes who undergoes a sex transformation operation to look like a female, might be classified as a female by an attending physician. Or a person with male genes and subdued male secondary characteristics might feel and act like a

---

[1] See, for example, Harold Garfinkle, "'Passing' as a Woman: A Study of Sex Change," in Arlene S. Skolnick and Jerome H. Skolnick, *Family in Transition* (Boston: Little, Brown, 1971).

woman (and consider himself to be a woman at heart) but be clinically classified as a man.

In deciding which measurement instrument to use, the researcher has to decide which *concept* is of interest. In the case of this author's research, two concepts (and thus two operationalizations) are used: in measuring the chronic stress of men and women, we're interested in sex as a social status. Therefore, the self-classification measurement instrument is closer to our needs. However, we also rely on death certificates filled out by physicians, in which case we're depending on a clinical, not a self-classification of sex. This would create measurement problems if there were not so few people for whom self-reported and clinical classifications would disagree.

This brings us to the first characteristic of measurement instruments. We want an instrument that, if applied to the same person or thing at two different points in time, or by two different observers at one point in time, yields the same result, assuming that the characteristic being measured hasn't changed. A ruler shouldn't expand or contract with changes in temperature to such a degree that the readings differ from one place to another; a car's gas gauge shouldn't move up and down erratically; an intelligence test administered at short intervals should give the same results each time. Without such constancy, we have a hard time telling whether a measured change reflects real change or some erratic process that has nothing to do with the concept being measured. This constancy of measurement instruments is called *reliability*.

It isn't enough to have an instrument that yields the same results each time a measurement is taken on a single person or thing; the results, themselves, must have a known meaning. Do our instruments measure what we think they do? Do they measure one thing for one respondent and something else for another? Or do they measure the same thing for all respondents, but something that we didn't intend and aren't aware of? When a measurement instrument measures what we think it does, it's *valid*. Validity is something we can rarely be sure of. For example, in recent surveys, people have been asked whether they would "mind having a black family move into their neighborhood." Many of those who answered, "Yes, I would mind," hastened to add that their answer did not reflect racial prejudice. What it does measure is their concern over the economic effects of blacks moving into all-white neighborhoods: "When blacks move in, property values go down."

Which meaning you give to the gesture "Yes, I would mind" will probably be influenced by your own politics and race, but it's hard to be sure just what the answer means without making assumptions. There certainly is no scientific way of establishing the absolute validity of this question as a measure of prejudice. We must rely on our own judgment.

A few more examples may give you a deeper feel for the idea of measurement validity. In trying to understand the causes of coronary heart disease, many social researchers have studied occupational differentials in the incidence of the disease. Most studies have found few consistent differences, and this has raised questions about the way in which occupation is measured.[1] Most studies have used broad categories of occupation such as "clerical and sales," "technical and kindred workers," and "professionals." If we suspect that the conditions of work affect health, then such categories may not be telling us what we want to know. "Professionals," for example, includes not only doctors and lawyers, but elementary school teachers, social workers, clergymen, and librarians. With the variable categorized in such gross terms, it's difficult to know just what it means. What we want to know is just where people are in the social structure and what they do. As it has been operationalized in most studies of coronary heart disease, occupation is an invalid measure for our purposes.

All of us at one time or another have been graded in school. There is a considerable body of research indicating that school grades do predict how well a student will perform in future schools (college, graduate school, etc.). There is another body of research, however, that strongly suggests that grades are not related to performance in settings other than school (e.g., being a lawyer as opposed to being a law student).[2] Thus grades can be viewed as *valid* measures of the ability to perform well in school settings, but as *invalid* measures of the ability to do well outside of school.

The idea of validity has other research applications you should be aware of. For example, an entire study may use a perspective that doesn't apply to the study population. If we used classical music to gauge the musical development of ghetto children, we might draw invalid conclusions since their experience of music derives from a cultural background different from that of many scholarly researchers. The same can be said of intelligence tests insofar as they reflect a culture in which the respondents do not live. The applicability of a research design to a study population is called *construct validity*.

A second application centers on the research design, too. For example, if we want to test a program designed to rehabilitate delinquents, we might send a sample through the program and then measure the recidivism rate (the rate at which they fall back into

---

[1] See, for example, Renee U. Marks, "Social Stress and Cardiovascular Disease: Factors Involving Social and Demographic Characteristics. A Review of Empirical Findings," *Milbank Memorial Fund Quarterly*, XLV, 2 (April 1967), part 2.

[2] See Michael A. Wallach, "The Psychology of Talent and Graduate Education," paper presented at the Invitational Conference on Cognitive Styles and Creativity in Higher Education, Montreal, November 1972 (to be published in a volume based on the conference, by Jossey-Bass).

delinquency). This result is not a valid basis for conclusions about the experimental program unless we have a comparison group that did *not* go through the program but resembles the experimental group in all other respects as closely as possible. This comparison group is called a *control group*. If the rates of recidivism are the same for both groups, we can conclude that the program doesn't make a difference. Without such comparisons, the results are *invalid*. This kind of validity is called *internal validity*.

When you read a research report, you have to decide for yourself whether or not the research design and the measurement instruments used are valid. You should be warned that reports do not always include the actual measurement instrument; they may refer instead to the concept they are trying to measure (e.g., "intelligence" instead of "scores on the ABCD Intelligence Test Battery"). You simply have to use your judgment. If, for example, you can think of several interpretations for a question and its answers, then any one interpretation becomes increasingly tenuous.

Let's return to our original problem, the sex differential in coronary heart disease. We've seen that in spite of the apparent simplicity of the variable "sex," any operationalization is based on conceptual assumptions. What of the second concept, "death from coronary heart disease"? The measurement task is not nearly so simple here.

First, when a person dies, it may be from several causes. For example, suppose Jeremy has a heart attack on Tuesday, enters the hospital that same day, seems to be stabilizing, then contracts pneumonia on Friday. Saturday he weakens steadily, and on Monday he finally dies. What was the cause of death? Coronary heart disease? Pneumonia? Some other condition the doctors didn't detect? When a physician fills out a death certificate, he must determine the primary cause of death as well as secondary causes. Since no one really *knows* what the "real" cause was, or whether or not it was primarily one cause, we must depend on the physician's judgment.

Or suppose that an ambulance physician responds to a call from Jeremy's wife, who has just come home and found her husband dead in the living room. How does the physician figure out the cause of death? An autopsy is perhaps the surest method, but it may not be performed and even if performed may not lead to absolute certainty. The physician must rely on certain observable signs as well as his expectations; he knows that, depending on the age, sex, and social status of the victim, some causes of death are statistically more likely than others. In arriving at his decision, he may use such knowledge perhaps unconsciously.

There are both reliability and validity problems in the measurement of cause of death. Some research suggests that most diagnoses, especially in recent times, are quite accurate and agree with the results of autopsies.[1] If doctors are just as likely to make errors with men as with women, and if those errors tend to be of the same type, then errors in diagnosis won't hurt our examination of sex differences in coronary heart disease.

When measurement is inaccurate, we have error. Error usually takes two different forms. The first is *random error;* the second — and by far the more serious — is called *bias.*

The word *random* has a specific and often misunderstood meaning. If I walk down the street and stop the first person I meet, this isn't a random selection of people. If I take all the people in an area, put their names on a list, assign a number to each name, and draw numbers out of a hat that contains all the numbers (well mixed up, of course), then I have a random selection. The difference? *Random* means that each possible alternative has an *equal* chance of happening. Certainly not everyone has an equal chance of walking down my street.

In our heart-attack problem, if attending physicians were equally likely to make one kind of diagnosis error or another, than the errors would be random, *and the errors would tend to cancel each other out in the long run.* For every heart attack that was misdiagnosed as something else, something else would be misdiagnosed as a heart attack.

If, however, doctors had a tendency to make certain kinds of misdiagnoses over and over again, the errors would accumulate and not cancel each other out. If, for example, doctors *expected* older men to die of heart attacks and therefore had a consistent tendency to report heart attacks too often, then the measurement of cause of death would be *biased.* Bias is error that tends to go in one direction.

There are many examples of bias in social science data. People tend to exaggerate their educational attainment and to report ages that end in 9, 0, or 1. There is some evidence that certain groups of people (such as the highly educated) have a slight tendency to give socially acceptable responses to certain attitudinal questions.[2] When measuring a number of attitudes, the matching of the races of respondent and interviewer can make considerable differences in the patterns of response. Whites are less likely to admit racial prejudice in the presence of blacks, even when the attitudes are recorded on anonymous written questionnaires.[3] Blacks are more likely to say that whites can be trusted if the interviewer is white than they are if he's black.[4]

---

[1] See Lewis Kuller, Abraham Lilienfeld, and Russell Fisher, "Quality of Death Certificate Diagnoses of Arteriosclerotic Heart Disease," *Public Health Reports,* vol. 82, no. 4, April 1967; and Iwao M. Moriyama, "Factors in Diagnosis and Classification of Deaths from CVR Diseases," *Public Health Reports,* vol. 75, no. 3, March 1960.

[2] See, for example, Douglas P. Crowne and David Marlowe, *The Approval Motive* (New York: Wiley, 1964).

[3] G. F. Summers and A. D. Hammonds, "Effect of Racial Characteristics of Investigator on Self-enumerated Responses to a Negro Prejudice Scale," *Social Forces,* 44 (1966): 515–518.

[4] Howard Schuman and J. M. Converse, "The Effects of Black and White Interviewers on Black Responses in 1968," *Public Opinion Quarterly,* 35 (1971): 44–68.

Good researchers always try to avoid bias in their measurement procedures. If it's unavoidable, the next best thing is to detect it, determine its direction, and gauge its magnitude.

The most important thing to keep in mind is that any measurement instrument is an operationalization of an underlying concept. The way in which survey questions are worded affects the distribution of responses. Suppose we want to measure the degree to which people hold the attitude that schools with mostly black students should have black principals. This was attempted in a survey of Detroit residents in early 1968.[1] Two questions were asked: first, "Some people say there should be Negro principals in schools with mostly Negro students because Negroes should have the most say in running innercity schools. Would you agree with that or not?" The second question was: "Suppose there is a public school that is attended mostly by Negro children; do you think the principal should be a Negro, a white person, or that his race should not make any difference?" In response to the first version, four out of ten respondents agreed that Negro principals should head mostly Negro schools; in the second version, only one in ten held this position. While both questions deal with the same problem, the first, by its strongly worded format, tends to elicit agreement; the second is easier to disagree with. By themselves, each is a reasonable question that might be used in a survey; it's only when we compare them directly that we see how wording can affect the responses.

Types of Variables

There are several different ways of classifying variables. First, variables may consist of the magnitudes of some characteristics (such as income, height, IQ, or age). Such variables are called *quantitative variables*, and allow us to speak in terms of "high" and "low" or "more" and "less." A second type of variable doesn't indicate the magnitude of a characteristic: these variables only allow us to say that one group is different from another. The variable "sex" consists of two categories, male and female. It makes no sense to speak of "male" and "female" in terms of "higher" and "lower" or "more" and "less." These variables measure *qualitative*, not quantitative differences, and are called *qualitative variables*. Other examples are race, religion, state of residence, and political party preference.

Among quantitative variables, we can make two further distinctions. Some variables can take on only certain values; for example, if we measure the number of children born to a woman during her lifetime,

---

[1] See A. Campbell and H. Schuman, *Racial Attitudes in Fifteen American Cities* (Ann Arbor, Mich.: Institute for Social Research, 1968), and H. Schuman and O. D. Duncan, "Questions about Attitude Survey Questions," in Herbert L. Costner (ed.), *Sociological Methodology 1973–1974* (San Francisco: Jossey-Bass Publishers, 1974), pp. 232–251.

we can get values of 0, 1, 2, 3, etc., but we can't get values of 0.6 or 2.37 children. Variables that can take on a limited number of values are called *discrete variables*. On the other hand, a variable such as age can take on any of an infinite number of values; we can express age in years, months, days, seconds, or milliseconds — the degree of detail possible is infinite. Variables that can take on any value within their range of values are called *continuous variables*.

Variables can thus be either quantitative or qualitative. Quantitative variables are either discrete or continuous.

There is another system for classifying variables that overlaps with the quantitative-qualitative distinction, but spells it out in more detail. Ideally, we'd like to be able to measure a concept on a numerical scale that has a natural zero point (such as age and income). Why? Because this would allow us to make precise comparisons between people. With age, for example, we can say that 45-year-old Joan and 30-year-old Beverly are of different ages; we can say that Joan is older than Beverly; if Susan is 15 years old, we can say that the *difference* between Joan's and Susan's ages is twice as great as the difference between Joan's and Beverly's ages (30 years versus 15 years); finally, and most importantly, we can say that Joan's age is three times as large as Susan's. You can see that with a variable such as age we can make every conceivable kind of comparison, the most powerful of which is the ability to take the ratio of one point on the scale to another. For this reason, the most powerful type of variable is called a *ratio-scale variable*.

With ratio-scale variables we can make four kinds of comparisons. We can talk in terms of *similarity* (Joan and Beverly are of different ages), *order* (Joan's age is higher than Susan's), the *magnitude of differences* (Joan and Susan are twice as far apart as Joan and Beverly are), and the *relative magnitudes of the scores* themselves (Beverly is twice as old as Susan). Note that each successive comparison in the above list allows us to make increasingly precise statements.

Suppose we had a variable that allowed us to talk in terms of similarity, order, and the magnitude of differences, but not in terms of the relative magnitudes of the scores themselves. The Fahrenheit temperature scale is such a variable. We can say that 40° and 60° are different temperatures; we can say that 60° is hotter than 40°; and we can say that the temperature difference between 40° and 60° is twice the difference between 80° and 90° (20° versus 10°). We *cannot* say that 80° is twice as hot as 40°, however, because 0° on the Fahrenheit scale does not represent zero heat or, more scientifically, absolute zero. If we used the Kelvin scale, whose zero point is absolute zero, we could say that 60° is twice as hot as 30°.

Thus, with such variables, the most powerful comparison we can make is that between the magnitudes of intervals between points on the scale. For this reason, these variables are called *interval-scale variables*. The only difference between a ratio-scale variable (such as degrees Kelvin) and an interval-scale variable (such as degrees Fahrenheit) is that an interval-scale variable does not have a natural zero point which indicates the complete absence of the characteristic being measured. You will rarely encounter interval-scale variables in the social science literature.

Now suppose we have a variable that allows us to talk in terms of similarity and order, but not in terms of the magnitude of either intervals or actual scores. Social class, degree of racial prejudice, agreement with a statement of attitudes: these are characteristics that can be ranked from high to low. We can say that upper-class George is different from lower-class Peter, and we can say that George's social class is higher than Peter's. We *cannot* say, however, that George's social class is "twice as great" as Peter's, nor can we compare the magnitude of the difference between upper and middle classes on the one hand and middle and lower classes on the other. When the most precise comparative statement we can make consists of ordering points on a scale from high to low, we have an *ordinal-scale variable*.

Finally, we may have a qualitative variable that allows us to go no further than noting differences. Sex, race, religion, and left- and right-handedness are all qualitative variables and are often called *nominal-scale* or *categorical variables*. They allow us to categorize on the basis of similarity, but our comparisons can go no further.

The properties of the four levels of measurement are summarized in Table 2-1.

Why do we make these distinctions between variable types? The distinctions are important because they dictate the kinds of statistical tools that can be applied to the data. The "higher" the level of measurement (i.e., the closer it is to a ratio scale), the more sophisticated are the statistical tools we can apply. Greater sophistication allows us to use greater precision in drawing answers from our data.

It's not too early to stress that statistical tools must be matched to levels of measurement. For example, if we have ordinal variables, it is

Table 2-1

Comparisons that can be made	LEVEL OF MEASUREMENT			
	Nominal	**Ordinal**	**Interval**	**Ratio**
Similarity or difference	Yes	Yes	Yes	Yes
Order	No	Yes	Yes	Yes
Magnitudes of differences	No	No	Yes	Yes
Magnitudes of scores	No	No	No	Yes

absolutely wrong to use statistical techniques designed for interval- or ratio-scale variables.[1] You'll occasionally encounter such abuses, and you should be alert. This will become clearer to you after you've read Chap. 6.

Summary

Regardless of what is being measured, social researchers must contend with the problem of what their observations mean. So must we as individuals. The moods we're in, the meaning we attach to what we see and hear, our prejudices and predispositions, our unpredictability, and our ability to empathize all combine to constantly challenge the interpretations we put on our experience. There's no substitute for critical thinking, common sense, and intelligent questioning.

When you read a report using data, remember these questions:

1 Exactly what measurement instrument was used (verbal questions, observing behavior, etc.), and what concept is it intended to operationalize? If the author doesn't give you the exact measure, then you should be careful about accepting his findings too readily. If the author did give the exact instrument, how many ways can you see to interpret it? Is the question ambiguous? Is it biased? Can the behavior being observed be readily interpreted in more than one way?

2 When was the information gathered? Especially with public-opinion polls, the timing of a question is very important, since events can change opinion quickly and decisively.

3 Who was taking the measurements? How might this affect the respondent? Were young people interviewing old people? men interviewing women? blacks interviewing whites? Such factors in the research design can make substantial differences in interpreting results.

4 What was the situation in which the measurement was taken? How might this affect the respondent's behavior? Think of other settings and how the respondent might behave in them.

If you do much reading, you're going to find frustration in two forms. First, the author may omit all kinds of information, especially that referred to in questions 1, 3, and 4. Second, when you sit down and try to think of alternative explanations of questions and observations, you may be dismayed to find that there are many in some cases.

I know of no satisfactory solution to the first frustration except to write to the author and request details. If you really care about the meaning of the results, this is one sure way to clear up at least some of the am-

---

[1] See Frank M. Andrews et al., *A Guide for Selecting Statistical Techniques for Analyzing Social Science Data* (Ann Arbor, Mich.: Institute for Social Research, 1974).

biguities. Barring this, you're left with the not altogether happy alternative of assuming that everything is fine and that the omitted information would not change the importance or the meaning of the results. Unfortunately, sometimes we're tempted to assume everything is fine if the results agree with our vision of the world but to insist on additional information if we don't agree with the results.

The second frustration has no easy solutions, either. Ambiguity is a matter of degree, and you must rely on your own good judgment to determine how valid the measure is. The greater the ambiguity, the more we must raise questions of validity. Beyond this, there is no greater precision available to consumers. Keep in mind that this is the same problem we encounter in our simplest human interactions, and beware of ignoring ambiguity when one of the possible explanations leads to an interpretation you agree with.

This chapter has not dealt with precise numbers and equations. Although what follows will contrast with this, let me repeat that social research is less precise than the numbers and tables often suggest. There is much judgment involved, and it's important that you never suspend your critical attention and questioning mind.

In this chapter I've tried to introduce you to (1) the process by which researchers (and the rest of us) make the transition from abstract things we'd like to know about to concrete ways of measuring them, (2) the main types of variables, (3) the general problem of discovering the meaning of what we hear and see, (4) some of the main sources of inaccuracy in gathering data, and (5) some of the kinds of questions you should be asking yourself when confronted with the measures used in research reports.

I've introduced several new terms and you should make sure you understand them. I've talked about *variables* and *constants*, *measurement instruments* and *operationalization*, *validity*, *random error*, *bias*, and schemes for classifying different types of variables. As I've suggested before, the best way to make sure you understand what these words *mean* is to explain them in your own words to someone else. (As part of your review, you might want to refer to the glossary, Appendix A.)

Problems

2-1 Define and give an example of each of the following:
  a. Measurement instrument
  b. Operationalization
  c. Variable
  d. Constant
  e. Reliability
  f. Measurement validity

    g. Construct validity
    h. Internal validity
    i. Random error
    j. Bias
    k. Quantitative variables
    l. Qualitative variables
    m. Discrete variables
    n. Continuous variables
    o. Ratio-scale variables
    p. Interval-scale variables
    q. Ordinal-scale variables
    r. Nominal-scale (or categorical) variables

2-2 Suppose we wanted to measure the degree to which someone can be considered to be "educated." How would you define the concept of "education"? How might you go about operationalizing it? What problems in validity and reliability might arise from the measurement instruments you construct?

Suggested Readings

1 Blalock, Hubert M., Jr.: *Social Statistics*, 2d ed., chap. 2. New York: McGraw-Hill Book Company, 1972.

2 _____: "The Measurement Problem: A Gap between the Languages of Theory and Research," in Hubert M. Blalock, Jr., and Ann B. Blalock (eds.), *Methodology in Social Research*, pp. 5–27. New York: McGraw-Hill Book Company, 1968.

3 Converse, Jean M., and Howard Schuman: *Conversations at Random: Survey Research as Interviewers See It*. New York: John Wiley & Sons, 1974.

4 Hyman, Herbert H.: *Interviewing in Social Research*. Chicago: University of Chicago Press, 1975.

5 You might want to take a look at a series of articles on problems in measurement to be found in Lieberman, Bernhardt: *Contemporary Problems in Statistics*, sec. 1. New York: Oxford University Press, 1971.

6 Loether, Herman J., and Donald G. McTavish: *Descriptive Statistics for Sociologists*, chap. 2. Boston: Allyn and Bacon, 1974.

7 Mueller, John H., Karl F. Schuessler, and Herbert L. Costner: *Statistical Reasoning in Sociology*, 2d ed., chap. 2. Boston: Houghton Mifflin Company, 1970.

3

distributions, comparisons, and learning from tables

Most of the data you'll encounter start out as many scattered observations of. the characteristics of everything from individual people to schools, factories, cities, or Ping-Pong balls. The researcher faces the problem of managing, organizing, and summarizing masses of information in meaningful ways. Your problem is to understand what the researcher puts out.

Frequency Distributions

We start with bits of information. In our example in Chap. 1 we had 798 answers that took the form of yes or no. The simplest way of presenting what we have is to count up the number of answers of each kind. This is called a *frequency distribution*.

Any arrangement of numbers in columns and rows (such as Table 3-1) is called a *table*. There are several things we can learn from this one:

1 When you look at a table, start with the description. Read it carefully. Next, examine the column and row headings so you're sure of the meaning of each number. In this case the first column lists the possible responses that women could have made. The second column lists the number of women who gave each response. So, 343 women said yes to the question and 455 said no, for a total of 798 women. The letter *N* (sometimes capitalized, sometimes not) usually stands for the number of

Table 3-1 Responses to the Question: "Would you approve of a woman who decided not to get married and have children because she wanted to do other things with her life?"

Response	Frequency
Yes	343
No	455
Total	$798 = N$

cases involved (number of women interviewed, number of cities studied, etc.). Also, the letter *f* often replaces the word *frequency*.

2 Sometimes a table has missing cases. The author may have said at one point, "We interviewed a total of 900 women"; then, you see a table with only 800 women represented. There should be an explanation in the text or in a footnote; if there is none, the table loses some of its meaning. The greater the number of missing cases, the less certain we are of whom the information represents. Properly done, a table with missing cases should look something like Table 3-2. This tells us there were 210 respondents, 60 of whom failed to answer the questions measuring alienation. The body of the table shows us how those who *did* answer the questions were distributed on the alienation measure. *Always* make sure the numbers in the table add up to the total number of respondents in the study. Sometimes the nonresponse to specific questions can be very large, and, as we'll see in Chap. 9, this raises serious questions about the representativeness of the recorded responses and the validity of their interpretation.

Table 3-2 Distribution of Alienation among Textile Workers (Hypothetical)

Level of alienation	Frequency
High	30
Medium	100
Low	20
Total	150
No response	60
	$210 = N$

3 Table 3-1 tells us that more women (112 more, to be exact) said no than said yes, and that we got a response from all women in the sample. As tables go, this one is about as simple as you're going to get. Even with such simple distributions, however, there's no substitute for starting at the top and carefully working your way through, making sure you know what each and every number means. It may sound too elementary, but even professionals have to crawl through tables if they want to be sure to get an accurate and full picture of what's in them. Running (even walking) through tables just doesn't pay off in most cases.

We often find that making a separate category for each possible response makes enormous tables. If we took exact incomes and made them into separate categories, we'd have thousands of rows in the table. Therefore, we abbreviate the table by lumping similar responses together. The resulting data are called *grouped data* and the procedure is called *grouping*. An income table might look like Table 3-3.

There are two things I'd like you to notice in this table. First, when we group data, we lose detail. Instead of knowing someone's exact income, we now know only that the person's income is somewhere, say, between $15,000 and $19,999. Second, when someone makes a table like this, there's no magic formula that solves the problem of how to group the

Table 3-3 Distribution of Family Income, United States, 1973

Total money income	Number of families
Under $1,000	628,000
$1,000 to $1,999	965,000
$2,000 to $2,999	1,755,000
$3,000 to $3,999	2,244,000
$4,000 to $4,999	2,491,000
$5,000 to $5,999	2,555,000
$6,000 to $6,999	2,640,000
$7,000 to $7,999	2,709,000
$8,000 to $9,999	5,515,000
$10,000 to $11,999	5,887,000
$12,000 to $14,999	8,152,000
$15,000 to $19,999	9,438,000
$20,000 to $24,999	4,962,000
$25,000 and above	5,112,000
Total	55,053,000

SOURCE U.S. Bureau of the Census, *Current Population Reports: Money Income in 1973 of Families and Persons in the United States*, ser. P-60, no. 93, Table A.

numbers. Often it's done arbitrarily; sometimes lines are drawn at substantively meaningful points, such as official poverty levels in the case of income.

We can see from these tables that a distribution shows how often a characteristic occurs in a group, and allows us at a single glance to see how the group looks on a given variable. Remember that a variable operationalizes a concept and allows us to assign people or things to categories, depending on their characteristics. A frequency distribution shows how many people or things are in each category. The purpose of frequency distributions is to reduce an unmanageable mass of information on individuals to a manageable description of a group.

Comparing Entire Distributions: Percentages and Proportions

It may have occurred to you that although frequency distributions are worth understanding, they don't help us answer the kinds of question we most often want to ask. We'd rarely be content to find out what the distribution on a particular variable looks like and stop there. We want to go on, usually to make comparisons between groups or of one group at different points in time. Do white men make more money than white women? Have black incomes increased in the last decade? Are northern schools as racially segregated as southern schools? Are cities losing population or gaining? We need a point of comparison to make distributions meaningful; we need to place them in some sort of comparative context.

The first step in making a comparison between two groups would be to compare their frequency distributions. As an example, let's look at another attitude measured in the Mexico City study mentioned earlier. "Would you approve of a mother holding a job outside the home if the family didn't really need the money, but the woman wanted to work anyway?" If a woman working outside the home because she wants to is a threat to a husband's masculinity, we'd expect the idea of women working outside the home under these circumstances to have less support in homes where the man dominates. To explore this expectation, we could first compare the distributions of this attitude for two groups: women whose husbands make most of the decisions and women whose husbands don't make most of the decisions. Table 3-4 shows these two frequency distributions as well as that for the entire Mexico City sample (i.e., both groups lumped together).

First, notice that this table has two "kinds" of numbers: the last column (4) and the bottom row ("total") show the numbers of women with each single characteristic (for example, 132 women answered yes). These four numbers (132, 666, 530, 268) are called *marginal frequencies*

Table 3-4 Responses to: "Would you approve of a mother holding a job outside the home if the family didn't really need the money, but the woman wanted to work anyway?" for Respondents Whose Husbands Do and Do Not Make the Majority of Family Decisions on Their Own

(1) Response	(2) Husband doesn't make most decisions alone	(3) Husband makes most decisions alone	(4) Total
Approve (yes)	112	20	132
Disapprove (no)	418	248	666
Total	530	268	$798 = N$

(or *marginals*, for short). Each number in the body of the table shows how many women hold a specific combination of characteristics (for example, 20 women *both* answered yes *and* live in marriages in which the husband makes most of the decisions). These numbers (112, 20, 418, 248) are called *cells*.

What kinds of comparisons can we make with a table like this? The first thing to do is to pick any number in it and explain its meaning to someone else's satisfaction. Twenty women in marriages dominated by the husband approved of the mother working outside of the home; 248 disapproved; 112 women from marriages whose husbands don't dominate approved and 418 disapproved. There are 268 women in husband-dominated marriages and 530 in marriages not husband-dominated. In the entire sample 132 women approved of the mother working and 666 disapproved. There are 798 women in the entire sample. All set? If not, read no further until you are.

We can make two comparative statements about Table 3-4. First, in both marriage types more women answered no than yes (418 versus 112 and 248 versus 20). Second, more women in marriages *not* dominated by husbands answered yes than in husband-dominated marriages (112 versus 20); on the other hand, more of the former than the latter answered no as well (418 versus 248).

We have a problem here. We want to answer the question: "Are women in husband-dominated marriages (column 3) more likely to *disapprove* of mothers working outside the home than other kinds of wives are (column 2)?" In terms of *frequencies*, fewer women in husband-dominated marriages disapprove (248 versus 418); but is this a valid comparison? Since there are only 268 women in husband-dominated marriages to begin with, it's *impossible* for the *number* who disapprove to reach 418, even if *all* such women disapprove.

The problem is that our sample doesn't include equal numbers of women in both types of marriages, and this is clouding the comparison. If we had equal numbers of each marriage type, then we could make

Table 3-5 Responses to: "Would you approve of a mother holding a job outside the home if the family didn't really need the money, but the woman wanted to work anyway?" for Respondents Whose Husbands Do and Do Not Make the Majority of Family Decisions on Their Own (Hypothetical)

Response	Husband doesn't dominate	Husband dominates	All
Approve (yes)	112	40	152
Disapprove (no)	418	490	908
Total	530	530	1,060

comparisons quickly and directly. For example, what if Table 3-4 had looked like Table 3-5?

Now a clear pattern emerges. Women whose husbands dominate are *more* likely to disapprove (490 versus 418) and less likely to approve (40 versus 112). Since both marriage types now have the same total number of women (530), the only explanation for these differences is a true difference in the *relative likelihood* of approval and disapproval.

So, if we want to make comparisons, it helps to have equal numbers of cases in each group. This, however, is virtually impossible to attain; it's hard to think of a group that would include equal numbers of all the subgroups we might be interested in comparing.

There's a much easier solution to this problem. The key word in the question we're trying to answer is "likely": are one kind of women more likely to disapprove . . . ? What does this mean? When we talk about the *likelihood* of whites having more education than blacks, for example, we're not talking about the absolute numbers of whites and blacks with college educations, but the number of whites with a college education *relative* to the number of whites in the country, and the number of blacks with college education *relative* to the number of blacks in the country. To get one number relative to another, we divide the first by the second. What results is a *proportion*. Multiply it by 100 and you have a *percentage*.

Now back to our original table, Table 3-4. What we need is the number of women in husband-dominated marriages, who approve and disapprove, relative to (i.e., divided by) the total number of women in husband-dominated marriages; and of the women in marriages *not* dominated by husbands, the number who approve and disapprove relative to the total number of women living in *that* kind of marriage. What was just stated looks like the material shown in Table 3-6. Before you go on, be sure you understand this last paragraph and be sure you see how Table 3-6 represents it.

Carry out these divisions and you get the *proportions* of women in

TABLE 3-6 Responses to: "Would you approve of a mother holding a job outside the home if the family didn't really need the money, but the woman wanted to work anyway?" for Respondents Whose Husbands Do and Do Not Make the Majority of Family Decisions on Their Own

Response	Husband doesn't dominate	Husband dominates	Total
Approve	112/530	20/268	132/798
Disapprove	418/530	248/268	666/798
Total	530/530	268/268	798/798

each group who approve and disapprove (Table 3-7). Multiply each of these *proportions* by 100 and you get *percentages* (Table 3-8).

Before we talk about what's in the table, note the following. First, percentages must add to 100.0 percent, and proportions must add to 1.00. If percentage *totals* are off by more than .1 percent (i.e., above 100.1 percent or below 99.9 percent) or if proportion *totals* are off by more than .001 (i.e., above 1.001 or below .999), then an error has been made somewhere. Check it out by adding it up yourself.

Second, if a percentage or proportional distribution is based on a small number of cases (under 25 to 30), the author is risking considerable inaccuracy. For example, if there are five cases, each case represents 20 percent (1/5 × 100). If a single error has been made at any point in the gathering or processing of the data, then the distribution is shifted by 20 full percentage points. Thus, one error can change a distribution from

60%		40%
40	to	60
100%		100%

Table 3-7 Proportional Distribution of Responses to: "Would you approve of a mother holding a job outside the home if the family didn't really need the money, but the woman wanted to work anyway?" for Respondents Whose Husbands Do and Do Not Make the Majority of Family Decisions on Their Own

Response	Husband doesn't dominate	Husband dominates	Total
Approve	.211	.075	.165
Disapprove	.789	.925	.835
Total	1.000	1.000	1.000
(N)	(530)	(268)	(798)

Table 3-8 Percentage Distribution of Responses to: "Would you approve of a mother holding a job outside the home if the family didn't really need the money?" for Respondents Whose Husbands Do and Do Not Make the Majority of Family Decisions on Their Own

Response	Husband doesn't dominate	Husband dominates	Total
Approve	21.1%	7.5%	16.5%
Disapprove	78.9	92.5	83.5
Total	100.0%	100.0%	100.0%
(N)	(530)	(268)	(798)

which reverses the majority. A single error makes too great a difference in the findings. So, don't rely on interpretations of such distributions when the number of cases gets down around 20 or so (at which point a single error makes a difference of 5 percent).

Now, what does Table 3-8 tell us? About 8 percent of women in the 268 husband-dominated marriages approve of mothers working, and 21 percent of women in the 530 marriages not dominated by the husband approve. Since each number (7.5 percent and 21.1 percent) is based on the same total (100.0 percent), we can be sure there is a real difference in the relative likelihood of approving and disapproving. Wives in husband-dominated marriages are more likely to disapprove of mothers working outside the home than wives in non-husband-dominated marriages. Notice that we would never have drawn such a conclusion from the frequencies in Table 3-4; we might have been tempted to draw the *opposite* conclusion.

Proportions and percentages allow us to make comparisons between groups even when the groups are of very different size. That's the sole reason for their existence and use.

When you read proportional and percentage tables, there's one very important thing to know and remember. When you're comparing two groups, the proportioning (or percentaging) is done *within* each group. (In our last example we percentaged within the two groups we compared: marriages where husbands dominate and marriages where they don't.) When you look at a table, you can tell immediately what's being compared; the groups that are percentaged are the ones being compared with each other. We'll talk more about this and its importance later.

Cross Tabulations

So far we've talked about comparing different groups on the basis of their distribution on a single variable. When the groups we're com-

Table 3-9 Approval of Mothers Working Outside the Home by Husband Dominance

Approval of mothers working outside the home	HUSBAND DOMINANCE		Total
	No	**Yes**	**Total**
Approve	112	20	132
Disapprove	418	248	666
Total	530	268	798 = N

paring are the categories of a second variable, we have what is known as a *cross tabulation*. We can look now at Table 3-4 in a new way. We have two variables: the first is a characteristic of the respondent; namely, does she approve of mothers working outside the home? The categories consist of two responses, approve (yes) and disapprove (no). The second variable is a characteristic of the respondent's marriage: does the husband dominate decision making? The variable consists of two possible responses, yes and no, where yes means the husband makes more than half the decisions and no means he makes half or less. If we look at Table 3-4 as a two-variable table, the numbers remain unchanged, but the labels look a bit different.

The word *by* in the title of Table 3-9 is simply a connecting word that links the two variables that define the table's columns and rows.

We now have *two* variables, and for each variable we have *two* distributions, one for each category of the other variable. In the previous section we compared distributions on the work attitude within two types of marriages. To do this, we percentaged within each marriage type (i.e., within each group involved in the comparison) and got Table 3-8. What if we had percentaged the other way? What if we had looked at the distribution of husband dominance within each category of the work attitude? How would the table look then, and what kinds of questions would it answer? (See Table 3-10.)

Table 3-10 Husband Dominance by Approval of Mothers Working Outside the Home

Approval of mothers working outside the home	HUSBAND DOMINANCE		Total	(N)
	No	**Yes**	**Total**	**(N)**
Approve	84.8%	15.2	100.0%	(132)
Disapprove	62.8%	37.2	100.0%	(666)
Total	66.4%	33.6	100.0%	(798)

We haven't rearranged anything in this table. The variables are still in the same position. All we've done is to divide each number by the total of its *row* instead of the total of its column. When you're comparing groups, remember that the percentaging is done *within* each group being compared. Using Table 3-10, we couldn't make the comparison we made in Table 3-8. In order to compare the two categories of husband dominance (as we did), we'd have to percentage the work attitude *within* each category of the husband-dominance variable (i.e., vertically). Since we've percentaged within the "approve" and "disapprove" groups, we can now compare only them in terms of the distribution of husband dominance.

We asked, "Are women in husband-dominated marriages more likely to disapprove of mothers working outside the home than are wives in marriages without dominating husbands?" We now can ask, "Are women who approve of mothers working outside the home more likely to live in husband-dominated marriages than are women who disapprove of mothers working outside the home?" It's important that you satisfy yourself that these are two different questions. The first describes women in husband-dominated and non-husband-dominated marriages in terms of their attitude on working; the second describes women who approve or disapprove of the work attitude in terms of the kind of marriage they live in.

When you look at a table that's in percentages or proportions, first check the direction of the percentaging or proportioning. *Establish firmly in your mind which groups are being compared and on what characteristic.* If you don't do this, you'll arrive at the right conclusion only by luck. I can't stress too much how important it is that you understand the connection between the direction of percentaging and the questions that can be answered from the table.

Just to prove that you can't be too careful, consider the case of a prestigious American sociological journal that published a paper in which almost all the tables were percentaged in the wrong direction.[1] This occurred in spite of readings by several equally prestigious reviewers and the journal's editorial staff. Although most of the paper's substantive conclusions were not altered when the percentages were run in the proper direction, several of the findings were, in fact, reversed. Even the most competent people make mistakes once in a while.

One more time: you have a two-variable cross tabulation in which percentages or proportions have been computed. First look for the "total" column (or row), the one with nothing but 1.00's or 100.0%'s in it. If

---

[1] See Jan Hajda, "Alienation and Integration of Student Intellectuals," *American Sociological Review*, 26 (October 1961): 758–777; and comments by David J. Bordua and Robert H. Somers, with Hajda's reply in *American Sociological Review*, 27 (June 1962): 416.

the columns have been percentaged (i.e., the column numbers add to 100.0 percent), then the categories of the column variables are the ones being compared, and the row-variable categories are the terms you're comparing them in (e.g., Table 3-8). If the row-variable categories are the ones that are percentaged, then everything holds in reverse (e.g., Table 3-10).

Now go back to Tables 3-8 and 3-10. Explain to someone who hasn't read this chapter just what the two tables tell us about attitudes and husband dominance in Mexico City. First, see whether you can get someone to understand your explanation. If they can, you've accomplished an important kind of learning. Then reread the text and see how your explanation compares with mine. Remember, being able to read someone else's explanation and say, "Yes, that makes sense," often gives you a false sense of security; it's a superficial kind of learning. To really understand, you must be able to reformulate the information in your own terms and be able to communicate your understanding to someone else.

More Complicated Tables

You're likely to run into more than simple two-variable cross tabulations before long. First, you can have more than two variables in a table. In Table 3-11 we have distributions of educational attainment by two other variables, sex and race. Tables such as this can look so imposing and complicated that they can scare you off at first. Remember to start at the top and carefully work your way through the table, making sure along the way you clearly understand the meaning of each number in the body of the table.

The table has seven columns (white men, white women, all whites, black men, black women, all blacks, and total of blacks and whites) and nine rows (seven for the categories of education, one for totals, and one for the number of cases the percentages are based on). Each *column* totals 100.0 percent, which tells you immediately that with the table percentaged in this way we can compare *columns only;* we can compare the educational distributions of white and black men and women. We cannot compare the sex or racial composition of groups with different educational attainments (i.e., we can't compare rows); to do this, we'd have to percentage across the rows, rather than down the columns. (Be sure not to just nod your head here; do you understand why this is so?)

You can find a lot in a table like this. Blacks are much more heavily loaded at the lower educational levels, whites more concentrated at the higher levels. White men and women have similar distributions up to high school graduation, but here differences emerge. White women are more likely to stop at high school graduation (40.2 percent versus 32.1

Table 3-11 Educational Attainment by Race and by Sex for Persons 14 Years Old and Older, 1972, United States

Years of school completed		WHITES			BLACKS			Total
		Men	Women	Total	Men	Women	Total	
Elementary	0–4	3.9%	3.4%	3.7%	15.6%	10.6%	12.8%	4.6%
	5–7	7.8	7.1	7.4	17.4	16.7	17.0	8.3
	8	12.4	12.0	12.2	9.6	9.7	9.6	11.9
High School	1–3	15.6	17.0	16.3	21.8	25.8	24.0	17.0
	4	32.1	40.2	36.4	23.7	25.8	25.0	35.3
College	1–3	12.0	10.9	11.4	6.4	6.6	6.5	10.9
	4+	16.2	9.4	12.6	5.5	4.8	5.1	12.0
Total		100.0%	100.0%	100.0%	100.0%	100.0%	100.0%	100.0%
N (000's)		47,133	52,410	99,543	4,635	5,768	10,403	109,946

SOURCES U.S. Bureau of the Census, *U.S. Census of Population: 1960*, vol. 1 *Characteristics of the Population*, part 1, United States Summary, 1964, table 173. U.S. Bureau of the Census, *Current Population Reports: Educational Attainment, March 1972*, ser. P-20, no. 243, 1972.

percent) and white men are more likely to go on to college (12.0% + 16.2% = 28.2% versus 10.9% + 9.4% = 20.3%). The pattern among blacks is different: black men are less likely to make it to high school (57.4 percent with high school or more versus 63.0 percent for black women), but there's little difference in the percentages who go to college and beyond (11.9 percent versus 11.4 percent). Thus, one finding is that at the upper educational levels there are both racial and sexual differences, but that the sexual differences depend on which race you're looking at. If you looked at data such as these for several points in time — for example, 1950 and 1960 as well as 1972 — you could make many revealing comparisons about changes over time in sex and racial differences in educational attainment. All it takes is patience and care on your part, and you can learn a lot from percentaged tables.

Could you use Table 3-11 *as it is presented* to answer the question: "Who dominates at the higher education levels, men or women?" How? Or why not?

Not all tables have frequencies in them, or percentages (or proportions) adding to 100 percent (or 1.00). In cases like this it's very important to read the title and footnotes carefully to make sure you understand what the numbers mean. For example, Table 3-12 has the percentage of people with different educational attainments who voted in the 1972 elections. These don't add to 100.0 percent because the percentage not voting is omitted.

Thirty-two percent of whites with 0 to 4 years of elementary school voted; 85 percent of whites with 4 years or more of college voted. At all levels but the two lowest, whites have a higher tendency to vote than blacks. With one exception ("high school 1–3") the higher one's education is, the more likely one's to vote.

Table 3-12 Of Those of Voting Age, the Percentage Voting in the 1972 Presidential Election, by Educational Attainment and by Race

Years of school completed		White percentage voting	Black percentage voting
Elementary	0–4	32.2%	35.9%
	5–7	43.5	48.5
	8	55.6	52.1
High school	1–3	53.1	46.9
	4	66.5	55.3
College	1–3	76.0	63.5
	4+	85.0	79.6
Total		64.5%	52.1%

SOURCE U.S. Bureau of the Census, *Current Population Reports: Voting and Registration in the Election of November 1972*, ser. P-20, no. 253, October 1973.

When you read a table like this, keep in mind that each cell refers to cases with the combination of characteristics formed by its row and column. So, the fourth number down in the second column (46.9 percent) represents the percentage of those who are black, have 1 to 3 years of high school, who voted in 1972. You have two things to do here: first, figure out what the number refers to; second, examine the row and column variables so that you understand what kinds of people each cell represents.

Ratios

If in a group of ten people there are eight whites and two blacks, we say there are "four times as many whites as blacks." We get this figure by dividing the number of whites (8) by the number of blacks (2); $8/2 = 4$. The quantity 8/2, or 8:2, is called a *ratio*; in this case we have the *ratio of whites to blacks*.

Ratios are commonly used for two purposes, both of which are subject to misinterpretation. In the first, we're comparing groups or individuals. For example, "Joe makes twice the money his wife does," or "There are nine times as many whites in the United States as there are blacks," or "The candidate won by a three-to-one margin." In the first example we divided Joe's income by his wife's; in the second the number of whites in the United States by the number of blacks; in the third the votes the candidate got divided by the votes his opponents got.

In the second case, ratios are used to indicate change over time. There are two basic variations of this. Suppose support for an amendment declined by 33 percent between February and October. Here we take the *difference* between the percentage supporting the measure in February and October (February % − October %) and divide it by the original figure (February %). The final ratio looks like this:

$$\frac{\text{February \% − October \%}}{\text{February \%}} = \frac{60 - 40}{60} = 33\%$$

The second variation is: "Support for the amendment in October was two-thirds its February level." In this case the ratio consists of October %:February % = 40:60 = 2:3.

All these uses of ratios suffer from the same problem: a ratio doesn't tell us anything about the *absolute* difference between two groups or the *absolute* change over time. Take the example of the income of Joe and his wife. Incomes of $15,000 and $7,500 make a ratio of 2:1, but so do incomes of $120 and $60. In the first case we're talking about a pretty impressive difference—$7,500—but in the second the difference is only $60. And yet the *ratio* in both cases is 2:1.

A candidate winning 800,000 to 400,000 votes wins by a 2:1 ratio; a candidate winning 4 votes to 2 votes is also winning by a 2:1 ratio, but it's not as impressive. As a final example, if support for the amendment dropped from 90 to 45 percent, this is a 50-percent drop [(90% − 45%)/90%] involving 45 actual percentage points (90 to 45); on the other hand, a drop from 2 to 1 percent is also a 50-percent drop [(2% − 1%)/2%], although the actual change is only one percentage point (2 to 1).

It should be clear by now that the problem is not one of misstatement. The problem is one of impact: *ratios can sound very impressive even when representing very trivial absolute differences between groups or changes over time.*

The solution for the reader is direct and simple: always convert ratios back to the original frequencies. This is the only way to determine the importance of the differences the ratios represent. If the author doesn't give you the original numbers, and if you have no idea of their magnitude, then you have to remember that the ratio could represent differences ranging from important to trivial.

Keep in mind that authors of articles, books, or speeches are mortals like the rest of us, and they like to feel that what they're saying is important. Saying "support tripled in 2 years" just sounds more impressive than "support rose from 1 to 3 percent in 2 years." The author isn't misstating the case; it's more a matter of stating information in the most dramatic form possible. So, be cool and calm and carefully work toward the truth.

Ratios, of course, can be very useful and revealing. We've spoken before of deaths from coronary heart disease. Suppose we wanted to compare the incidence of heart attacks in 1950 and 1971. In 1950, 535,705 people died of coronary heart disease; in 1971, 674,316 people died of coronary heart disease. Does this mean that coronary heart disease was more of a problem in 1971 than it was in 1950? The problem here is the same one we encountered before in dealing with comparisons among frequencies: if we want to determine the likelihood of dying from coronary heart disease in 1950 and compare it with the likelihood for 1971, we must take into account the differing numbers of people who were eligible to die. Thus, what we want is the number of deaths in 1950 *relative* to the number of people alive during 1950, and a comparable ratio for 1971. In 1950, there were 152,378,000 people in the United States; in 1971, there were 206,782,000. The proportions who died of coronary heart disease in those years are:

1950: 535,705/152,378,000 = .003516
1971: 674,316/206,782,000 = .003261

As you can see, people in 1950 were *more* likely to die of coronary heart disease than people in 1971. We never could have seen this from the absolute numbers of deaths.

You will also notice that the proportions above are very small and, for this reason, somewhat unwieldy. They represent "deaths per person." In the case of death data, we usually use a larger denominator (for example, 100,000), giving us "deaths per 100,000 people." These numbers are called *rates*. For example,

$$\frac{.003516 \text{ deaths}}{\text{person}} \frac{100,000}{100,000} = \frac{351.6 \text{ deaths}}{100,000 \text{ people}}$$

The coronary heart disease rates for 1950 and 1971 are, therefore, 351.6 and 326.1, respectively. The rate in 1971 was lower than the rate in 1950, in spite of the fact that a greater *number* of people died in 1971.

You'll find another example of the usefulness of rates in Table 3-13. Here we've taken the ratio of male death rates to female death rates, for all causes of death. For example, in 1960, among those 15 to 24 years old, men were two-and-one-half times as likely to die as women (check the table and make sure you see where this number came from). If you examine each age group and go across its row, you can see how the gap between men's and women's death rates grew between 1950 and 1970. For example, among those 65 to 74 years old, in 1950, the men were one-and-one-half times as likely as women to die (a ratio of 1.47 in column 1); in 1970, men were almost twice as likely to die (a ratio of 1.89). The use of ratios allows us to compare men and women directly and tell a revealing story about time trends.

What about the problem raised earlier about the inability of ratios to tell us the absolute differences? How does that apply here? The absolute differences in the death rates are not very large (for example, see the comparison between overall death rates in 1950 and 1971 cited earlier), but this doesn't concern us here because we aren't interested in the absolute differences. The death rates reflect the likelihood of death, and the ratios of death rates indicate the likelihood of death for men relative to women. In this case, the ratios tell the whole story: men are more likely than women to die, and this gap has been growing since 1950.

The importance of knowing absolute differences thus varies with the problem at hand. You, as a reader, have to examine just what the author is trying to accomplish through the use of ratios, and evaluate their use in those terms.

Keep in mind the fact that proportions are ratios, as percentages are, and we've already established their usefulness.

Table 3-13 Ratios of Male Death Rates to
Female Death Rates, from All Causes, by
Age, United States, 1950 to 1970

Age	1950	1960	1965	1970
Fetal[1]	1.15	1.11	1.11	[2]
Infant[3]	1.29	1.30	1.29	1.30
1–4	1.15	1.20	1.25	1.12
5–14	1.40	1.50	1.67	1.67
15–24	1.89	2.50	2.67	2.71
25–34	1.52	1.73	1.82	2.20
35–44	1.48	1.61	1.70	1.74
45–54	1.67	1.87	1.87	1.85
55–64	1.70	1.92	2.04	2.07
65–74	1.47	1.71	1.82	1.89
75–84	1.24	1.33	1.40	1.50
85+	1.13	1.11	1.09	1.15

[1] Deaths to fetuses who have gestated at least 20 weeks, per 1,000 live births. Includes all those with no stated gestation age. Sex not stated is distributed proportionately.
[2] Data not available.
[3] Deaths under 1 year of age, excluding fetal deaths, per 1,000 live births.
SOURCES Sam Shapiro, Edward R. Schlesinger, and Robert E. L. Nesbitt, Jr., *Infant, Perinatal, Maternal, and Childhood Mortality in the United States* (Cambridge, Mass.: Harvard University Press, 1968), tables I.1b, I.1c, I.12a, I.12b, III.1a, III.2a, all in appendix tables.
For 1965 and 1970, annual volumes and yearly summaries, *Vital Statistics of the United States*, National Center for Health Statistics, Public Health Service, Washington, D.C.

Describing Distributions with Pictures

Sometimes we use pictures to describe a group in terms of a variable. Keep in mind that these pictures contain the same information as the tables. They're used to add drama and interest to presentations of data. They catch a reader's attention and often can be more easily grasped than tables. Unfortunately, for this very reason they can be a greater source of exaggeration and misunderstanding than tables. We can look at them so quickly that we're less critical than we should be.

Take, for example, the most commonly used *graphic* method of presenting distributions, the *bar graph* (Fig. 3-1). Both parts *a* and *b* represent the same data. In many bar graphs the left-hand side (or *axis*, as it is called) shows the number (or proportion or percentage) of people who hold the characteristic described on the horizontal axis.

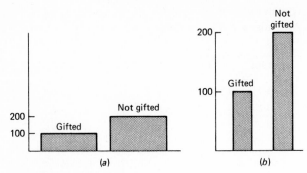

Figure 3-1 A bar graph representing hypothetical distributions of gifted and ungifted children.

In this example we have two characteristics (being a gifted child and not being gifted), and on the vertical axis we have the number of children (or a total of 300) who hold one of these traits. In most bar graphs, the height of the bar indicates the number of people holding that characteristic. The bars are of equal width. Occasionally the relative numbers in each category are indicated by the *area* of the bar, but this is less common.

Now, what do the graphs tell us? In both cases, the "gifted" bar reaches a height of 100, indicating that 100 children have this characteristic. The "not gifted" bar goes up to 200, indicating that 200 of the 300 children have this characteristic. In both cases the not-gifted children outnumber the gifted children by a ratio of 2:1, but I think you'll agree that the difference seems more pronounced and dramatic in the right-hand graph than in the left. The difference isn't actually greater, it just feels that way.

The only way to read a graph of any kind is to look carefully at the scales on the vertical and horizontal axes to determine independently of the graph just what the picture means. If you rely solely on the visual effect you can run the risk of drawing conclusions more extreme than the facts warrant. Remember the graphs don't create new information; they express a table in pictorial form. It's a lot harder to be misled by a table than by a picture. When in doubt, translate the picture back to the original.

Another kind of picture is the line graph, such as those depicting stock averages or trends in the percentage of unemployed. Again, the way in which the numbers are marked off on the axes affects our interpretation. For example, consider the hypothetical trends in the percentage of unemployed (Fig. 3-2).

First, notice the broken lines on the vertical axes of parts *a* and *b*. These always should be used when the vertical (or horizontal) scale

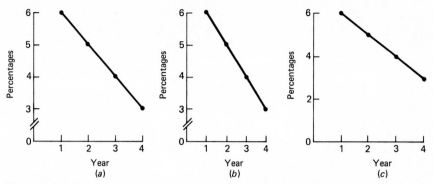

Figure 3-2 A line graph representing percentages of unemployed.

doesn't begin at zero. Without this there would be the false impression that unemployment approached zero in year 4.

All three graphs show the same trends over the same 4 years, but clearly the drop in part *b* is more impressive than in *a* or *c*, and that in *a* more impressive than in *c*, *unless* we look at each vertical axis and see that the *actual* drops in the percentage of unemployed are identical in all three graphs. Why the different appearance? First, in part *b* the horizontal scale has been compressed (the distance representing 1 year in parts *a* and *c* equals 1.5 years in *b*). Second, the vertical scale in *c* has been compressed: a 2-percent change in *c* corresponds to a 1.5-percent change in *a* and *b*. If you want to know what's going on in a graph, you have to look at the scales.

The problem with all graphic handling of data is that there are many ways to represent one set of precise bits of information. Your task as a reader is to cut through the visual image to the underlying set of facts. The visual image can't be allowed to stand on its own; you have to pick it apart.

By now you're probably recalling the good old phrase "lying with statistics." You should keep in mind that there is no formula that tells us what an objective picture of any set of data should be; there is no "naturally" best way. The only readers who will draw unwarranted conclusions will be those who don't bother to do more than read the text and glance at the graph. If you care about the meaning of the information, you owe it to yourself to take the time to dig deeper.

I've often heard and read the assertion that one can "prove anything with statistics." This simply isn't true, no more so than that one can "prove anything with words." This is no more the fault of the statistics than lying with words is the fault of language.

If we are more easily deceived by statistics and data, I think it's because so many of us are untrained or impatient or both. Even professionals sometimes skim carelessly through tables and graphs because the text is more interesting and the process of verifying the author's interpretation requires patience and care. I can sensitize you somewhat in a book like this, but I can't teach you patience; you have to care enough about truth to take the time and effort to examine evidence carefully and thoroughly.

There are numerous ways of displaying data graphically, and, when properly done, they allow the reader to grasp readily what's going on in a body of data. Line graphs can be particularly useful. In Fig. 3-3 we have a graph displaying death rates (per 1,000 people) by age. By using a graph, we can quickly see that death rates are relatively high at birth (age 0), drop sharply by age 4, remain very low until age 10, begin a very gradual upward climb through age 40, and then start rising precipitously. At a glance we can see how death rates vary through the life cycle.

Another common graphic display is similar to the bar graph, but rather than representing qualitative data (such as being gifted), it represents quantitative data (such as income). This is called a *histogram*. Figure 3-4 shows the percentage distribution of age at menopause for American women. The horizontal axis shows the age at menopause; the vertical axis shows the percentage of women experiencing menopause at a given age. We can see immediately that most women (54 percent) experience menopause between their 45th and 55th birthdays, and that

Figure 3-3 A line graph representing death rates (per 1,000) by age in the United States in 1960.

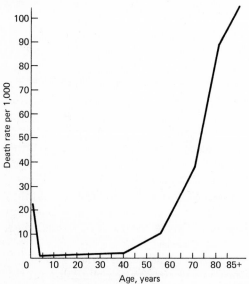

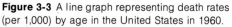

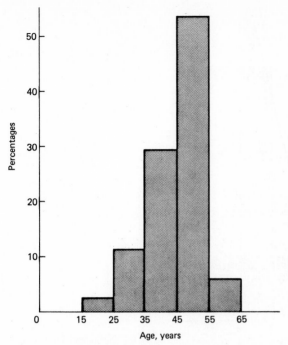

Figure 3-4 A histogram representing age at menopause
for American women, 1959 to 1961. (*Source: U.S. Health
Examination Survey, 1959–1961*, U.S. Department of
Health, Education, and Welfare.)

a small percentage (2 percent) experience menopause before their 25th
birthday. The histogram tells the story quickly and clearly.

Sometimes an author will fit a line graph to a histogram by connecting the midpoints of the tops of each bar, as in Fig. 3-5. This is called
a *frequency polygon*.

The same data could be displayed in yet another way. We could
have plotted, for each age, the percentage of women who had experienced menopause *before reaching that age*. This is called a *cumulative
distribution*, and the graphic form is called an *ogive*. Figure 3-6 shows
the data in Fig. 3-4 in cumulative form. We can immediately see that by
age 25 very few women have experienced menopause, but that after
age 25 the percentages increase sharply. By age 55, 96 percent of all
women have experienced menopause.

Authors have shown great ingenuity in devising graphic modes for
presenting data, and it's not this author's intent to describe them all.
You'll find suggested readings at the end of this chapter if you want to
become familiar with other techniques. The important thing to re-

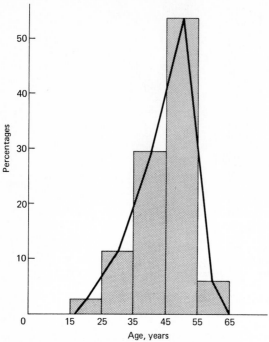

Figure 3-5 A frequency polygon representing the age at menopause of American women, 1959 to 1961.

member when you encounter any graphic display of data is that there's a table somewhere behind it. You must scrutinize a graph carefully, noting what the vertical and horizontal dimensions stand for. Graphic displays can be most useful, but only in the hands of competent authors and critical, alert readers.

Looking Back

The message of this chapter is an important one: you've got to get down on your hands and knees and get dirty, figuratively at least. Tenacity is one of the most important factors in learning from tables, especially with some of the doozies you're likely to run into.

You should be able to explain in your own words what a frequency distribution is and what a cross tabulation is and what they're good for. Also, where do percentages and proportions come from, and what are they good for? Most importantly, you should be able to approach a table and work your way through it and understand what's going on. Don't get discouraged if you find it difficult; we *all* do. There are no formulas that make table or graph reading easy. The only way to get to be good at it is to do it a lot.

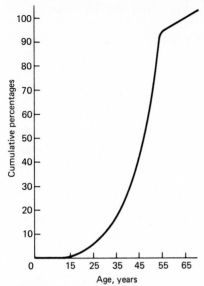

Figure 3-6 Ogive representation of the cumulative percentages by age of American women experiencing menopause, 1959 to 1961. (*Source: U.S. Health Examination Survey, 1959–1961*, U.S. Department of Health, Education, and Welfare.)

Problems

Refer to Table 3-14 in answering Probs. 3-1 to 3-5.

3-1 What people are *not* represented in this table?

3-2 How many variables are there in the table? What are they?

3-3 Why don't the numbers add up to 100 percent anywhere?

3-4 Using Table 3-14 as it's presented, can you answer the following questions? *If yes*, what's the answer? *If no*, how would you have to change the table so you could answer the question? (Problems 3-4a to g refer to wives, 18 to 39 years old only.)

    a. In 1965, who was more likely to have ever used contraception — whites or nonwhites?

    b. In 1965, who was better educated — whites who had ever used contraception or nonwhites who had ever used contraception?

    c. In 1965, what proportion of all wives 18 to 39 years old had ever used contraception?

    d. If we compare whites and nonwhites who had ever used contraception in 1965, which group had the highest percentage with "some college"?

Table 3-14 *Percentage* of Wives 18 to 39 Years Old Who Have Ever Used or Expect to Use Contraception, by Educational Attainment and race

	WHITE				NEGRO AND OTHER RACES	
	HAVE EVER USED		HAVE EVER USED OR EXPECT TO USE		HAVE EVER USED	HAVE EVER USED OR EXPECT TO USE
Educational attainment	**1965**	**1955**	**1965**	**1955**	**1965**	**1965**
Elementary school or less	65%	49%	75%	59%	58%	71%
High school, 1 to 3 years	83	66	88	76	79	87
High school, 4 years	86	74	92	83	83	91
Some college or more	88	85	94	88	85	88
Total	84%	70%	90%	79%	77%	86%

SOURCE U.S. Bureau of the Census, *Current Population Reports: Fertility Indicators: 1970*, ser. P-23, no. 36, 1971, table 31.

　　e. How did the use of contraception among white wives change between 1955 and 1965? Did this change occur at all educational-attainment levels? Did it occur more at some levels than at others? Which?

　　What are the answers to these questions for nonwhites?

　　f. For 1965, at what educational-attainment level is the difference in contraceptive use between whites and nonwhites the greatest? What is the difference?

　　g. In 1955, what percentage of white wives with high school diplomas had ever used or expected to use contraception?

3-5 What important information is missing from Table 3-14?

3-6 "Over half of the respondents favored the proposition, a finding that surprised us considerably."

Response to Proposition

Response	**Percentage**
Favor	60%
Oppose	40

Total   100%   ($N = 10$)

　　a. Does anything bother you about the reported finding?

3-7 "As the data indicate, whites are over twice as likely as nonwhites to have at least some college education."

Percentage Supporting Jones, by Race
and by Education

	Whites	**Nonwhites**
High school or less	40%	60%
At least some college	75	35

a. Is this what the table tells us? If not, what does it tell us?

3-8 "Support for Jones among urban lower-class workers increased from 2 to 6 percent, a 300-percent jump that should bring a smile to Jones's face. Not many candidates could hope to triple their support in only a year's time."

a. If you were Jones, would you be happy with your 300-percent increase in support? Why or why not?

Suggested Readings

1 Blalock, Hubert M., Jr.: *Social Statistics*, 2d ed., sec. 4.3. New York: McGraw-Hill Book Company, 1972. This is a very brief but competent look at the same techniques covered here.
2 Loether, Herman J., and Donald G. McTavish: *Descriptive Statistics for Sociologists*, chap. 4. Boston: Allyn and Bacon, 1974. This is by far the most extensive discussion on graphic techniques I've ever seen. I highly recommend it to you.
3 Mueller, John H., Karl F. Schuessler, and Herbert L. Costner: *Statistical Reasoning in Sociology*, 2d ed. Boston: Houghton Mifflin Company, 1970. A cut below Loether and McTavish in terms of comprehensiveness, but very much worth your while.
4 You should also look at the many examples to be found in Tanur, Judith M., et al. (eds.): *Statistics: A Guide to the Unknown*, p. xix of the index. San Francisco: Holden-Day, 1972.

4

summarizing
whole
distributions

It's not uncommon to hear people talking about the practice of "reducing people to statistics," as if it were an inhuman thing to do and had nothing to do with people. You may have noticed that in Chap. 3 we never talked about individuals: individuals got lost somewhere in the frequency and percentage distributions. By their nature, the kinds of data we're talking about never focus on individuals. Statistics is the study of groups; it's the study of individuals only insofar as they take on the characteristics of the groups they belong to.

You may be inclined at this point to mutter something about individuality and mass society. Those who use statistics don't (or at least shouldn't) pretend that their data allow them to make precise statements about individuals; what they claim is that many problems can't be approached on an individual level and we can often learn a great deal about the situations facing individuals by examining the groups they belong to in comparison with other groups.

The issue here boils down to the difference between clinical psychology and sociological research. If a person goes to a job interview and is turned down, a clinical psychologist might be interested in how that individual handles the resultant feelings of disappointment. If the person is black, indicating membership in a social category, a sociologist might be interested in the ways in which membership in that social category affected the outcome of that interview and others like it. The questions, although related, are qualitatively different and call for different analytical techniques. The sociologist's question is more amenable to statistical analysis than the psychologist's is, and even though we're talking about groups rather than John or Jane Doe, knowledge that membership in a particular social category may bring about discrimination in employment is important for those in that category.

For example, are women discriminated against in pay for the same jobs? We could go out and find Mary Hall and compare her with a man working at the same job, but how would we know that we hadn't just picked an exceptional case, a fluke? We wouldn't. If we want to talk about Mary, all we have to do is check out Mary: if we want to talk about working women, we've got to study all working women or a representative sample of them. There are many research questions that have implications for individuals, but they often affect individuals because of characteristics those individuals share with others. If being a woman causes discrimination, we'll never be able to prove it unless we compare women as a group with men as a group.

I'm not suggesting that statistical analysis on the group level is the only way to learn about the world, far from it. I am suggesting that to validate our ideas we'll have to shift to a group-level perspective sooner or later. The confusion of group-level analysis with the problem of the submersion of the individual in mass society is unfortunate and unwarranted.

The idea of a distribution is going to start assuming more and more importance in the chapters to come, and it's important that you start getting a more comfortable feel for what distributions are all about and what forms and uses they can have. In this chapter we're going to talk about ways of summarizing entire distributions. We'll try to concentrate not on complicated computation formulas and complex mathematical derivations, but on what the numbers mean and how their interpretation can help us or mislead us.

The Mythical "Average Person": Means and Medians

As we suggested in Chap. 3, there's little interest in confining our attention to a single distribution. We're more likely to be interested in making comparisons between groups or of groups over time. We saw how difficult it is to make comparisons between groups when they're unequal in size, a problem we solved by using proportions and percentages. Most of our examples, however, involved variables with only a few categories (such as "agree" and "disagree"); comparing distributions with many categories can be very cumbersome. If the variables are nominal or ordinal, all we can do to simplify things is to combine categories, a practice that sacrifices detail for simplicity. If we have an interval or ratio variable, however, we can simplify our intra- and intergroup comparisons in other ways. For example, consider the distributions shown in Table 4-1.

If we're interested in knowing which group tends to have the largest number of children, percentage distributions don't provide a very clear answer. One thing we could do is to see which group has the largest total number of children. For example, group 1 has five people who are childless $(5 \times 0 = 0)$, five with one child $(5 \times 1 = 5)$, etc., for a total of $(5 \times 0) + (5 \times 1) + (25 \times 2) + (10 \times 3) + (2 \times 4) + (2 \times 5) + (1 \times 6) = 109$ children for the entire group. The same procedure for group 2 yields 456 children for the entire group. So, group 2 has roughly four times as many children as group 1, but as you may have noticed, this isn't a fair comparison, since group 2 also has four times as many respondents (200 versus 50). We've got the same problem we had with comparing frequency distributions: in order to compare the two groups fairly, we have to allow for the different numbers of cases involved. The best way to do this is to divide each total number of children by the number of cases they came from (that is, 109/50 and 456/200). This gives us the number of children in each group relative to the number of respondents. These numbers (2.18 and 2.28) are called *means* (or *averages*). The symbol for a mean of a sample is usually a capital X with a bar over it, such as $\bar{X}$; population means are represented by the Greek letter mu (μ).

Notice that no person in either group has the mean number of children (and in the case of this variable, it's impossible to have the mean number). This may strike you as strange, but it's not if you remember that means are numbers that describe groups, not individuals. To say "the average person in the group has 2.18 children" misstates the case by unjustifiably implying that means say something precise about individuals. The correct interpretation is this: group 2 has relatively more children than group 1. We can't use means to infer things like "most people in group 2 have more children than people in group 1."

Table 4-1 Distributions of Number of Children, Groups 1 and 2

Number of children	GROUP 1		GROUP 2	
	f	Percentage	f	Percentage
0	5	10%	22	11%
1	5	10	24	12
2	25	50	80	40
3	10	20	48	24
4	2	4	10	5
5	2	4	8	4
6	1	2	8	4
Total	50	100%	200	100%

Table 4-2 Incomes
of Five Men

Person	Income
John	$ 8,000
Jose	7,500
Harry	1,000,000
Bill	9,000
Curt	8,250
	$1,032,750

Notice also that the mean can be affected by extremely large or small numbers. Consider the distribution shown in Table 4-2. The mean income for this group is $1,032,750/5 or $206,550. If we leave Harry out, the mean is $8,187.50 (that is, $32,750/4). Including Harry in the group makes the mean much higher than most of the individual incomes and much lower than Harry's. Again, by definition, we can't use means as indicators of individual characteristics.

We can use a physical analogy to improve your understanding of the mean. Let's return to Table 4-1 and use the distribution of number of children for group 1. Imagine a long piece of wood laid out on the ground, whose length has been divided into six equal sections:

We ask each of our respondents to stand at the point that corresponds to his number of children (forcing a number of people to stand on others' heads, of course). Now, we're going to place a fulcrum under the beam in such a way that it exactly balances (with all our 50 people standing on it). Assume that everyone has the same weight. It would look something like this:

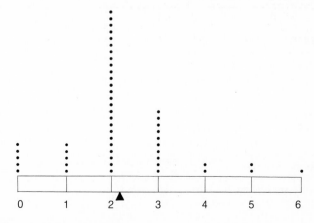

The point at which we'd have to place the fulcrum in order to balance the beam is exactly equal to the mean. You can now see how extreme scores affect the mean: one individual with, say, 50 children, will force us to move the fulcrum to the right. Even though it's just one person, the great distance produces considerable leverage, forcing us to move the fulcrum a disproportionate amount. If we added such a score to the distribution, the new mean would be 3.12, a shift that shows how much a single deviant case can affect a mean.

To summarize, a mean is a number that describes a group. It's calculated by adding up a bunch of numbers (one for each case in the group) and dividing by the number of numbers you added up. Notice that we've replaced an entire distribution with a single number. We can't help risking the loss of important information when we do this.

While the mean can be misleading in drawing conclusions about individuals, it's a very useful measure for characterizing groups. The mean *locates* a *distribution* along a continuum going from the lowest possible score to the highest. It allows us to compare groups on the basis of the amount of a characteristic possessed by groups, relative to their size.

Let's look at an example to see how means can be useful. In 1971 and 1974, the U.S. Bureau of the Census interviewed a representative sample of married American women. They asked the women how many children they already had and how many additional children they expected to have during their lifetime. Adding the two numbers together tells us the total number of children expected by these women. Table 4-3 shows the means, by age, race, and year.

Means allow us to compare the numbers of children expected by groups such as "whites" and "blacks," taking into account the size of the groups. There's a great deal we can tell from this table. For example, if

Table 4-3 Mean Total Number of Children Expected by Currently Married American Wives, 1971 and 1974, by Age and by Race

Age	WHITES		BLACKS		SPANISH		TOTAL	
	1971	1974	1971	1974	1971	1974	1971	1974
14–17	2.4	2.2	*	*	*	*	2.5	2.1
18–24	2.4	2.2	2.6	2.2	*	2.4	2.4	2.2
25–29	2.6	2.3	3.1	2.8	*	2.7	2.6	2.3
30–34	2.9	2.7	3.7	3.2	*	2.9	3.0	2.7
35–39	3.2	3.0	4.2	3.6	*	3.9	3.3	3.1
Total	2.7	2.5	3.3	2.9	*	2.9	2.8	2.5

* No reliable data available.
SOURCE U.S. Bureau of the Census, *Current Population Reports: Fertility Expectations of American Women: June 1974*, ser. P-20, no. 277, February 1975, table 1.

we look at the columns, we see that regardless of age or race, women in 1971 expected to have more children than women in 1974. Note that the absolute drop is greater for blacks than it is for whites.

We can also use this table to compare the expected fertility of whites and blacks in 1971, and of whites, blacks, and people of Spanish origin in 1974. In 1971, black fertility expectations were higher than those for whites (find the appropriate figures in the table and see if I'm right). By 1974 black expectations among 18- to 24-year-olds equaled those for whites, but were still larger at the older ages. In 1974, the expectations for Spanish people were lower than those for blacks at ages 25 to 29 and 30 to 34, greater at the other ages, and greater than those for whites at all ages.

You'll also note that older women have higher birth expectations than younger women (reading down the columns). This could mean two things. First, it might be that younger women will have fewer children than women who grew up in a different historical period (a generational effect); worries about overpopulation, for example, might be entering into fertility decisions. Second, it may also be that younger women tend to underestimate their total fertility (by overestimating their ability to control their fertility) and that older women, who are very close to the end of their fertile years, can make more accurate estimates. Only time will tell which of these factors produces these age patterns, but there is some evidence that younger women do, in fact, tend to underestimate their future fertility.

Did black and white fertility expectations grow more similar between 1971 and 1974? A handy way to find out is to take the ratio of black means to white means for 1971 and 1974. (See Table 4-4.)

Table 4-4 Total Expected Number of Children: Ratios of Black Means to White Means, United States, 1971 and 1974, by Age

Age	BLACK/WHITE RATIO	
	1971	**1974**
18–24	1.08	1.00
25–29	1.19	1.22
30–34	1.28	1.19
35–39	1.31	1.20
Total	1.22	1.16

SOURCE Table 4-3.

Notice first that the racial gap was strongest at the oldest ages in 1971, but not in 1974. Also, by 1974, the black expectations had moved closer to the white at all ages except 25 to 29. Overall (the "total" row), black expectations were closer to those of whites in 1974 than they were in 1971.

By using several techniques—cross tabulations, means, and ratios—we can answer a number of different questions clearly and definitively. In spite of the drawbacks of group measures, means are very valuable tools in social research.

Medians

An alternate way of summarizing an entire distribution is to find the "middle" of the distribution. For example, suppose we have the group 1 distribution in Table 4-1. If we lined everyone up, starting with those with the fewest children and working our way up, we'd have a list starting with 0, 0, 0, 0, 0, 1, 1, 1, 1, 1, 2, 2, . . . and ending with 5, 5, 6. The middle of this list would be the number of children had by the person halfway between 1 and 50, the person who has an equal number of people above him and below. With an even number of people (50) there is no such person, but we can use a point midway between the 25th and 26th persons, or the 25.5th person. Well, as we can see from the distribution, the 25th and 26th people each have two children. Therefore, the 25.5th person (imaginary, of course) can have only two children as well. If the two people had different numbers of children, the "middle" would be the average of the two. This number, the score corresponding to the middle case in an ordered distribution, is called the *median*.

If we had 51 people instead of 50, then the median case would have been the 26th person, since 25 lie below and 25 lie above.

As we did with the mean, we can use a balance-beam analogy to clarify the concept of median. We arrange our 50 people from high to low and ask them to sit on a beam that is just long enough to hold them all. Everyone has the same weight. Since we've uniformly increased the weight of the bar along its entire length, the fulcrum will always balance the beam when placed at its exact center. The median is the *score* of the person sitting right above the fulcrum:

If the highest person's score (a 6 above) is changed to 50, the median won't change at all *since his distance from the center of the beam remains the same.*

A second example illustrates how the value of the median, unlike that of the mean, is unaffected by extremely low or high scores. Consider the income distribution we had in Table 4-2; the median income is the income of the third person when we rank them from low to high (or from high to low):

$$
\begin{array}{r}
\$ \quad 7,500 \\
8,000 \\
8,250 \\
9,000 \\
1,000,000
\end{array}
$$

This income of $8,250 has as many cases above it as below and is therefore the median income. If we doubled the high income to $2 million, the median would still be $8,250; if we lowered the bottom income to $0, the median would remain the same. Only by changing the income of the middle person can we change the median without actually adding new cases to the distribution. Because the median is insensitive to extreme scores, it's considered a better measure of the "typical case" than the mean is. Remember, however, that the median, like the mean, is a summary descriptive measure that applies to groups, not individuals. In the final analysis, the best procedure is to look at *both* measures.

Two examples demonstrate quite clearly, I think, why means and medians should never be relied upon too heavily. If we have a distribution of income at one point in time (say the mean is $8,000 and the median is $7,500) and another distribution at a later time (with a mean of $8,000 and a median of $7,500), we might be tempted to conclude that income hasn't changed for people in the group. However, if the rich got richer and the poor got poorer, the gains and losses might cancel each other out (leaving the mean unchanged), and as long as the middle case remains unchanged, the median will remain constant. So, even though conditions are changing, the means and medians suggest stability.

Second, suppose we had two income distributions like these:

Income in dollars	Group 1	Group 2
0–1,000	111	0
1,001–2,000	110	0
2,001–3,000	7	0
3,001–5,000	4	190
5,001–7,000	9	83
7,001–9,000	6	0
9,001–10,000	160	0
Total	407	273

In both groups the mean income is $4,608. Can we use this to infer that both groups are equally well off? Group 1 has more people at the high end, but many more at the low end as well. Group 2 has no rich people, but it has no poor people, either. Clearly, the decision you reach cannot be based on means alone. We need to consider the entire distribution.

The Mode

The score or characteristic that is the most frequent in a distribution is called the *mode*. For example, the *modal* race in the United States is "white," the modal marital status for adults is "married." In some cases there is more than one characteristic frequently encountered; in such cases the distribution may be bimodal or multimodal. For example, if we look at the completed fertility of married women in the United States, we find that women tend to have two or three children much more than none, one, or more than three. Such a distribution is bimodal (2 and 3 each being a mode).

In general, the median is preferred whenever the distribution has a relatively small number of extreme scores (as in the case of income), since it's not affected by a relatively small number of very high or very low scores. If the distribution is symmetrical, of course, the two measures are equal and either can be used. The mean is usually used because reliable techniques for making statistical inferences about medians have not been developed. For purely descriptive purposes, however, the median is the best bet. With qualitative data, the mode is the only measure to use.

Measuring Variation:
Standard Deviations and Variance

An obvious but important fact about any distribution is that not all people are alike; there's variation. If we compare groups with each other, one difference we're likely to find is in the degree of homogeneity (or heterogeneity). Table 4-5 shows extreme examples. I think you can see that in group 1 there is much less diversity in prior arrest records than there is in group 2, even though the means are the same. How might we go about expressing this difference?

If we're going to talk about how heterogeneous groups are, we have to handle the question: "Heterogeneous relative to what?" There has to be some point relative to which we measure deviation. The most convenient point is the mean, since every distribution has one. One could always use the median, but in general practice this isn't done, primarily because using the mean leads to certain mathematical situations that help us in statistical inference (more on this later).

Table 4-5 Distribution of Number of Prior Arrests, Groups 1 and 2

Number of prior arrests	GROUP 1		GROUP 2	
	f	Percentage	f	Percentage
0	0	0%	20	10%
1	0	0	16	8
2	15	25	20	10
3	30	50	88	44
4	15	25	20	10
5	0	0	16	8
6	0	0	20	10
Total	60	100%	200	100%
Mean = 3.0			Mean = 3.0	

So, at some point we want to take the score of each person and note how far away it is from the mean (i.e., subtract one from the other). We call each of these differences a *deviation from the mean*. We could calculate a difference between each score and the mean and add up those differences, but there's a problem with this: *The sum of the differences between scores and the mean is always* zero. For example, consider the following distribution of people in group 2 taken from Table 4-5:

Group 2

(1) Number of prior arrests	(2) f	(3) Difference from mean, (1) − 3.0	(4) (2) × (3)
0	20	−3	−60
1	16	−2	−32
2	20	−1	−20
3	88	0	0
4	20	+1	+20
5	16	+2	+32
6	20	+3	+60
Total	200		0

Columns 1 and 2 look familiar. In column 3 we've subtracted the mean (3.0) from each possible score (0 through 6). But, we need to add up 200 such differences, one for each person. Since 20 people, for example, had a deviation of −3 from the mean, we need to add in a −3 twenty times (which is what we've done in column 4). As you can see, the sum of the deviations of all 200 people is zero.

The way we get around the problem of the pluses and minuses canceling each other out is to square each difference. What results is the following:

Group 2

(1)	(2)	(3)	(4) Squared	(5)
Arrests	*f*	Difference	Difference	(2) × (4)
0	20	−3	9	180
1	16	−2	4	64
2	20	−1	1	20
3	88	0	0	0
4	20	+1	1	20
5	16	+2	4	64
6	20	+3	9	180
Total	200			528

We've taken the difference between each score and the mean, squared the difference, and added up the 200 squared differences. If we do the same thing for group 1, we get the following:

Group 1

(1)	(2)	(3)	(4) Squared	(5)
Arrests	*f*	Difference	Difference	(2) × (4)
0	0	−3	9	0
1	0	−2	4	0
2	15	−1	1	15
3	30	0	0	0
4	15	+1	1	15
5	0	+2	4	0
6	0	+3	9	0
Total	60			30

Now, the sum of the squared differences is 528 for group 2 and only 30 for group 1. But we've again run into the problem of unequal numbers of cases (200 versus 60). To compensate for this, we divide each sum by the number of cases it's based on (that is, 30/60 for group 1 and 528/200 for group 2) and get two *average squared differences*, .5 for group 1 and 2.64 for group 2. These average squared differences of scores from the mean of a distribution are called *variances*. The square root of a variance is called a *standard deviation* (.71 for group 1 and 1.62 for group 2). The symbol for a variance in a *population* is the Greek letter sigma squared (σ^2); in a *sample* it's s^2. The corresponding symbols for standard deviation are the same, without the superscript 2.

OK, you ask, what's so special about the average squared difference, not to mention the square root of the average squared difference? First of all, although the actual numbers (.5, 2.64, .71, 1.62, etc.) have a statistical meaning, in practical usage they are most meaningful in comparison with each other. Thus we can say that group 1 is more homogeneous (smaller variance) than group 2 (larger variance).

Second, it just so happens that standard deviations and variances help us describe some very important theoretical distributions that we use in statistical inference. Because of this, we use these summary measures as comparative indicators of variability in distributions. When we look at theoretical distributions (Chap. 10), you'll see this in more detail.

As with means and medians, variances and standard deviations are descriptions of groups, not individuals.

It's very important that you understand the concept of variation in a distribution. If you find it difficult to explain in your own words, go back over what we've done. An understanding at this point will be very valuable later on.

Putting It Together:
Pictures and Numbers

The relevance of means, medians, and measures of variability to distributions is clearest when we use pictures. In Figs. 4-1 to 4-4, we have four of the infinite number of ways a variable such as income might be distributed. Notice that these are smoothed frequency polygons.

Along the horizontal axis we have income. The height of the curve at any point corresponds to the proportion of people who have that particular income level. Take some time to look at these graphs, because this way of presenting the distribution of a ratio-scale variable will become increasingly important as we go along.

Figure 4-1

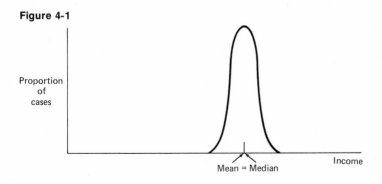

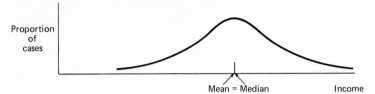

Figure 4-2

Notice that although the mean is the same in all four distributions, they don't look alike at all. In Fig. 4-1 everyone is tightly clustered around the mean, and there are equal numbers of people above and below the mean (i.e., the distribution is symmetrical); this tells us that the median and the mean will be equal. In Fig. 4-2 the distribution is also symmetrical, but the cases are more spread out than in Fig. 4-1. In Fig. 4-3, there's a big proportion of cases just below the mean and a small proportion of cases at the extremely high income levels. The distribution is loaded at the low end and stretches out at the high end. We call such a distribution *skewed;* this one is skewed to the right, or positively skewed, since the right end is the high end. Notice that here the median is below the mean. The mean is being pumped up by a few extreme scores while the median sticks to the center of the distribution. Finally, in Fig. 4-4 we have a distribution that is skewed to the left (or negatively skewed). Here the bulk of the cases lie above the mean and a smaller number stretch out below the mean. Here the median is above the mean, since the extremely low scores are pulling the mean down while the median once again follows the center of the distribution. All these distributions have only one hump, and we call them *unimodal.* Distributions can have two humps (*bimodal*) or many humps.

Roughly, the mean and median tell us where along the horizontal axis the distribution is located. For example, if we compared black and white income in the United States, the distributions might look like *a* and *b* in Fig. 4-5. Both distributions are skewed to the right, but the white distribution (*b*) is in general farther up the income scale than the black dis-

Figure 4-3

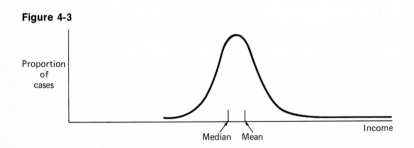

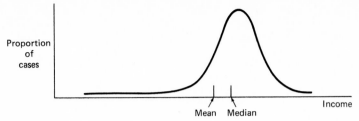

Proportion
of
cases

Income

Mean   Median

Figure 4-4

tribution (*a*). While there are certainly some blacks who make more money than some whites (where the distributions overlap), the whites as a group are better off than the blacks as a group. The difference between the group means ($6,000 versus $10,000) tells us that the white distribution is located to the right of the black, but *only if the distributions are similarly shaped*. If the white distribution were skewed to the right (as it is Fig. 4-5) and the black distribution skewed to the left, the picture might be like that shown in Fig. 4-6. What's happening here is that the black mean is being pulled down by extreme low scores and the white mean is being pulled up by extreme high scores. If we look at white and black *medians*, I think you can see that there wouldn't be much difference, since the centers (medians) of the black and white distributions aren't very far apart. The fact of the matter is that white and black incomes are distributed in much the same way (as in Fig. 4-5), but I hope you can see the trouble you can get into by inferring too much from means and medians in the absence of the entire distributions.

There are, of course, an infinite number of shapes distributions can assume. We've already mentioned skewness, and there is another characteristic that is worth our attention. All the distributions we've looked at in this chapter are without breaks in them; they're *continuous*. Suppose we're looking at a bar graph representing responses to an attitude on

Figure 4-5 Hypothetical comparison of incomes for blacks and whites in the United States using group means of $6,000 versus $10,000.

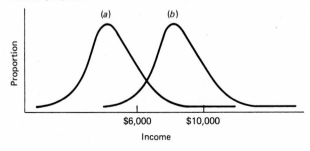

Proportion

(*a*)   (*b*)

$6,000 $10,000

Income

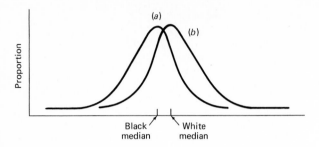

Figure 4-6 Skewed distributions of hypothetical incomes for blacks and whites.

which everyone is either in favor or opposed. In such a case, the middle of the distribution simply won't be there: all the cases will be at the polar extremes (Fig. 4-7).

The distribution in Fig. 4-7 is *discontinuous* because there's a break in the middle. To be discontinuous, the break need not be in the middle, but this often happens in the case of attitudes over which there's strong polarization in a population.

If you're feeling a bit confused at this point, there's good reason. There's a lot going on here, and it's hard to keep track at first. A distribution, as we've just seen, has three important characteristics, and no single one of them tells the whole story. First, there's the general position of the distribution along the horizontal axis (measured by means and medians). Then there's the shape of the distribution (symmetrical, skewed, etc.). Finally, the scores can be bunched up at the middle or spread out (the difference between Figs. 4-1 and 4-2, for example, mea-

Figure 4-7 Bar graph of a discontinuous distribution of a hypothetical attitude.

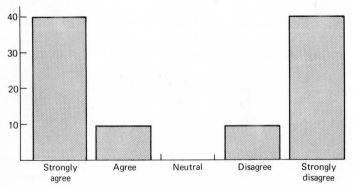

sured by standard deviations and variances). In order for means and medians to have real significance in making comparisons, the other features of the distributions (variability and shape) have to be pretty much the same. If they're not, then it's hard to interpret differences between means and medians. Often the distributions do look quite similar, but there's nothing inherent in means and medians that makes them so.

The problem we're running into here should be getting to be a familiar one by now. Summary measures make things neater, but we pay a price. We lose details that can alter the importance if not the nature of our conclusions. There's a constant, unresolvable tug-of-war going on between the desire to simplify data (called "data reduction") and the need to retain significant details.

The Range

Suppose you're a graduate of a 4-year college, and you're interested in a career in chemistry. You've majored in chemistry and have a job offer from a good laboratory. You've also received a fellowship from a good graduate school and could go on to get your Ph.D. A friend points out to you that with your training, the starting salary without your Ph.D. isn't much less than it would be if you had a Ph.D., and, besides, you'd be earning money instead of studying! Suppose the average salary for this position is $11,000 without a Ph.D. and $11,500 fresh out of graduate school with a Ph.D.

Before making your decision, there's an additional fact you might want to know about salaries. The means tell you where the two distributions lie on the money continuum. What if you found out that the highest salary you could ever hope to achieve without a Ph.D. was $15,000, but that *with* a Ph.D. you could go as high as $35,000? What we're referring to here is the *range* of salaries in a distribution. While you may start off just about as well as someone with a new Ph.D., there are constraints on how much money you can eventually earn.

The difference between the highest and lowest scores in a distribution is called a range. Although rarely used in the social sciences, it clearly provides one more valuable piece of information about a distribution.

Percentiles

A median is a *percentile*. The 60th percentile is that score which cuts off the lower 60 percent of the cases. The median is the 50th percentile, cutting off the lower half of the cases. The 90th percentile is the score that cuts off the lower 90 percent of the cases when we rank the cases from low to high. Thus, if the 90th percentile for income is $15,000, this means that 90 percent of the people make less than $15,000 and 10 percent make $15,000 or more.

However, there's a hitch. If my income is in the 80th percentile and your income is in the 90th, then you make more money than I do. We can't tell from this, however, how much lower my income is: we could be quite close in income, or we could be quite different from each other. It all depends on how the cases are distributed.

Trends

Means and medians are often used to study changes in a variable over time. There are two ways to measure trends. In the first, we gather information on a group of individuals at one point in time and then gather the same information on the *same* group at a later time. This is called a *panel* study.

In the second case, we gather information on a sample of individuals at one time and then gather the same information on a comparable sample of individuals at a later time. The two samples are usually unique, especially if the population is large. This is how the comparisons are made: if the interviews are 10 years apart, we can compare those 20 to 24 years old in the first sample with those 30 to 34 years old in the second. What we have is two representative samples of a population at two different points in time (minus those who have died or otherwise left the population). Since we don't have information on the same individuals, we can't look at change on an individual level. We can only compare changes on a group level (e.g., changes in the mean income of the population). We're thus confined to examining "net" change, without being able to determine the nature of the individual changes comprised in it.

Sometimes researchers will try to use the results of a single survey to draw conclusions about change over time. This is a mistake for the following reason. Suppose we find in a single survey that old people are politically more conservative than young people. This could be explained in two ways. First, the process of aging might make one more conservative (an aging effect). Second, the old people's relative conservatism might have resulted from the fact that they grew up in other historical circumstances than those of the young people in the sample. As long as we're confined to the results of a single sample, there's no way to determine which factor is operating.

As a final note, there's a critical problem associated with trying to describe the nature of a trend. Figure 4-8 shows a hypothetical measurement of the incidence of a disease at three points in time over a span of 20 years. It appears (and might be tempting to conclude) that conditions

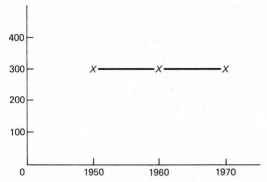

Figure 4-8 Hypothetical measurement of the incidence of disease X per 100,000 for 1950, 1960, and 1970.

have been completely stable over time. The danger lies in using only a few points in time to describe a trend. If we had taken measurements every 2 years (versus every 10), we might have found the distribution shown in Fig. 4-9.

By omitting the intervening years we overlooked an enormous amount of variation over time. Indeed, conditions have been quite erratic (note that the original three points are circled).

Whenever you encounter a table or graph that tries to describe a trend, make sure the points in time are not so widely spaced that considerable variation might be hidden. If you feel there is too much time between data points, then you must consider this in evaluating the findings.

Figure 4-9 Hypothetical measurement of the incidence of disease X per 100,000 for the years 1950 to 1970.

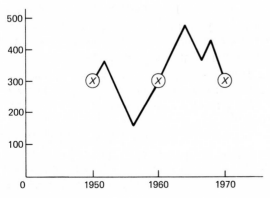

Here's an example of an effective presentation of trends. Table 4-6 shows the trends in birthrates for the United States from 1820 through 1974. You can see that birthrates have dropped a great deal in the last 150 years, from a high of 55.0 per 1,000 population to a current low of 15.0 births per 1,000 population. If we make a line graph, the trend is even easier to grasp (see Fig. 4-10). The rates dropped steadily between 1820 and 1860, paused for a decade (which included the Civil War), steadily declined for 70 years, rose after the Second World War (the famous "baby boom"), and continued the downward trend around 1960. Trends displayed in this manner are particularly useful because they provide us with a picture of history. If, for example, we looked at the death rates for the Soviet Union through the last 100 years, the devasta-

Table 4-6 United States Birthrates, 1820 to 1974

Year	Births per 1,000
1820	55
1830	53
1840	52
1850	48
1860	44
1870	45
1880	40
1890	36
1900	32
1910	30
1920	28
1930	21
1940	20
1950	24
1960	24
1970	18
1974	15

SOURCES Irene B. Taeuber and Conrad Taeuber, *People of the United States in the 20th Century* (Washington, D.C.; U.S. Department of Commerce, 1971), table VIII-1. Also, National Center for Health Statistics, *Monthly Vital Statistics Report*, vol. 22, no. 11, "Summary Report: Final Natality Statistics, 1970," and vol. 23; no. 12, "Births, Marriages, Divorces, and Deaths for 1974."

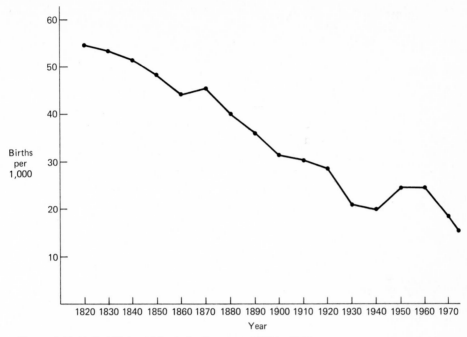

Figure 4-10 United States birthrate for the years 1820 to 1974.

tion caused by the Second World War would be clearly and dramatically shown by the sharp rise in the curve after 1940.

Summarizing

What I hope you're starting to get from all this is the idea that variables have distributions that can be described in several ways, and that once they're fully described, we can make comparisons between the whole distributions. But we have to be careful, because our methodology can get in the way. In later chapters we're going to talk about more distributions in terms of their means and variances and shapes, so it would be worth your while to spend some time thinking about distributions in the terms we've used.

You should be able to think about distributions in terms of their three describing characteristics (means and medians, variation, and shape). You should be able to explain to someone what these measures mean and how they can be misleading as well as informative. You should be able to explain the meaning of a percentile. In all cases, you should be developing an awareness of the need to examine entire distributions, rather than relying on summary measures alone.

Problems

Use the data below to answer Probs. 4-1 to 4-5.

	Number of close friends
Cleo	1
Bert	0
Ernie	2
Chris	3
Josh	2
Jesse	3
Joan	3
Charlotte	2
Paula	4
Emily	1
Paul	1

4-1 For the group, what is the mean number of friends?

4-2 For the group, what is the median number of friends?

4-3 What is the standard deviation for number of friends?

4-4 Is it valid to use the mean or the median to describe individuals in the group? Why or why not?

4-5 Describe the use of a standard deviation in descriptive statistics.

4-6 "The Morrisville schools were in the 30th percentile on standardized achievement test results. Clearly, Morrisville students are way behind the rest of the state as far as test performance is concerned."
   a. Do the data support the conclusion?
      Why or why not?

4-7 "In 1960 the median income of this group was $6,500; in 1965 the mean income was $8,000. We can conclude that the typical member of this group has enjoyed a substantial income increase during this period."
   a. Is the comparison between a median at one time and a mean at another valid? Why or why not? Under what circumstances is it valid?
   b. Is the conclusion about the "typical member" valid? Why or why not? Under what circumstances would it be valid?

4-8 "Even though the mean incomes for groups 1 and 2 are identical, the standard deviation in group 1 is twice that in group 2. This tells us that there is less homogeneity in income in group 1 than in group 2." Do you agree with the conclusions? Why or why not?

4-9 Describe the distributions given in Fig. 4-11 in terms of: modality, relation of mean to median, skewness, symmetry, continuity, variation.

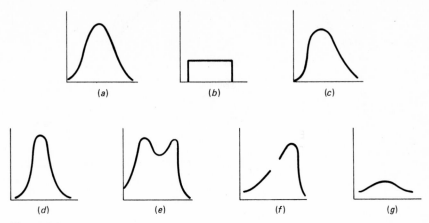

Figure 4-11

Suggested Readings

1 Blalock, Hubert M., Jr.: *Social Statistics*, 2d ed., chaps. 5 and 6. New York: McGraw-Hill Book Company, 1972.
2 Hays, William L.: *Statistics for the Social Sciences*, 2d ed., Secs. 6.1–6.7, 6.15–6.20, 6.25. New York: Holt, Rinehart and Winston, 1973.
3 Loether, Herman J., and Donald G. McTavish: *Descriptive Statistics for Sociologists*, chap. 5. Boston: Allyn and Bacon, 1974.
4 Mueller, John H., Karl F. Schuessler, and Herbert L. Costner: *Statistical Reasoning in Sociology*, 2d ed., chaps. 5 and 6. Boston: Houghton Mifflin Company, 1970.

5

elementary
probability
theory

If you're going to understand the rest of this book, it's important that you gain some familiarity with the basics of probability theory. Probability underlies the idea of relationships between variables and is crucial in statistical inference. Most of the ideas are comprehensible to someone with common sense, and this chapter has been written with that kind of person in mind. Be sure to take your time, study each idea, *thoroughly* familiarize yourself with new terms and symbols; and don't move on to a new idea before you've fully grasped previous ones. The material in the chapter is cumulative and you need to proceed patiently, step by step.

Some Key Terms

When you flip a coin, two things can happen (assuming it won't land on its edge): you'll get either heads or tails. In probability theory, each flip is called a *trial*, and each of the possible outcomes is called an *event*. If we draw one person at random from a group, and it's a man, then the event "drawing a man" has occurred. If we also note that the man is white, then the event "drawing a man *and* drawing a white" has occurred. This latter kind of event is called *joint* because it consists of more than one event ("drawing a man" and "drawing a white"). "Drawing a man" is a *simple event*.

When we're determining the probability of a particular event (e.g., drawing an ace from a deck of cards), it's conventional to call that event a *success* when it occurs and to label all other possible outcomes as *failures*. This has nothing to do with the terms as commonly used: being mugged during the coming year can be labeled a success, as winning the lottery can.

We can use two perspectives to understand the idea of a *probability*. Suppose we have ten people in a room, five men and five women. We're going to draw one person at random, and we're interested in the probability that our selection will be a woman. In this case, "drawing a woman" is called a success and "drawing a man" is called a failure. What's the probability of a success? There are ten people in the room, and thus ten possible outcomes. Five of these outcomes will be successes and five will be failures. The probability of success is defined as the number of potentially successful outcomes divided by the total number of possible outcomes, or 5/10 = .50. The probability of drawing a woman at random from a group of five men and five women is .50. By convention, the probability of an event is symbolized by $p(A)$, which reads "the probability of event A."

We can also define probability from a long-run perspective. Suppose we flip a fair coin over and over again. If the coin is fair, then a head is just as likely as a tail. If we flipped the coin twice, we could get two heads in a row; but if we flipped it 1,000 times, we'd expect the proportion of heads (and the proportion of tails) to be quite close to .50, since each outcome is equally likely. Thus, the probability of flipping a coin and getting a head is equal to the proportion of heads expected in the long run.

When we flip a coin once (or pick a single person from a group) and say, "The probability is .50 of getting a head on this flip" (or "The probability is .12 of drawing a nonwhite person"), what we're really saying is "If I flipped this coin repeatedly, in the long run I'd expect the proportion of heads to be .50" (or "If I repeatedly drew people from this group, in the long run I'd expect the proportion of blacks to be .12"). Behind all statements about the probability of a single event lies the idea of long-run probabilities.

The Basic Types of Probabilities

In Table 5-1 we have the cross tabulation of·three variables—educational attainment, attitudes toward racial segregation (favoring versus not favoring), and region of residence (south versus nonsouth). The rest of this chapter will use these data for illustration, so begin by going over the table carefully, making sure you understand what the labels and numbers refer to.

Table 5-1 contains seven simple events: having a grammar school education, high school education, or college education; being in favor or

Table 5-1 Favoring Racial Segregation, by Highest Level of Educational Attainment and Region of Residence, United States, 1968

Educational attainment	SOUTH			NONSOUTH			TOTAL		
	Favors	Doesn't favor	Total	Favors	Doesn't favor	Total	Favors	Doesn't favor	Total
Grammar school	49	49	98	39	101	140	88	150	238
High school	44	114	158	59	363	422	103	477	580
College	14	92	106	10	245	255	24	337	361
Total	107	255	362	108	709	817	215	964	1,179 = N

SOURCE *American National Election Study*, conducted by the Political Behavior Program, Institute for Social Research, University of Michigan, Ann Arbor, Mich., 1968.

not being in favor of racial segregation; and living in the south or living in the nonsouth. To calculate the probabilities for these simple events, we divide the number of possible outcomes that constitute successes by the total number of possible outcomes. The probabilities for the seven simple events are given in Table 5-2.

Before you go any further, satisfy yourself that you understand where the numerators and denominators in the calculations came from. This is most important.

We've divided the events into three groups, one group for each variable. Within each group, the events are *mutually exclusive*, which means that it's impossible for more than one to occur at the same time (we can't select a person who both went to college and never went beyond grammar school). The events in *different* groups, however, are not mutually exclusive (because logically we could draw one person who was a college graduate, in favor of segregation, and living in the south).

When we have a group of events that exhausts the logical possibilities (i.e., each person is included in one and only one event) and when we have the probabilities associated with each event, then we have what is known as a *probability distribution*. Note that the probabilities for the simple events must sum to 1.000 in a probability distribution.

We calculated each of the simple-event probabilities by dividing a *marginal* (e.g., the total number of southerners) by the total number of people in the sample. We calculated the probability of living in the south without specifying any other details (such as being in favor of racial segregation). Because we placed no *conditions* on the event, these probabilities are called *unconditional probabilities*.

We might have calculated the probability of being in favor of racial segregation *given* that one lives in the south. When we say, "given that one lives in the south," we're going to consider *only* southerners in calculating the probability of favoring racial segregation.

Table 5-2 Simple-Event Probabilities
from Table 5-1

p(grammar school)	= 238/1,179 =	.2019
p(high school)	= 580/1,179 =	.4919
p(college)	= 361/1,179 =	.3062
		1.0000
p(favors segregation)	= 215/1,179 =	.1824
p(doesn't favor)	= 964/1,179 =	.8176
		1.0000
p(lives in south)	= 362/1,179 =	.3070
p(lives in nonsouth)	= 817/1,179 =	.6930
		1.0000

There are 362 southerners in the sample, and of these, 107 favor racial segregation. Therefore, the probability of favoring racial segregation *given* that one is a southerner is 107/362 = .2956 (be sure you see where these numbers came from and why we used them). The probability of being in favor of segregation given that one lives outside the south is 108/817 = .1322. Thus, southerners are more likely than nonsoutherners to be in favor of racial segregation.

These last probabilities were *conditional* on a second factor (residence) and are therefore called *conditional probabilities*. The general symbolic form for conditional probabilities is $p(A|B)$ which means "the probability of event A (being in favor of racial segregation) given event B (that one lives in the south)." The vertical line means "given."

Just as there can be conditional probabilities, there can be conditional probability distributions. If we'd calculated the first two probability distributions in Table 5-2 for southerners only, then we'd have two conditional probability distributions (conditional on living in the south). Table 5-3 shows the unconditional probability distribution for education and two conditional probability distributions, one conditional on living in the south, the second conditional on living in the nonsouth.

This should look familiar to you. All we've done is to cross tabulate education and region of residence, and compute the proportional distribution down the columns.

Before going on to the next section, be *sure* you understand (and can illustrate with examples) the following: trial, simple event, joint event, success, failure, probability, unconditional probability, conditional probability, mutually exclusive events, nonmutually exclusive events, unconditional probability distribution, and conditional probability distribution.

Joint Probabilities

Suppose we want to calculate the probability of drawing from our sample a person who went to college *and* favors racial segregation.

Table 5-3 Probability Distribution for Highest Level of Educational Attainment, for the Entire Sample (Unconditional), Conditional on Living in the South, and Conditional on Living Outside the South, United States, 1968

Educational attainment	South	Nonsouth	Total
Grammar school	.2707	.1714	.2019
High school	.4365	.5165	.4919
College	.2928	.3121	.3062
Total	1.0000	1.0000	1.0000

We're looking for the probability of a joint event, and this is one example of a *joint probability*. A joint probability is denoted by the symbol $p(A,B)$, which reads "the probability of event A *and* event B occurring."

There are 24 people in the sample who both went to college and favor racial segregation (check Table 5-1 and see for yourself). There are 1,179 people in the sample. Therefore, we can use the table directly to calculate the joint probability: $24/1,179 = .0204$.

There's another way of calculating joint probabilities. We proceed in two steps: first, the probability of being a college graduate is $361/1,179$; now, *given* a college education, the conditional probability of favoring racial segregation is $24/361$. The probability for the *joint* event is the probability of being a college graduate multiplied by the probability of favoring racial segregation *given* that one is a college graduate:

$$p(A,B) = p(A) * p(B|A) = \left(\frac{361}{1,179}\right)\left(\frac{24}{361}\right) = \frac{24}{1,179} = .0204$$

where event A is "being a college graduate" and event B is "favoring racial segregation." This is the same answer we arrived at above. The joint probability is thus the product of an unconditional and a conditional probability. Note that

$$p(A) * p(B|A) = p(B) * p(A|B)$$

$$\left(\frac{361}{1,179}\right)\left(\frac{24}{361}\right) = \left(\frac{215}{1,179}\right)\left(\frac{24}{215}\right) = .0204$$

Therefore,

$$p(A,B) = p(A) * p(B|A) = p(B) * p(A|B)$$

Suppose now that we wanted to draw *two* people from the sample. How would we calculate the probabilities of the different possible outcomes? Here we have another kind of joint probability, $p(A,B)$, where, for example, event A is "drawing a high school person on the first draw" and event B is "drawing a grammar school person on the second draw."

The situation here is comparable to the previous one, but it is complicated by the fact that there are two ways of drawing two people from the group. First, we could draw one person, note his education, *replace* him, and then draw a second person. Or we could draw two people in a row *without replacing* the first person. In the first case, the first person drawn has a chance of being drawn a second time; in the second case, once drawn, the first person is not considered on subsequent selections.

First, let's consider drawing them *with replacement*. What's the probability of drawing a high school person *followed* by the selection of a person who never went beyond grammar school?

$$p(A,B) = p(A) * p(B|A)$$

The probability of drawing a high school person on the first draw is

$$p(A) = \frac{580}{1,179} = .4919$$

After the first selection, we return the chosen person to the sample and make another selection. By replacing the first draw, we've returned the sample to its initial composition. *Therefore, the outcome of the first draw in no way affects the outcome of the second.* This means that

$$p(B|A) = p(B) = \frac{238}{1,179} = .2019$$

The above formula is a very important one in probability and its social science applications, for it defines *independence* between events. When occurrence of event *A* in no way alters the probability of occurrence of event *B*, then the two events are *independent*.

The probability of drawing a high school person and *then* drawing a person who never went beyond grammar school, *with replacement*, is thus

$$p(A)p(B|A) = (.919)(.2019) = .0993$$

What if we had made our selections *without* replacement? The probability of drawing a high school person on the first draw remains the same: $p(A) = 580/1,179 = .4919$. The probability of drawing a grammar school person on the second draw, *given* that we've removed the high school person from the population, is $p(B|A) = 238/1,178 = .2020$, slightly higher than the unconditional probability of .2019. The probability is higher because the number of people available for selection on the second draw (the denominator) has been reduced by 1. The joint probability is $p(A)p(B|A) = .0994$, slightly higher than the joint probability selecting *with* replacement.

With large groups, the denominators of the probabilities will be so large that selecting without replacement won't have a great effect on the probabilities (as you can see from the above example). If, however, the groups are quite small, the differences between probabilities associated with replacement and nonreplacement will be appreciable, because the reduction of the denominator by one case will be proportionately larger.

Note that if B is independent of A, then A is also independent of B. Knowing that we selected a grammar school person on the second draw doesn't help us at all in predicting what happened on the first draw. Therefore,

$$p(A|B) = p(A) = .4919$$

By defining independence in this way, we can then look at pairs of events in Table 5-1 and see if they're independent. For example, is being in favor of racial segregation (A) independent of being a southerner (B)? If we know the respondent is a southerner, does this help us predict his racial attitude?

Without knowing region of residence, the probability of being in favor of racial segregation is $p(A) = 215/1,179 = .1824$. If we know the respondent lives in the south, however, the *conditional* probability is $p(A|B) = 107/362 = .2956$ (again, be sure you see where these numbers come from and why). The conditional probability is quite different from the unconditional probability and the two events are, therefore, not independent. They are *dependent*.

Consider another example. The probability of a newborn child being a male is approximately .50; the probability of a newborn being black is approximately .10. So, for a hypothetical group of newborns, the cross tabulation between sex and race might look something like that shown in Table 5-4. Whites and blacks have the same distribution by sex at birth. Thus, knowing that a newborn is white doesn't improve our ability to predict its sex, and vice versa. For example, the probability of a newborn being female (A) *given* that it's white (B) is

$$p(A|B) = \frac{90}{180} = .5000$$
$$= p(A)$$

Therefore, the two events are independent of one another.

Notice what happens to the formula for a joint probability when the two events are independent:

$$p(A,B) = p(A) * p(B|A)$$
$$= p(A) * p(B)$$

since, when independent, the probability of B conditional on A is equal to the probability of B unconditional on A: $p(B|A) = p(B)$. The formula for

Table 5-4 Sex by Race for Newborn
Children (Hypothetical Data)

| | RACE | | |
Sex	White	Black	Total
Male	90	10	100
Female	90	10	100
Total	180	20	200 = N

a joint event under conditions of independence is an important one to understand. Be sure you do before moving on.

We can calculate the probability for a joint event involving more than two events. For example, consider the probability of drawing someone who lives in the nonsouth (*A*), went to college (*B*), and doesn't favor racial segregation (*C*). From Table 5-1 we can see directly that there are 245 people with this combination of characteristics. The probability of drawing such a person at random is thus 245/1,179 = .2078. We could obtain the same result by extending our formula for joint events to cover three events:

$$p(A,B,C) = p(A) * p(B|A) * p(C|A,B)$$

First, go through the formula and be sure you can translate it into words (and understand your translation).

The first two terms on the right are familiar:

$$p(A) = \frac{817}{1,179} = .6930$$

$$p(B|A) = \frac{255}{817} = .3121$$

The third term is the probability of not favoring racial segregation given that one is a nonsoutherner who went to college. There are 255 nonsoutherners who went to college, of whom 245 do not favor segregation. Therefore, $p(C|A,B) = 245/255 = .9608$. The joint probability is the product of these three probabilities:

$$p(A,B,C) = (.6930)(.3121)(.9608) = .2078$$

which is exactly what we got above.

Adding Probabilities

Suppose we're going to select one person at random from our sample, and we're interested in the probability that our selected person is *either* a southern resident or in favor of racial segregation (in probability, the word or is *inclusive*, meaning that we'd accept as a success someone who had *both* characteristics). We first find the number of people who constitute a success; there are 362 residents of the south, and there are 215 people who favor racial segregation (find these numbers in Table 5-1 and confirm for yourself that I've used the right ones). We might be tempted to add these numbers together to get the number of potential successes, but there's a problem here: the 107 people who *both* favor segregation *and* live in the south *were counted twice*. They're included in the "southern" group *and* in the "favors" group. Since we've counted them twice, we have to subtract them from the total so that they'll be counted only once. The total number of potential successes is, therefore, $362 + 215 - 107 = 470$. The probability of drawing someone who is either a southern resident, in favor of segregation, or both, is $470/1,179 = .3986$.

You can see this more clearly if we calculate the probability in another way. We want the total number of possible successes. First, we count the number of southern residents: there are 362. We also want the number of people who favor segregation. Since we've already counted the southerners who favor segregation, we need only count the non-southerners in favor: 108. The total number of potential successes is thus $362 + 108 = 470$, which is what we got above.

In probability, the probability of event A or event B occurring is denoted by the symbol $p(A$ or $B)$. The formula reflects what we've done above:

$$p(A \text{ or } B) = p(A) + p(B) - p(A,B)$$

or the probability of being a southerner, or in favor of segregation, or both is the probability of being a southerner *plus* the probability of being in favor of segregation *minus* the probability of being *both*.

Now, suppose we wanted to calculate the probability of being either someone who stopped his schooling at high school graduation or a person with college experience. In this case, it's impossible to select a person with both characteristics since they're mutually exclusive. Thus, $p(A,B)$ is zero and the formula becomes

$$p(A \text{ or } B) = p(A) + p(B) = \frac{580}{1,179} + \frac{361}{1,179} = .7981$$

This holds for any two mutually exclusive events.

Expected Values

Suppose we're drawing a sample of 1,000 Americans and we know the probability of being white is .88. This means each selection carries with it a probability of being white (.88) and a probability of being nonwhite (.12). The first two selections might both be nonwhite, which is not in line with the actual probabilities. However, the long-run nature of probabilities is reflected in a mathematical law called the law of large numbers. It states that as we make more and more selections (more trials), the proportion of people with a given characteristic will approach the actual proportion in the population. Thus, with two people the proportion of nonwhites might be 1.00; but with 100 it's more likely to be closer to .12; and with 1,000 it's likely to be very close to .12.

If we draw 1,000 people at random, the expected proportion of nonwhites is .12. Therefore, the *expected value* for the *number* of nonwhites is $(.12)(1,000) = 120$. In general, if we make N selections and the probability of success is p on any one selection, then the expected number of successes is $p * (N)$. Thus, if we make only 10 selections, we'd expect to get $(.12)(10) = 1.2$ nonwhites and 8.8 whites, or, rounding off, 1 nonwhite and 9 whites. Since expected values are based on long-run probabilities, we wouldn't expect to achieve one in a small number of trials.

Betting provides an easily grasped application of expected values. Suppose we flip a fair coin. If it comes up heads, I pay you \$5; if it comes up tails, you pay me \$5. You'll expect to lose \$5 half the time [an expected value of $(.50)(-\$5) = -\$2.50$]; you'll also expect to win \$5 half the time [an expected value of $(.50)(+\$5) = +\$2.50$]. In the long run your expected value is $\$2.50 - \$2.50 = 0$. In other words, you'd expect to break even.

In the *short* run, however, you might not do so well (nor might I). You might get three tails in a row, losing \$15 to me. In Las Vegas, the long-run odds are in favor of the house. Over a period of time (and thousands of betting "trials") the house wins much more than it loses. When someone walks in and "breaks the bank," he's demonstrating that probabilities apply *in the long run* and that the short run may yield outcomes that aren't in line with expected values. Casinos are living proof, however, that probabilities work in the long run.

Conclusion

Understanding the rest of this book will be helped greatly by understanding this chapter. You owe it to yourself to get to a point where you feel comfortable with elementary probability and can do the problems at the end of this chapter. As you do these problems, take your time and be sure you understand the question before you dive into the data. *Think* about the problem, and decide not only what you're going to do, but why you're going to do it, *before* you do it.

Problems

In answering Probs. 5-1–5-7 use the data in Table 5-5.

5-1 How many simple events are there in this table? What are they? Compute their probabilities.

5-2 How many joint events are there in this table? What are they? Compute their probabilities using the appropriate formula; then verify your answer by using the table directly.

5-3 We're going to draw two people from this group and note their sex. Make a list of the possible outcomes, being sure to specify the order in which the events occur. Now, for each possible outcome, calculate the probability, using the appropriate formula. Verify your result by using the table directly.

5-4 If we draw one person at random from this group, what's the probability that our selection will be either a male or someone in favor of racial segregation? Use the appropriate formula and then verify your answer by using the table directly.

5-5 Explain the short-run and long-run approaches to probability and give an example of each.

5-6 Define a "conditional probability distribution" and cite an example from the table above.

5-7 Is "being a male" independent of "being in favor of racial segregation"? Be sure to explain what is meant by "independence" in this context.

5-8 If the probability of drawing a male (event M) from the population of newborns is .51, of 1,000 newborns, what's the *expected value* for the number of newborn males?

Table 5-5 Favoring Racial Segregation, by Sex, United States, 1968

	Sex	(C) Favors	(D) Doesn't favor	Total
(A)	Female	13	53	66
(B)	Male	9	44	53
	Total	22	97	$119 = N$

Suggested Readings

1 Blalock, Hubert M., Jr.: *Social Statistics*, 2d ed., chap. 9 and chap. 10, sec. 10.1. New York: McGraw-Hill Book Company, 1972.
2 Feller, William: *An Introduction to Probability Theory and Its Applications*, 2d ed., vol. 1. New York: John Wiley & Sons, 1957.
3 Hays, William L.: *Statistics*, chaps. 1–5. New York: Holt, Rinehart and Winston, 1963.
4 Kemeny, John G., J. Laurie Snell, and Gerald L. Thompson: *Introduction to Finite Mathematics*, 2d ed., chap. IV. Englewood Cliffs, N.J.: Prentice-Hall, 1966.
5 Loether, Herman J., and Donald G. McTavish: *Inferential Statistics for Sociologists*, chap. 2. Boston: Allyn and Bacon, 1974.
6 Mueller, John H., Karl F. Schuessler, and Herbert L. Costner: *Statistical Reasoning in Sociology*, chap. 8. Boston: Houghton Mifflin Company, 1961.
7 Look through the collection of illustrative articles in Tanur, Judith M., et al. (eds.): *Statistics: A Guide to the Unknown*, p. xxi of the index. San Francisco: Holden-Day, 1972.

6

relationships
between two
variables

The building blocks of social science are concepts and ideas that specify how those concepts are related to each other. These ideas and theoretical frameworks are devised to answer questions of importance to the researcher, such as "Why do men die younger than women?" "Why do blacks make less money than whites?" "Are old people more likely to be prejudiced than young people?" Each of these questions involves concepts (race, income, age, and prejudice), and the questions deal with the ways in which these concepts are related to each other. In each case, the research question suggests that people with one characteristic (e.g., being a male) tend to have another characteristic (e.g., young age at death) more than other kinds of people (e.g., females).

When we come to the problem of empirical research, we've seen that it's necessary to operationalize our concepts and turn them into *variables*, which, as measurement instruments, specify how to observe the characteristic (interview questions, direct observation, etc.) and how to interpret and categorize the results.

There are several ways to define the idea of a relationship between two variables, two of which we'll describe here. Consider, for example, the variables "occupation" (defined as "white-collar" and "blue-collar") and "being in favor of racial segregation" (defined in terms of responses to the question: "In general, are you in favor of racial segregation, racial desegregation, or something in between?"). What would it mean to say that these two variables are or are not related to each other?

We could look at it in terms of the general question: "Do white-collar people differ from blue-collar people in their support for racial segregation?" Or because people differ in their occupations, does this go along with a tendency to differ in their racial views, and does this tendency take on some meaningful, identifiable pattern? Let's look at the data and see what this means (Table 6-1).

Before going on, you should recognize this type of table as something you've seen before (in Chap. 3) and familiarize yourself with it thoroughly. Read the title, be sure you understand what the variables stand for, and note the direction of percentaging. *Before starting the next paragraph*, go through the table and determine what each percentage means, which percentages we can legitimately compare with which, and what those comparisons tells us about occupation and this racial-attitude variable. *Stop* reading until you've done this.

Now that you've done some analysis of your own, let's see how your reading compares with mine. We percentaged the table across the rows: within each category of occupation we calculated the percentage distribution for the racial attitude. This means we can compare the racial attitudes of white- and blue-collar workers. We *cannot* use this table as it is to compare the occupational composition of people with different racial attitudes. If you don't see why this is true, then go back to Chap. 3 and brush up.

Table 6-1 shows that white-collar workers are less likely than blue-collar workers to favor racial segregation (11.1 percent versus 25.0 percent). There is, therefore, a *relationship* between one's occupation and the *tendency* to favor racial segregation as measured in this study (or the social attitude is *dependent* on occupation). This does not mean that one's occupation *causes* racial attitudes. These data show a statistical relationship; the data cannot tell us what that relationship means. Only

Table 6-1 Support for Racial Segregation by Occupation, United States, 1968

	SUPPORT FOR RACIAL SEGREGATION			
Occupation	**Favors**	**Doesn't favor**	**Total**	*N*
White-collar	11.1%	88.9	100.0%	422
Blue-collar	25.0%	75.0	100.0%	332
Total	17.2%	82.8	100.0%	754

SOURCE *American National Election Study*, conducted by the Political Behavior Program, Institute for Social Research, University of Michigan, Ann Arbor, Mich., 1968.

sound theoretical reasoning and controlled experiments can deal with the question of interpretation.

What would it mean to have *no* relationship? If the two variables were not related to each other, then blue- and white-collar workers, while differing in occupations, would not differ in their racial attitudes. Thus, the percentages of blue- and white-collar workers favoring racial segregation would be identical.

Table 6-2 is hypothetical; given the marginal distribution (i.e., keeping the same total number of people with each of the characteristics), how would the *cells* of the table look if there were no relationship between the two variables (i.e., how would the combinations of characteristics be distributed?). In this table, there are no differences between white- and blue-collar attitudes, and the variables are *independent* of each other. Notice that when there is independence, the distribution of racial attitudes within each occupation is identical with that for the entire group (total). Do you know why this is always true? (Think about it; there's nothing tricky here. Try to imagine its *not* being true.)

The idea of a relationship between two variables thus rests on the ideas of dependence and independence. It may help your understanding to approach these latter two from a probability perspective (be sure you feel comfortable with conditional probabilities before reading on). If we put Table 6-1 in the form of proportions, we then have probabilities (Table 6-3).

What does this table tell us? First, the probability of being in favor of racial segregation is .172 and that of not being in favor is .828 (be sure you see this from the table and understand why it's true). What about the cells of the table? These cells represent the probability of being either in favor or not in favor of racial segregation *given* the fact that one is either a white- or a blue-collar worker. When we calculated proportions within an occupational category (such as white-collar workers), we restricted ourselves to that group of people. Since those probabilities (.111 and .889) apply only to white-collar workers, they are

Table 6-2 Support for Racial Segregation by Occupation, Assuming No Relationship (Hypothetical)

Occupation	SUPPORT FOR RACIAL SEGREGATION		Total	N
	Favors	**Doesn't favor**		
White-collar	17.2%	82.8	100.0%	422
Blue-collar	17.2%	82.8	100.0%	332
Total	17.2%	82.8	100.0%	754

Table 6-3 Support for Racial Segregation by Occupation, United States, 1968

| | SUPPORT FOR RACIAL SEGREGATION | | | |
Occupation	Favors	Doesn't favor	Total	N
White-collar	.111	.889	1.00	422
Blue-collar	.250	.750	1.00	332
Total	.172	.828	1.00	754

conditional on that characteristic. The marginals (bottom row) thus tell us how likely *anyone* is to favor racial segregation; the cells tell us how white- and blue-collar workers compare in their tendencies to favor segregation. The rows in the table are therefore probability distributions, one for each of two occupational groups and one from everyone combined.

When the probability distribution of the dependent variable (favoring segregation) is the same for each category of the independent variable, then the two variables are independent of each other. This is exactly what we have in Table 6-2. This is called *stochastic independence.*

Go back and look at Table 6-2 for a moment. Notice again that when the variables are independent, the percentages within occupation are the same as the row for everyone (total). In terms of probabilities, this is the crucial fact in defining statistical independence: the total percentage (17.2 percent) is the same as the comparable percentage for each occupational group; but the cells are *conditional* probabilities (the probability of favoring segregation *given* that one is white-collar, for example) and the marginal is an *unconditional* probability. *Thus, two variables are independent of each other if and only if the conditional probabilities are the same as the unconditional probabilities.*

The probabilistic definition of independence is not simply another way of looking at things (although at this point it may seem like that to you). When we talk about making inferences about relationships in the population, you will see that this definition is the keystone of one of the most frequently used statistical tools. So, it's to your advantage to get a firm grasp on it now; let it sink in and not catch you by surprise later on.

Types and Characteristics of Relationships

Relationships have two statistical characteristics. The *direction* of a relationship refers to the pattern by which the probability distributions differ from one another. For example, if we examine the relationship between income and education, we find that the higher education is, the higher income tends to be. In such a case, the relationship is *positive*. However, if we look at the relationship between educational achievement and the number of siblings in the respondent's family, we find that people who come from larger families tend to spend fewer years in school. Here high values on one variable (family size) tend to go with low values on the other (years in school) and the relationship is *negative*. A third type of relationship is found when we relate social class to the incidence of large families. Middle-class people are the least likely to have large families; both lower- and upper-class people are relatively more likely to have large families. Thus, as class level goes higher, the likelihood of large families goes down but then up again. Such a relationship is curvilinear, as you can see in Fig. 6-1.

The fourth type of relationship is the most difficult to interpret and can best be characterized as messy. This happens when there is a relationship (i.e., the probability distributions are different across categories of the independent variable), but there's no neat pattern to the differences. Suppose we gathered data on educational attainment and attitudes toward a political candidate, the latter measured as "in favor" and "opposed" and the former measured in years of schooling. Suppose we get the results shown in Table 6-4a.

It would be impossible to give any quick description of this relationship other than "erratic." Support for candidate A goes up with schooling for a while, then sharply down, up, and then down again. While we would be accurate in saying that it's curvilinear, you can see that the curve is going to have a lot of bumps in it, making it difficult to characterize the relationship in substantively meaningful terms. Sometimes the "bumps and squiggles" in relationships are very small and can be ignored, but in this instance there's clearly something messy going on and we can't make statements like "support increases with education." To say the relationship is curvilinear doesn't tell us anything at all. In such cases, the author has to dive in and describe differences

Figure 6-1 Incidence of large families by social class.

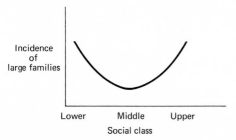

Table 6-4a Attitudes toward Candidate A by years of Schooling

		ATTITUDE TOWARD A			
Years of schooling		**In favor**	**Opposed**	**Total**	*N*
Elementary	0–4	20%	80	100%	100
	5–7	25%	75	100%	90
	8	30%	70	100%	150
High school	1–3	10%	90	100%	130
	4	50%	50	100%	150
College	1–3	75%	25	100%	100
	4+	35%	65	100%	50
Total		35%	65	100%	770

between levels of schooling in detail. There's no shorthand substitute for this (except to call it irregular or messy and give up).

One could clean up the mess by dichotomizing the education variable into "less than high school graduate" and "high school graduate or higher." We'd then get the results shown in Table 6-4b. This table shows a positive relationship between education and political attitudes, but it does so at the cost of hiding the true messy relationship in Table 6-4a. This is *not* a legitimate way to handle an irregular relationship between two variables. If a relationship is already negative or positive, it's acceptable to dichotomize; it's never acceptable to dichotomize in order to commit what amounts to a misrepresentation of the relationship's direction.

You should be particularly alert for this form of abuse. When you encounter a table in which a clearly multicategory variable has been dichotomized, you should ask yourself, "Would the relationship look different if the variable had not been dichotomized? Would the strength be the same? The direction?" It's the author's responsibility to justify such practices, to demonstrate that he isn't thereby hiding any messes that complicate (or contradict!) the conclusions drawn from the data.

The *strength* of a relationship refers to the degree to which the proba-

Table 6-4b Attitudes toward Candidate A by Educational Attainment

	ATTITUDE			
Educational attainment	**In favor**	**Opposed**	**Total**	*N*
Less than high school graduate	21%	79	100%	470
High school graduate or higher	56%	44	100%	300
Total	35%	65	100%	770

SOURCE Table 6-4a.

Table 6-5 Support for Racial Segregation by Occupation, (Hypothetical)

Occupation	RACIAL SEGREGATION		Total	N
	Favors	Doesn't favor		
White-collar	0%	100	100%	422
Blue-collar	39%	61	100%	332
Total	17%	83	100%	754

bility distributions differ from each other. Going back again to Table 6-1, suppose the relationship looked like that shown in Table 6-5.

Here the difference between white- and blue-collar workers is much stronger than it was before (i.e., occupational group makes a much greater difference in racial attitudes) and the relationship between the two variables is thereby stronger than it was in Table 6-1. Later we'll see that sometimes the direction of the relationship (especially if it's curvilinear) can confuse the determination of how strong the relationship is.

The statistical literature contains many *numerical measures of association* that reflect strength of relationship; in addition, there are two ways of characterizing the direction of relationships. In both cases, a great deal depends on the nature of the variables involved, specifically the scale of measurement they represent. There are different measures of association for relationships using nominal-scale variables, ordinal variables, and ratio- and interval-scale variables (not to mention relationships involving two variables of different scales, such as one nominal and one ratio); in addition, the nominal case presents a problem when it comes to characterizing relationships as negative, positive, or curvilinear. In the next three sections we'll talk about relationships involving different kinds of variables, introduce you to some of the more commonly used measures of association, and through examples show you more about the directions relationships can take.

Relationships between
Nominal-Scale Variables

In the last section we encountered an example of a relationship between two nominal-scale variables, occupational group and being in favor of segregation. (See top of p. 88.)

First let's talk about the direction of the relationship. With nominal-scale variables, the description of direction is arbitrary, and it doesn't matter how we do it as long as we're consistent. When the variables are

Support for Racial Segregation by Occupation,
United States, 1968

SUPPORT FOR
RACIAL
SEGREGATION

Occupation	Favors	Doesn't favor	Total	N
White-collar	11.1%	88.9	100.0%	422
Blue-collar	25.0%	75.0	100.0%	332
Total	17.2%	82.8	100.0%	754

nominal, the idea of one variable taking on greater values as the other increases or decreases doesn't make much sense, since the variables don't measure characteristics in quantitative terms. We handle this by arbitrarily assigning ordinal characteristics to the categories of the two variables (usually in the form of pluses and minuses whenever there are only two categories). (See Table 6-6.)

In this context, a positive relationship is one in which pluses tend to go with pluses and minuses tend to go with minuses; a negative relationship has pluses tending to go with minuses and minuses tending to go with pluses (make sure this is clear to you before going on). In our example, white-collar workers (+) have a greater tendency than blue-collar workers (−) to not favor segregation (−). Thus pluses tend to go with minuses and the relationship is negative. We could say, "There's a negative relationship between being white-collar and favoring segregation." An equivalent description would be: "There's a *positive* relationship between being *blue*-collar and favoring segregation." We get this by simple assigning different signs to the occupational categories (giving a + to blue-collar and a − to white-collar). We then have pluses going with pluses and minuses going with minuses. The *results* are the same; what varies is the use of "positive" and "negative" to artificially

Table 6-6 Support for Racial Segregation by Occupation, United States, 1968

	RACIAL SEGREGATION			
Occupation	(+) Favors	(−) Doesn't favor	Total	N
(+) White-collar	11.1%	88.9	100.0%	422
(−) Blue-collar	25.0%	75.0	100.0%	332
Total	17.2%	82.8	100.0%	754

order the categories of the two variables. The author of an article should make it clear just how he set up the table.

You should be sure you understand that saying "there's a positive relationship between white-collar and *not* favoring segregation" is equivalent to saying "there's a *negative* relationship between being *blue*-collar and *not* favoring segregation," "there's a negative relationship between being white-collar and favoring segregation," and "there's a positive relationship between being blue-collar and favoring segregation." For each arbitrary arrangement of pluses and minuses there are four ways of stating the results. They all describe the same relationship.

It might be a good idea to take a blank piece of paper at this point and draw two versions of Table 6-1, assigning pluses and minuses in the two different ways possible. (Do not make the mistake of assigning new signs to *both* variables, since this will not change things at all. Do you see why?) Then, work your way through each table and describe the results in four ways for each—as both positive and negative relationships. When you're all done, reread the above paragraph and see how your verbal descriptions square with those above.

Of course, it's possible to have relationships between nominal-scale variables of more than two categories. In this case, we can't arbitrarily assign pluses and minuses to transform the variable into an ordinal scale. The characterization of the relationship's direction in such cases is not possible. The only way to proceed is via a detailed description of the differences within the table. (For example, there's a relationship between religious affiliation and suicide: Protestants are the most likely to commit suicide, Catholics the least, and Jews are in between. Such a relationship could never be described in terms of "positive" and "negative" without dichotomizing the religion variable.)

Measures of Association

So, according to Table 6-6 we have a negative relationship between being white-collar and favoring segregation. (What's another acceptable verbal description for Table 6-6?) We've described the relationship in terms of its direction; now we want to get some idea of how *strong* it is. How great are these positive (or negative) "tendencies"?

We're looking for a quantitative description of the strength of a two-variable relationship, preferably a number that has some useful meaning. These are called *measures of association*, and social scientists have devised many. We'll concentrate on three that are used most often with nominal-scale variables: Yule's Q, Pearson's phi coefficient, and Goodman and Kruskal's tau.

Yule's Q

Social scientists have agreed that measures of association should conform to several standards in order to make them of greatest value. A measure should have a value of zero when there is independence (as in Table 6-2); it should have a value of -1.00 when there's a perfect negative relationship (e.g., when *all* white-collar workers are not in favor of segregation and *all* blue-collar workers are in favor); it should have a value of $+1.00$ when there is a perfect positive relationship; and it should have some meaningful interpretation in terms of independence and dependence.

Yule's Q is a measure that meets these standards fairly well. It might help explain where it comes from if we repeat Table 6-1, replacing the marginals and cells with letter symbols (see Table 6-7). Note that the marginal totals are simply the sum of the appropriate row or column frequencies.

In order to determine what kind of relationship exists, we have to convert the frequencies to proportions (see Table 6-8). Table 6-8 is simply Table 6-3 in symbolic terms. In what follows, refer to both Tables 6-3 and 6-8. Take your time and be sure you understand each sentence before going on to the next.

In Table 6-3 there's a negative relationship between being white-collar and favoring racial segregation. We know this because the proportion of white-collars favoring segregation is lower than the comparable proportion for blue-collar workers (.111 versus .250) and the difference is reversed for not favoring segregation (.889 versus .750). In terms of Table 6-8, $a/(a + b)$ is less than $c/(c + d)$ and $b/(a + b)$ is greater than $d/(c + d)$. If the relationship is negative, the last sentence will always be true in a 2×2 table. If the relationship were positive, then the direction of the differences would be reversed.

What we want is a measure that reflects the size of the differences between the proportions for white- and blue-collar workers. Now let's

Table 6-7 Table 6-1 without Cells and Marginals

| Occupation | RACIAL SEGREGATION | | Total |
	(+) Favors	(−) Doesn't favor	
(+) White-collar	a	b	$a + b$
(−) Blue-collar	c	d	$c + d$
Total	$a + c$	$b + d$	$a + b + c + d$

Table 6-8 Table 6-7 in Proportional Terms

| Occupation | SUPPORT FOR RACIAL SEGREGATION | | Total |
	(+) Favors	(−) Doesn't favor	
(+) White-collar	$a/(a + b)$	$b/(a + b)$	1.00
(−) Blue-collar	$c/(c + d)$	$d/(c + d)$	1.00
Total	$(a + c)/N$	$(b + d)/N$	1.00

take a look at Yule's Q and see how it accomplishes this. Yule's Q is calculated by the following formula,

$$Q = \frac{(a*d) - (b*c)}{(a*d) + (b*c)}$$

and is used in 2 × 2 tables only. It can be calculated with frequencies, proportions, or percentages. We've computed the products (called *cross products*) *within* each of the two diagonals ($a*d$ and $b*c$) and have taken the difference between them for the numerator and the sum for the denominator. To see why this is a good measure of association, we need to change the frequencies in our formula into proportions (which we can do without changing the value of Q since we're dividing each by the same quantity, as you can see below):

$$Q = \frac{\left(\dfrac{a}{a+b}\dfrac{d}{c+d}\right) - \left(\dfrac{b}{a+b}\dfrac{c}{c+d}\right)}{\left(\dfrac{a}{a+b}\dfrac{d}{c+d}\right) + \left(\dfrac{b}{a+b}\dfrac{c}{c+d}\right)}$$

Each of the cross products in the formula has in effect been divided by the same quantity, $(a + b)(c + d)$. In order for Q to be negative, the right-hand side of the numerator has to be larger than the left. Since we've already seen that $c/(c + d)$ is larger than $a/(a + b)$ and $b/(a + b)$ is larger than $d/(c + d)$, then the product on the right must be larger than that on the left. The numerator must be negative for these data. (At this point you might want to go back over what we've just done and be sure you understand everything so far.)

The stronger the relationship is, the greater will be the imbalance between the term on the right and that on the left in the numerator of Q. Thus, as the relationship gets stronger, Q gets larger. If there is independence, then $a/(a + b)$ will equal $c/(c + d)$ and $b/(a + b)$ will equal $d/(c + d)$ (as in Table 6-2). In this case the numerator of Q (and Q itself) will be zero. If the relationship is positive, then $a/(a + b)$ will be greater than $c/(c+d)$ and $d/(c+d)$ will be greater than $b/(a+b)$). In this case the left side of the numerator would be greater than the right and the numerator would be positive, making Q positive. In our example, using proportions, Q is

$$Q = \frac{(.111)(.750) - (.889)(.250)}{(.111)(.750) + (.889)(.250)} = \frac{-.1390}{.3055} = -.4550 = -.46$$

The highest value that Q can attain is 1.0, either positive or negative. This will occur whenever one of the cells in a 2×2 table has no cases in it (as in Table 6-5). In our example, a *substantively* perfect relationship would be one in which no blue-collar workers failed to support segregation and no white-collar workers favored segregation (i.e., both d and a are zero in Table 6-7). In this case, knowing one's occupational group tells us everything there is to know about whether or not the respondent favors racial segregation.

You'll note in Table 6-5, however, that Q is -1.0 even though there are a number of blue-collar workers who do not favor racial segregation (61 percent). This is called a *conditional association*. If we know the respondent is a white-collar worker, and use the hypothetical results in Table 6-5, we can predict the racial attitude with no error whatsoever. Thus, *conditional on being white-collar*, the relationship is perfect. Yule's Q can achieve a value of 1.0 whenever the relationship is either substantively or conditionally perfect. Because of this, it's worth your while to examine the original table to be sure of Q's meaning in a particular case.

Q is a useful and widely used measure. While the numerical value of Q ($-.46$ in our example) lacks a precise mathematical interpretation, Davis's assignment of verbal labels to Q's of different sizes is a good guide:

Value of Q	Appropriate phrase
$+.70$ or higher	A very strong positive association
$+.50$ to $+.69$	A substantial positive association
$+.30$ to $+.49$	A moderate positive association
$+.10$ to $+.29$	A low positive association
$+.01$ to $+.09$	A negligible positive association
$.00$	No association
$-.01$ to $-.09$	A negligible negative association
$-.10$ to $-.29$	A low negative association
$-.30$ to $-.49$	A moderate negative association
$-.50$ to $-.69$	A substantial negative association
$-.70$ or lower	A very strong negative association

SOURCE James A. Davis, *Elementary Survey Analysis* (Englewood Cliffs, N.J.: Prentice-Hall, 1971), p. 49, reprinted by permission of the publisher.

In our example, we have a moderate negative association between being white-collar and favoring racial segregation.

The Phi Coefficient

Pearson's phi (ϕ) coefficient (also known as the *index of mean-square contingency*) is another measure of association we can use to measure the strength of relationships between nominal-scale variables. For 2×2 tables, phi is calculated as follows, using the same cell and marginal symbols we used in Table 6-7:

$$\text{phi} = \frac{(a*d - b*c)}{\sqrt{(a + b)(c + d)(a + c)(b + d)}} = \phi$$

The numerator is identical to that for Yule's Q; the denominator is the square root of the product of the marginals. Phi can be calculated *only* with frequencies. Let's look at some of its characteristics.

When the variables are independent of each other (as in Table 6-2), phi will equal zero, since $a*d$ will equal $b*c$ (as is the case with Yule's Q). Phi differs from Yule's Q in that it will take on values of $+1.0$ and -1.0 only when the relationship is *substantively* perfect. In Table 6-5 we had a relationship that was not substantively perfect, since 61 percent of blue-collar workers were not in favor of racial segregation. The value for Q in those data is -1.0. Phi, on the other hand, has a value of

$$\phi = \frac{0*203 - 129*422}{\sqrt{129*625*332*422}} = -.51$$

Thus, while Yule's Q is sensitive to the conditional associations in Table 6-5, phi indicates that the relationship, while substantial, is not substantively perfect.

With 2×2 tables, phi has a very useful characteristic that should be noted. If we square phi (ϕ^2), the resulting quantity is the *proportion of the variation in the dependent variable that is explained by the independent variable*. What does this mean? We know there is variation in racial attitudes: some favor segregation, some oppose it. We want to explain why some do and some don't. In a substantively perfect relationship, the independent and dependent variables vary together completely; in a situation of independence between variables, as the independent variable changes in value, there is no patterned change in the dependent variable; the two variables do not vary together at all. The quantity ϕ^2 tells us the exact degree to which the two variables vary together, and the proportion of the variation in attitudes that is statistically due to their relationship with occupation. This is a very powerful measure and is the most precise statement we can make about the strength of a relationship. In our case, $\phi^2 = .26$, telling us that about a quarter of the variation in attitudes is statistically accounted for by occupation.

Pearson's phi can be calculated with tables larger than the 2×2 table,[1] but there are problems associated with this practice. First, the resulting quantity has no positive or negative sign; second, the value of phi in larger tables often is greater than 1.0, which makes interpretation all but impossible.

In general, you'll find that values for phi will be lower than Q for the same set of data. For example, if we calculated phi for Table 6-1, we'd get a value of $-.18$, lower than the Yule's Q of $-.45$ calculated for these same data. Thus, while both measures of association have values of zero when there's independence and range between -1.0 and $+1.0$ in 2×2 tables, as the relationship gets stronger, the values of Q tend to rise much faster than those of phi, making phi a more conservative measure of association.

Assume that we have a 2×2 table in which the marginals for both variables are split fifty-fifty. As the relationship gets stronger, values of Yule's Q would compare to phi as follows:

Value of Q	Value of ϕ
.08	.04
.38	.20
.69	.40
.88	.60
.98	.80
.997	.92
.999	.96
1.00	1.00

Yule's Q rises very sharply at first and then levels off; phi, on the other hand, rises more smoothly.

One reason for Q's wide use is that it's better known. Another, however, is that it gives larger values than phi, which may exaggerate the strength of the relationship. While Q has many useful properties, phi would seem to be a scientifically preferable measure of association.

Goodman and Kruskal's Tau

Relationships can be viewed in terms of increasing our ability to predict one characteristic from knowledge of another. If income and education

---

[1] See William L. Hays, *Statistics for the Social Sciences*, 2d ed. (New York: Holt, Rinehart and Winston, 1973), p. 743.

are related, then knowing education tells us something about what income is likely to be. Knowing where someone stands on the independent variable thus improves our ability to predict scores on the dependent variable. If there's no relationship (independence), then knowing the value of the independent variable doesn't add anything to our knowledge of the dependent variable. In terms of probabilities, a relationship means that the conditional probabilities are different from the unconditional probabilities (the marginals of the dependent variable).

Goodman and Kruskal's tau is a measure designed for nominal variables and deals directly with the question: "If I want to predict Y (political preference, for example), how much is my accuracy improved by knowing X (religious affiliation, for example)?" Let's take our original example and apply tau to it (Table 6-9).

Suppose for the moment that we don't know occupation; i.e., we have no information except the marginal distribution for the segregation attitude (the bottom row). Suppose that given this information we wanted to take each of the 754 people in the sample—at random—and assign them to one of the attitudes, either "favors" or "doesn't favor" racial segregation. *We're interested in estimating how many errors we can expect to make in our assignments; i.e., how inaccurate our predictions will be, given no information about occupation.*

We might randomly assign numbers to everyone in the group (1 to 754) and then assign all those with numbers 1 through 130 to the "favors" group and the rest to the "doesn't favor" group (we'd never do this in practice; this hypothetical procedure is simply an illustration of the rationale behind tau). How many mistakes are we likely to make?

Well, we're going to put 130 people in the "favors" group. Since the probability that any one of those is actually *not* in favor of segregation is $624/754 = .8276$, then we can expect 83 percent of our assignments *to be in error.* We'd thus expect to make a total of $(.8276)(130) = 107.6$ errors. In the same way, we're going to assign 624 people to the "doesn't favor" group; the probability that any one of those is actually in *favor*

Table 6-9 Support for Racial Segregation by Occupation, United States, 1968

Occupation	SEGREGATION ATTITUDE		Total
	(+) Favors	(−) Doesn't favor	
(+) White-collar	47	375	422
(−) Blue-collar	83	249	332
Total	130	624	754

of segregation is $130/754 = .1724$. We'd thus expect to make $(.1724)(624) = 107.6$ errors in assigning people to the "doesn't favor" group. The total number of errors we'd expect to make is $107.6 + 107.6 = 215.2$ errors. Thus, in randomly assigning 754 people, we can expect to be wrong on 215, or 29 percent of the time.

What if we knew occupation as well? If we knew what each person's occupation was *at the time of random selection*, would this improve our accuracy in predicting racial attitudes? To answer this, we repeat the above process of assigning 754 people to racial attitudes, *but we now do it within each occupational group.* Insofar as the two variables are related to each other, the distributions within occupational groups should differ from one another. Insofar as they differ, they alter the probabilities of error in our predictions. These altered probabilities constitute useful information. The more information we have, the more accurate should be our predictions.

We start with the white-collar workers. We'll assign 47 people to the "favors" group with a probability of error of $375/422 = .8886$, giving us $(.8886)(47) = 41.8$ expected errors. We'll assign 375 people to the "doesn't favor" group with a probability of error of $47/422 = .1114$, giving us $(.1114)(375) = 41.8$ expected errors. In making assignments of white-collar workers to racial attitudes, we can expect to make $41.8 + 41.8 = 83.6$ errors.

We now repeat the process for blue-collar workers and get an expected number of errors of

$$83(249/332) + 249(83/332) = 83*.75 + 249*.25 = 124.5 \text{ errors}$$

(Make sure you see where these numbers came from.)

Without knowing occupation, we expect to make 215.2 errors in predicting the racial attitude; *knowing* occupation, we expect to make $83.6 + 124.5 = 208.1$ errors. *Goodman and Kruskal's tau is the proportional reduction in prediction error that results from knowing the independent variable.*

$$\frac{215.2 - 208.1}{215.2} = .03$$

I hope you're saying to yourself, ".03 doesn't look so hot," because you're right. Even though $Q = -.45$ for this same table, knowing occupation improves our ability to predict this attitude by only 3 percent. Tau is equal to ϕ^2 in a 2×2 table and is itself a ratio-scale variable: we can say that a tau of .50 represents a relationship twice as strong as one of .25. We can't make such statements about Yule's Q, or phi, although we can about ϕ^2.

Tau will be zero when there's no relationship (you might take Table 6-2 and demonstrate this for yourself). It can never be negative, and will equal 1.0 when the relationship is perfect. For example:

	Y		
	(+)	**(−)**	**Total**
(+)	0	100	100
X			
(−)	100	0	100
Total	100	100	200

Without knowing X we'd expect to make $100 * .5 + 100 * .5 = 100$ errors in predicting Y. Knowing X, however, we make no errors whatsoever and tau will be

$$\frac{100 - 0}{100} = 1.0$$

In our example above, we tried to predict a racial attitude from knowledge of occupational class. We could have done the reverse, predicting occupational class from racial attitudes. Because tau can be computed for predictions in both directions, two symbols are often used. If we have two variables A and B, and want to predict variable A from variable B, the symbol for tau is tau-a. If we predict B from A, the symbol for tau is tau-b. In general, the numerical values for tau-a and tau-b will not be the same.

There are other measures of association for nominal-scale variables in the social science literature. These three, however, are used widely and serve, I hope, to get your feet wet in the most interesting part of social science, relationships between variables.

Relationships between Ordinal-Scale Variables

In cross tabulations of ordinal-scale variables one of the most frequently used measures of association is Goodman and Kruskal's gamma. In a 2×2 table, gamma is identical to Yule's Q. In larger tables, the computation is somewhat more complex. First, gamma uses only frequencies in its calculation (except in the 2×2 case); second, in order for gamma to make any sense, the categories of each variable must be arranged in order. If you're going to use the computational procedure outlined below, you must also arrange the variables in a symmetrical fashion, as in the tables below:

	VARIABLE B					VARIABLE B	
	High	Medium	Low		Low	Medium	High

Variable A	High Medium Low	or	Variable A	Low Medium High

Both variables should start in the upper left corner with the same end of their ordinal scale (i.e., either both high or both low, as in the above examples). If you have one starting at "high" and the other starting at "low," and use the computational procedures presented here, the sign of the measure of association will be opposite to the actual direction. This is simply a matter of adopting and following a convention.

In the Mexico City fertility study cited earlier, we gathered data on educational attainment and the residential background of the respondent's parents. Since educational attainment in Mexico is very low by American standards, we dichotomized the variable into two categories, "greater than primary school" and "primary school or less." The parents' residential background consisted of replies to the question: "Where did your parents spend most of their married life?" This was coded in three ordinal categories, going from the most urban to the least urban. The relationship looks like that shown in Table 6-10a.

If we convert the table to percentages, we see immediately that the size of the parents' main married residence is positively related to the daughter's educational attainment (Table 6-10b).

Gamma flows from the same logic as Yule's Q: we're essentially comparing diagonals. In the 2 × 2 table we calculated cross products going from the upper-left to the lower-right cell and from the upper-right to the lower-left cell ($a*d$ and $b*c$). Gamma uses the same logic, except that there's more work involved.

Table 6-10a Educational Attainment of Married Mexican Women by Parents' Main Type of Residence While Married, Mexico City, 1971

Parents' main married residence	EDUCATION		Total
	Greater than primary	Primary or less	
City	176	233	409
Town	57	256	313
Village	7	69	76
Total	240	558	798 = N

SOURCE Allan G. Johnson, "Modernization and Social Change: Attitudes toward Women's Roles in Mexico City," unpublished Ph.D. dissertation, University of Michigan, Ann Arbor, Mich., table 4.5.

Table 6-10b Educational Attainment of Married Mexican Women by Parents' Main Type of Residence While Married, Mexico City, 1971

Parents' main married residence	EDUCATION		Total (N)
	Greater than primary	Primary or less	
City	43%	57	100% (409)
Town	18%	82	100% (313)
Village	9%	91	100% (76)
Total	30%	70	100% (798)

SOURCE See Table 6-10a.

To get the cross product comparable to $a*d$, we start in the upper left-hand cell and multiply it by the *sum* of all the cells to the right and down [that is, $(176)(256 + 69)$]. We do this for all cells that have a cell down and to the right of them. In this case there are two, the second of which is $(57)(69)$. The first cross product is the sum of these two cross products, or

$$(176)(256 + 69) + (57)(69) = 61,133$$

This is comparable to the $a*d$ cross product in the formula for Yule's Q. To get the $b*c$ cross product, we repeat the procedure, starting in the upper *right* cell and multiplying the sum of cells down and to the left:

$$(233)(57 + 7) + (256)(7) = 16,704$$

Once we have the two cross products, we proceed as before:

$$\text{Gamma} = \frac{61,133 - 16,704}{61,133 + 16,704} = +.57$$

This tells us that there are substantial differences in educational attainment between women of differing parental backgrounds.

Gamma, like Q, can attain a value of 1.0 when there is a conditionally perfect but not substantively perfect relationship. Also, like Q, it's not a conservative measure of the strength of association and tends to give higher values than more conservative measures for the same relationship. It is, nonetheless, quite useful and widely employed in the social science literature.

Rank-Order Measures of Association

Sometimes we have data on individuals that rank them from high to low on several variables. For example, suppose we have four members of a statistics class. Over the course of the semester we keep track of how often members participate in class discussions, and at the end of the semester we rank the students on their overall achievement. Suppose we obtained the data shown in Table 6-11. We've ordered the students by their rank on class participation. If participation and achievement are related, then we would expect the two columns to look similar. In this section we'll discuss two measures commonly used to measure the degree of association between two variables such as these.

The first of these is *Spearman's* r_s. To calculate it, we directly compare the two columns of ranks by taking the difference between each pair of ranks (one pair for each student), squaring each difference, and adding them up. We then fiddle with the measure to force it to equal $+1.0$ when the ranks are in complete agreement, -1.0 when they are in complete disagreement, and zero when there is no relationship. We do this by multiplying the sum of the squared differences by 6 and then dividing by the quantity $N(N^2 - 1)$, where N is the number of cases. We then subtract this from 1.0. In our example, the sum of the squared differences is

$$(1 - 2)^2 + (2 - 1)^2 + (3 - 3)^2 + (4 - 4)^2 = 2$$

Spearman's r_s is then

$$1 - \frac{6(2)}{4(16 - 1)} = 1 - \frac{12}{60} = 1 - .20 = .80 = r_s$$

This indicates a strong tendency for people ranked high on class participation to rank high also on achievement. If the two columns of rank were identical, each of the differences would be zero and r_s would be

$$1 - \frac{6(0)}{60} = 1.0 = r_s$$

Table 6-11 Ranks of Four Students on Class Participation and Achievement

Student	Participation rank	Achievement rank
Ramona	1	2
Steve	2	1
Jean	3	3
Charles	4	4

If there's a perfect negative relationship, the second term in the formula will always equal 2, making $r_s = 1 - 2 = -1.0$. To illustrate, in our example, had there been a perfect negative relationship, the table would have looked like this:

Student	Participation	Achievement
Ramona	1	4
Steve	2	3
Jean	3	2
Charles	4	1

The sum of the squared differences is

$$(1 - 4)^2 + (2 - 3)^2 + (3 - 2)^2 + (4 - 1)^2 = 20$$

Spearman's r_s is then

$$1 - \frac{6(20)}{4(16 - 1)} = 1.0 - 2.0 = -1.0 = r_s$$

When there's no relationship, the second term in the formula will equal 1.0.

Occasionally individuals are tied on one of the variables. For example, suppose Ramona and Steve were tied for first place on class participation. In this case we assign them both the average of the two ranks involved (first and second), or 1.5. If the number of ties is small, Spearman's r_s can be calculated as we've done above. If the number of ties is substantial, however, a correction factor must be used, but we'll not bother to describe it here.[1]

It's difficult to describe particular values of r_s in terms of "weak," "moderate," "strong," etc. This is a frequently encountered problem with many measures of association applied to nominal- and ordinal-scale variables, and you'll have to get used to some vagueness.

The second measure is *Kendall's tau* (symbolized by the Greek letter τ, not to be confused with Goodman and Kruskal's tau, τ_a, τ_b, etc.). It's applied to the same kind of data but in a slightly different way. We first put the cases in perfect order for one of the variables (as we've done with class participation in Table 6-11). We then determine to what extent the students are in the proper order on the second variable, achievement. We take all possible pairs of *students* and, for each, score it $+1.0$ if the order is correct and -1 if it's the reverse of what it was on class participation. For example, Ramona has a higher rank on class partici-

---

[1] See Sidney Siegel, *Nonparametric Statistics* (New York: McGraw-Hill Book Company, 1956), pp. 206–210.

pation than Steve, but she has a lower rank on achievement; this means we score the Ramona-Steve pair with a −1.0. On the other hand, Steve has a higher rank than Jean on class participation and a higher rank on achievement. Since the orders for this pair of students are the same for the two variables, we score the Steve-Jean pair with a +1.0. We do this for all six pairs of students and sum the assigned scores:

Student pair	Assigned score
Ramona-Steve	−1.0
Ramona-Jean	+1.0
Ramona-Charles	+1.0
Steve-Jean	+1.0
Steve-Charles	+1.0
Jean-Charles	+1.0
Total	+4.0

Since the sum is positive, we know that the ranks on achievement agree with those on participation more than they disagree. To force tau to have a range of values between −1.0 and +1.0, we divide the above sum by the maximum that it could be. The largest number we could get would occur when each pair was in the proper order on achievement and was assigned a +1.0. Since there are six pairs, the maximum possible sum is 6. A shorthand formula for calculating the maximum possible value is given by $N(N − 1)/2$. In our example, $N = 4$, and so we divide 4 by $4(4 − 1)/2 = 6$. Kendall's tau is thus

$$\frac{4}{4(4 − 1)/2} = .67 = \tau$$

If all the pairs are in the same order on achievement as they are on participation, each student pair will have a value of 1.0 and tau will equal +1.0. If the ranks on achievement are exactly the opposite of those on participation, all the student pairs will have a value of −1.0 and tau will equal −1.0. If there is no relationship, there will be as many +1.0's as −1.0's and tau will equal zero.

You'll notice that the value of tau is lower than r_s (.67 versus .80). This happens because r_s relies on *squared* differences, giving extreme differences in ranks a relatively large impact on the overall measure of association. Tau treats all differences equally, assigning a +1.0 or −1.0 regardless of the size of the difference in ranks.

Relationships between Interval- and Ratio-Scale Variables

In previous sections of this chapter, we talked about the strength and direction of relationships between nominal and ordinal variables. All we could say about direction was that it was positive, negative, or curvilinear; in addition, the measures of association rarely had an exact meaning. *Regression analysis* is a technique that allows us to describe relationships between interval- and ratio-scale variables with greater precision and meaning than we could with nominal and ordinal variables. We do this by finding the mathematical function that most closely describes a set of data.

Volumes have been written on regression analysis. The area is much too large to be covered thoroughly in this kind of book. What I will try to do is acquaint you with the logic and procedures so that you can understand research reports that use regression analysis.

Nuts and Bolts Regression Analysis: Linear Regression

We start with two variables, both of which occur as numbers, such as years of schooling completed and the number of children desired. Any two-category variable (such as sex) can be used in regression analysis by assigning a one to one category (e.g., female) and a zero to the other. We interview a sample of 20 people and get the results shown on Table 6-12. In regression analysis, we're interested in both the form and the strength of the relationship. To get a better picture of this, it helps to plot the data on a *scattergram* (Fig. 6-2). On the horizontal axis we have the

Figure 6-2 Scattergram of number of children desired, by years of schooling (from Table 6-12).

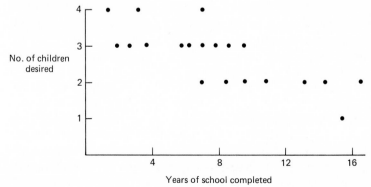

Table 6-12 Raw Data on Years of Schooling Completed and Number of Children Desired

Respondent number	Years of schooling completed (X)	Number of children desired (Y)
1	3	4
2	3	3
3	4	3
4	2	3
5	1	4
6	7	4
7	7	3
8	8	2
9	6	3
10	5	3
11	7	2
12	8	3
13	5	3
14	9	3
15	11	2
16	13	2
17	9	2
18	14	2
19	16	2
20	15	1
Total	153	54
	$\bar{X} = 7.65$ years	$\bar{Y} = 2.70$ children

number of years of school completed, and on the vertical, number of children desired. Each point on the scattergram represents one of the respondents in Table 6-12.

You can see that as the years of schooling increase, the number of children desired *tends* to go down. From the graph alone we can tell there's a negative relationship between schooling and desired family size. With regression analysis, we can describe the relationship in more detail.

Linear-regression analysis tries to describe a set of data (i.e., the scattergram) with a straight line. We fit a line to the points in such a way that on the average the squared vertical distances between the points and the line are minimal (called for this reason the *least-squares regression line*). There is only one such line (Fig. 6-3).

In algebra, a straight line is described by a formula, called a *function*. The general form of the function is $Y = a + bX$, where Y is the predicted value of the dependent variable (on the vertical axis), and X is the in-

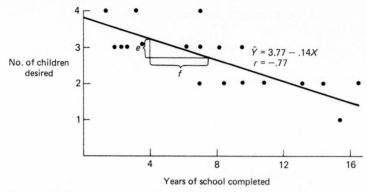

Figure 6-3 Scattergram of number of children desired, by years of schooling, with least-squares linear-regression line superimposed (from Table 6-12).

dependent variable (on the horizontal axis).[1] The a is the point where the line crosses the vertical axis (i.e., when X equals zero) and is called the *regression constant*. The b is the number of units that Y changes for every unit change in X, and is called the *slope* (also called the *regression coefficient*). In our example, the slope is the change in the number of children desired associated with each additional year of schooling. Look at Fig. 6-3. The bottom of the small triangle represents a distance of 4 years of schooling (f). With 4 years of schooling, the number of children desired drops by $-.56$ (e), according to the straight line that best fits these data. The slope is thus $-.56$ per 4 years, or $-.56/4 = -.14$ child per year of schooling.[2]

A negative slope goes from the upper left to the lower right of the graph (as in Fig. 6-3); a positive slope goes from the lower left to the upper right of the graph. A slope of zero is a straight horizontal line, parallel to the X axis. A slope that is perfectly vertical (perpendicular to the X axis) has an infinite slope, but this occurs only when there is only one value of X (i.e., X is a constant). In this rare case, there's no point in using regression analysis since there's only one variable (Y).

We begin with the data in Table 6-12. From the raw data we calculate the slope (b) and Y intercept (a) of the best fitting linear-regression line.

---

[1] In math courses you may have been taught that the general form of a linear function is $Y = mX + b$, where Y and X are the dependent and independent variables, respectively, m is the slope, and b is the regression constant. In the social sciences we use slightly different symbols (b for the slope, rather than m, and a for the constant rather than b). The idea is the same; don't let the new arrangement and symbols confuse you.

[2] If X is the independent variable and Y is the dependent variable, we refer to the regression as "the regression of Y on X" and the slope is symbolized by b_{yx}; if we performed the regression of X on Y (where X would now be the dependent variable), the symbol for the slope would be b_{xy}.

The formula for the slope might be somewhat intimidating, so I've omitted it from the text.[1]

From our data, $b = -.14$. The formula for the best-fitting line is now $Y = a - .14X$. Since the line will always pass through the point $(\overline{X}, \overline{Y})$, we substitute the two means to get a:

$$\overline{Y} = a - .14\overline{X}$$
$$2.70 = a - .14(7.65)$$
$$2.70 + 1.07 = a$$
$$3.77 = a$$

The formula for the best-fitting line is thus

$$\hat{Y} = 3.77 - .14X$$

and is shown superimposed on the scattergram in Fig. 6-3.[2]

Notice that most of the points do not lie on the regression line. Technically, regression analysis approaches relationships between variables from a *prediction* perspective. In our problem, we want to describe the relationship in terms of our ability to predict someone's desired number of children from knowledge about their educational experience. If all the points lay on the line, we'd be able to predict perfectly: tell me someone's education and I could tell you with no error the number of children they want. The more scattered the points are about the line, the more error there will be in our predictions.

In regression analysis we use a correlation coefficient to measure the extent to which the points "hug" the regression line. It's called the *Pearson product-moment correlation coefficient* and is symbolized by the letter r. It ranges from -1.0 to $+1.0$.

It might help our understanding of r if we examine its formula:[3]

$$r = \frac{\Sigma(X - \overline{X})(Y - \overline{Y})}{\sqrt{[\Sigma(X - \overline{X})^2][\Sigma(Y - \overline{Y})^2]}}$$
$$= \frac{\text{covariance}}{(\text{standard deviation of } X)(\text{standard deviation of } Y)}$$

---

[1] The slope (b) is calculated with the following formula: $b_{yx} = \dfrac{N\Sigma XY - (\Sigma X)(\Sigma Y)}{N\Sigma X^2 - (\Sigma X)^2}$

The Σ symbol is called a summation sign. It tells us to add up all the scores of variables to the right of the sign. Thus, ΣXY tells us to multiply years of schooling times number of children desired for each respondent and then add up those 20 products. If you're interested in an analysis of the origin and derivation of this formula, I recommend looking at Hubert M. Blalock, Jr., *Social Statistics*, 2d ed. (New York: McGraw-Hill Book Company, 1972), sec. 17.1.

[2] The "hat" mark (∧) over the symbol for the dependent variable signifies that the values generated by the equation are *predictions*.

[3] Again, the Σ sign tells us to add up the quantities to the right of the sign for each case (20 in our example). So, the algebraic expression $(X - \overline{Y})(Y - \overline{Y})$ tells us to multiply the difference between each person's education and the mean education times the difference between each person's desired children and the comparable mean. For respondent 1 we'd have $(3 - 7.65)(4 - 2.70)$. We'd add up 20 products.

The numerator of the coefficient is a number which measures the extent to which X and Y vary together, and is called the *covariance*. By "vary together," we mean that as X varies, there's a pattern to the way Y changes (as in Fig. 6-3). If the relationship is positive, then when X is above its mean, Y will tend to be above its mean also; when X is below its mean, Y will tend to be below its mean. In both cases, the product $(X - \overline{X})(Y - \overline{Y})$ will be positive most of the time (the product of either two positive or negative numbers). If the relationship is negative, then when X is above its mean, Y will *tend* to be below its mean, and when X is below its mean, Y will tend to be above its mean. In both cases the product $(X - \overline{X})(Y - \overline{Y})$ will tend to be negative (the product of one positive and one negative number). When the relationship is zero, then no matter what X is, Y will have an equal tendency to be above or below its mean. The product $(X - \overline{X})(Y - \overline{Y})$ will be positive as much as it is negative, and the sum of such products (the covariance) will be zero.

The denominator is the product of the standard deviations of X and Y, and measures the *total* amount of variation in the data. The correlation coefficient thus measures the proportion of the total variation that consists of covariation. If all the variation in the data is covariation, then the variables are perfectly related (the points all lie on the regression line) and the correlation is either $+1.0$ or -1.0, depending on the direction of the relationship. (See Figs. 6-4 and 6-5.)

What does independence look like in a regression analysis? You'll recall that two variables are independent when the distribution of one variable is the same within all categories of the other. This was called stochastic independence. In regression analysis, we encounter a second type of independence. (See Fig. 6-6.)

If we fit the least-squares line to this set of data, both the slope and the correlation coefficient will be zero. The overall mean of Y is 5.0, and, for each value of X, the values of Y are just as likely to be above the mean of Y as they are to be below (look at the figure and verify this for yourself). The result is that the mean of Y is the same for all categories of X. Since our prediction of the *mean* of Y is the same for all values of X, knowing X doesn't improve our ability to predict at all, and the two variables are independent. When the *mean* of Y is the same for all values of X, we say the two variables are *mean-independent*.

Figure 6-4 Example of a perfect positive correlation.

Figure 6-5 Example
of a perfect negative
correlation.

What's the difference? With stochastic independence, the conditional probability distributions of Y are the same for all values of X; with mean independence, the conditional *means* (which summarize the conditional probability distributions) are the same for all values of X. When we calculate a mean, we lose information. Therefore, knowing that the *means* are the same doesn't tell us whether or not the *distributions* are the same.

You can see from Fig. 6-6 that although knowing X doesn't make any difference in our predictions of the *mean* of Y, the distributions of Y for each value of X are *not* identical. Thus, although X and Y are mean-independent in Fig. 6-6, they are not stochastically independent. If we know X, we *do* improve our ability to predict specific values of Y (e.g., if X is 1.0, we'd never predict a value of 9.0 for Y, but if X is 4.0, a value of 9.0 is possible for Y).

Figure 6-6 Example of mean independence and stochastic dependence.

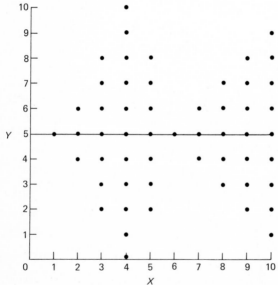

Note that if two variables are stochastically independent, they will also be mean-independent.

You can now see that regression analysis uses the independent variable to predict mean values of the dependent variable. If the slope and correlation coefficient are zero, we only know about X's ability to improve our predictions of mean values of Y. The only way we can verify the existence of stochastic independence is to examine the scattergram.

The correlation r for the data in Table 6-12 and Fig. 6-3 is $-.77$, indicating that, in this sample, "years of schooling" is a powerful predictor of the number of children desired, and that as education increases, "children desired" tends to decrease. We have thus described the relationship in quite precise terms: schooling is a powerful predictor in these data ($r = -.77$); each additional year of schooling is associated with a *decrease* of .14 child desired ($b = -.14$), and the linear function that predicts children desired with the least amount of error is

$$\hat{Y} = 3.77 - .14X$$

The product-moment correlation coefficient has one additional property that's very useful. If we square r, the resulting number r^2 represents the proportion of the variation in Y that is "explained" by the relationship with X as described by the regression line (called the *coefficient of determination*). To understand what this means, first consider the variation in Y. The variance of desired number of children represents the fact that not all people have the same desires. The purpose of relating Y to an independent variable is to explain this variation: why do some people desire more or fewer children than others? The regression line is the best linear predictor of Y from X. It's not perfect; many points don't lie on the line, although on the average they're pretty close. This means there's variation in Y that the regression line fails to account for. The square of the correlation coefficient is the proportion of the total variation in Y(as measured by the variance) that is accounted for (or "explained") by the linear relationship with X. Mathematically, it is the ratio of the variance of Y on *the regression line* to the total variance of Y (on and off the regression line). This is equivalent to ϕ^2 in a 2×2 table: if we assigned values of 0 and 1 to each variable's categories, r would equal ϕ.

In our example, r^2 is $(-.77)^2 = .59$. This tells us that by using a *linear*-regression line, we can account for 59 percent of the variation in children desired by using years of schooling as an independent variable. By subtraction, 41 percent of the variance in desired children is left unexplained. (The square root of this, that is, $\sqrt{1 - r^2}$, is called the *coefficient of alienation*.)

Don't be misled into thinking that a correlation coefficient r of $+.50$ (or

—.50) is "halfway to a perfect correlation of +1.0 (or −1.0)" or, by implication, that an r of .60 is "twice as strong" as one of .30. This isn't true, and you can see why if you square the r's and look at the proportion of the variation in Y explained by X:

$$(.60)^2 = .36 \quad \text{and} \quad (.30)^2 = .09$$

Thus, a correlation of .60 represents *four* times as much explained variance as an r of .30. As a *measure*, r is an ordinal-scale variable, strictly speaking; r^2 is a ratio-scale variable and gives us much more meaningful information.

Keep in mind that the use of the term *explained* does not imply causality. This is a statistical explanation, not a causal one. At best, such an analysis will lend empirical support to a theoretical causal argument. You should also keep in mind the distinction between explanation and prediction. With explanation, we want to discover the causal mechanisms lying behind a particular phenomenon. With prediction, we want to discover those independent variables that yield accurate predictions of the dependent variable, regardless of causal connections. So, if by knowing the number of bathrooms in one's house, I can accurately predict an election voting decision, I'd be happy from a prediction standpoint, but not so happy from an explanation standpoint.

Interpreting Slopes and Correlation Coefficients

There are important interpretive distinctions between slopes (regression coefficients) and correlations that you should learn to appreciate. The correlation coefficient tells us how accurately we can predict Y from X. The slope tells us how much of a change in Y is associated with each unit change in X. The correlation thus reflects the usefulness of the linear regression line as a prediction rule. The slope, on the other hand, is a direct reflection of the *impact* of X on Y.

For example, suppose we correlate education and income for two samples and find the following:

Sample *A*	Sample *B*
r = .85	r = .85
b = $500	b = $50

In both samples the relationship between education and income is very strong, with education explaining 72 percent [or $(.85)^2$] of the variation in income. This tells us that education is an accurate predictor of income in both groups. The slopes, however, tell a very different story.

Each additional year of schooling brings with it an increment of $500 in group A, but only $50 in group B. The *impact* of education is 10 times as great in group A as in group B. The payoff of additional years of schooling is much higher in sample A.

If we drew graphs of the regressions in samples A and B, they might look something like those shown in Fig. 6-7. As you can see, in both samples the points lie very close to the line ($r = +.85$); we can accurately use education to predict income in these samples. However, in sample A, additional years of schooling have a much greater effect on income ($b = +\$500$) than in sample B ($b = +\$50$).

Whenever you come across a statement that refers to the impact of one variable on another in a regression analysis, you should immediately start looking for regression coefficients (slopes). If the author uses correlation coefficients to support statements about impacts or effects, he's misusing the correlation coefficient. The *strength* of a relationship is a function of the ability to predict accurately; the *impact* or *effect* of X on Y is a function of the steepness of the regression line. This is a very important distinction to understand and remember.

Figure 6-7 Scattergram (with least-squares linear-regression lines) for the regression of income on years of schooling completed for two hypothetical samples.

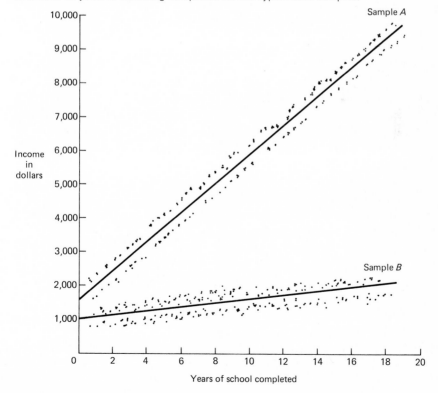

There's a second distinction between slopes and correlations that we should mention. If the correlation between X and Y is, say, .45, then the correlation between Y and X is also .45. In other words, correlations are symmetric: we can use X to predict Y with the same accuracy that we can use Y to predict X. Slopes, on the other hand, are asymmetric: in general the number of units Y changes for every unit change in X will not be the same as the number of units X changes for every unit change in Y. If we return to the data in Table 6-12, while the slope for the regression of Y on X is $-.14$, the slope for the regression of X on Y is -4.19: for every additional year of schooling there is a decline of .14 child; for every additional child desired there's a decline of 4.19 years of schooling. Thus, the value of the slope depends on which variables we designate as dependent and independent, while the value of the correlation coefficient does not.

A Note on Curvilinear Regression

Linear regression assumes that a set of data can best be described by a straight line. Certainly not all relationships take this form. There is a set of techniques for finding the best-fitting *curve* for a set of data, but they are rarely used in the social sciences, and we won't go into them here.

It's important for researchers to avoid blindly assuming that a relationship is linear (and linear-regression techniques assume just that). For example, the relationship in Fig. 6-8 represents a perfect curvilinear relationship (i.e., we could perfectly predict Y from X; all the points lie on a line that can be described by a mathematical function).

But if we apply linear-regression techniques to these data, the best-fitting line (shown on the graph) will show a slope and correlation of zero, suggesting no ability to use X to predict Y. This is clearly a false conclusion which occurs because of a false assumption about the shape of the relationship between X and Y.

Figure 6-8 A curvilinear relationship with the least-squares *linear*-regression line superimposed.

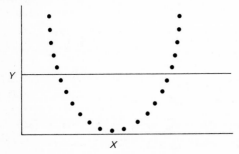

We should note that a relationship has to be sharply curvilinear in order to justify the use of curvilinear techniques. In other words, for mildly curvilinear relationships a straight line yields predictions that are only slightly less accurate than a best-fitting curve.

We've seen that linear-regression techniques may show no relationship when in fact a curvilinear relationship does exist. We've also seen that although regression analysis is sensitive to *mean* independence it is insensitive to *stochastic* independence. The lesson here is clear: before attempting to use linear-regression techniques on a set of data, you must first examine a scattergram to be sure that linear techniques are appropriate and that, if we find mean independence, there is stochastic independence as well.

Summary

In any research problem we start with concepts. We've seen the necessity for moving from concepts to operationalizations that allow us to move our research efforts to an empirical level. We then talked about the first results of such research, the distributions of single variables. In this chapter we've combined both the descriptive and explanatory functions of empirical research by looking at relationships between two variables. The crux of this task is the examination of differences between and among groups defined by the category system of an independent variable. It's in this chapter that we've expanded out from purely descriptive statistics into explanatory statistics. Here we're trying to discover the causes of a dependent variable. So far we've dealt only with one-cause situations—relationships between one dependent and one independent variable. In the next chapter we'll explore the explanation of relationships themselves: for example, why is it that whites make more money than blacks? Why do men die younger than women? Here we start with a two-variable relationship and try to understand it on a deeper level.

In Chap. 8 we'll take up the case of trying to explain a dependent variable using more than one independent variable. We'll have then finished our look at descriptive and explanatory statistics, and we'll move on to the problem of using sample data to accomplish the tasks of description and explanation.

You should come away from the present chapter with a good feel for what a relationship between two variables is. You should have some appreciation of the fact that the characterization of relationships in terms of direction and particularly strength is in part a function of the level of measurement of the variables involved. Most importantly, you should begin to see how relationships form the basis for scientific investigation.

Problems

6-1 Consider the data of Table 6-13 in answering Probs. 6-1a to d.

Table 6-13 Answers to the Question:
"Under most circumstances, do you think
it inappropriate for *you* to cry if you're
feeling very sad?" by Sex

Sex	CRYING ATTITUDE		Total
	Won't cry	Will cry	
Men	8	2	10
Women	1	9	10
Total	9	11	20

    a. Describe the relationship between the variables sex and attitude toward crying in terms of direction. Describe it both as a positive and as a negative relationship (i.e., describe it in two ways).

    b. Measure the strength of the association by computing Yule's Q, Goodman and Kruskal's tau, *and* phi (*show your work*). What do the resulting numbers tell us? How does the choice of a measure of association (in this case) affect the description of the relationship?

    c. What characteristics should all measures of association ideally have?

    d. Can gamma be used with nominal-scale variables having more than two categories? Explain your answer.

6-2 In answering Probs. 6-2a and *b*, consider the data of Table 6-14.

Table 6-14 Answers to the Question: "Under
most circumstances, do you think it inappropriate
for *you* to cry if you're feeling very sad?" by
Social Class

Social class	CRYING ATTITUDE		Total
	Won't cry	Will cry	
Upper	4	6	10
Middle	3	3	6
Lower	2	2	4
Total	9	11	$20 = N$

    a. Describe the relationship's direction, both as a positive relationship and as a negative relationship.

   b. Use gamma to measure the strength of the relationship (*show your work*). State the results in a sentence that gives meaning to the number you compute.
6-3 Consider the following data and problem:
   Five people are competing for awards. Their performances have been ranked by two judges. Use *two* measures of association to determine how closely the judges agree (*show your work*):

Contestant	Judge 1	Judge 2
Sue	4	3
Marc	1	2
Bill	2	1
Peggy	5	4
John	3	5

   Describe and interpret your results.
6-4 "When we graph the relationship between education and income for group 1, we find that the correlation is very strong ($r = .75$). Education has a large impact on income for members of this group." (See Fig. 6-9.)
   a. Do you agree with the conclusion that "education has a large impact on income for members of this group"? Why or why not?
   b. What does the "very strong" correlation of .75 tell us about the relationship between education and income?
6-5 We examine the relationship between income and the number of years on the job. The best-fitting regression line is

$$\hat{Y} = 8,000 + 500X \qquad r = +.63$$

   where Y is yearly income and X is the number of years on the job.
   a. What is the *impact* of years on the job on income?

Figure 6-9 Regression of income on years of schooling (hypothetical).

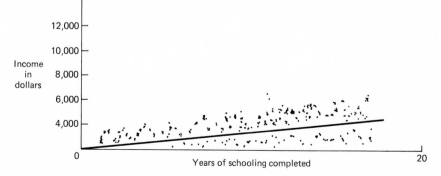

   b. How accurately can we predict Y from X?
   c. How much of the variation in income is explained by years on the job?

6-6 We examine the relationship between two variables X and Y, within three different groups, with the following results:

Group 1	Group 2	Group 3
$r = +.42$	$r = -.15$	$r = +.20$
$b = +.56$	$b = -.37$	$b = +.92$

In detail, compare the relationships found in these groups with each other. Try to use your own words, and concentrate on the *meaning* of the information. Try your explanation on someone else.

6-7 Consider the following regression equation which represents the relationship between number of siblings (X) and IQ (Y) (fictitious data):

$$\hat{Y} = 100 - 3X \qquad r = -.20$$

   a. *Briefly* explain the meaning of:
   (1) The equation as a whole
   (2) Each separate symbol and number
   (3) The value of r
   b. What does the quantity r^2 tell us?
   c. In this example, calculate the coefficient of alienation. What does it measure?

6-8 a. Can we say that a relationship with $r = .60$ is twice as strong as one with $r = .30$? Why or why not?
   b. Can we say that a relationship with $r^2 = .36$ is twice as strong as one with $r^2 = .18$? Why or why not?

Suggested Readings

1 Blalock, Hubert M., Jr.: *Causal Inferences in Nonexperimental Research*, Chap. I and II. Chapel Hill: University of North Carolina Press, 1964.
2 _____: *Social Statistics*, 2d ed., sec. 15.3. New York: McGraw-Hill Book Company, 1972.
3 Davis, James A.: *Elementary Survey Analysis*, chaps. 1–3. Englewood Cliffs, N.J.: Prentice-Hall, 1971.
4 Draper, Norman, and H. Smith: *Applied Regression Analysis*. New York: John Wiley & Sons, 1966.
5 Ezekiel, Mordecai, and Karl A. Fox: *Methods of Correlation and Regression Analysis: Linear and Curvilinear*, 3d ed., chaps. 1, 3, 4, 5, 6, 8, and 9. New York: John Wiley & Sons, 1967.

6 Goldberger, Arthur S.: *Topics in Regression Analysis*, chaps. 1–3. New York: The Macmillan Company, 1968.

7 Hays, William L.: *Statistics for the Social Sciences*, 2d ed., secs. 15.1, 15.2, 15.5, 15.6, 15.7, 15.9, 15.11, 15.12, 15.14, 15.16, 15.23, 15.29, 15.30, 18.12–18.17. New York: Holt, Rinehart and Winston, 1973.

8 Loether, Herman J., and Donald G. McTavish: *Descriptive Statistics for Sociologists*, chaps. 6 and 7. Boston: Allyn and Bacon, 1974.

9 Mueller, John H., Karl F. Schuessler, and Herbert L. Costner: *Statistical Reasoning in Sociology*, 2d ed., chaps. 9–11. Boston: Houghton Mifflin Company, 1970.

10 Siegel, Sidney: *Nonparametric Statistics*, chap. 9. New York: McGraw-Hill Book Company, 1956.

11 The examples of correlation and regression to be found in Tanur, Judith M., et al. (eds.): *Statistics: A Guide to the Unknown*, p. xxii of the table of contents. San Francisco: Holden-Day, 1972.

7

relationships
of more than
two variables:
controlling

There are occasions when two-variable relationships suffice to answer a research question. For example, a relationship between the use of birth-control pills and the incidence of fatal blood clotting might be enough evidence for the Food and Drug Administration to issue warnings to physicians and users of the pill. Or the relationship between background characteristics of potential jurors and prejudice against young left-wing radicals might be enough information for attorneys to affect jury selection in favor of their cause. If we ask respondents to tell us how stressful they feel, we can test the validity of such questions by relating the replies to physiological measurements of stress, such as blood pressure, electrocardiogram readings, and cholesterol levels. Finally, finding *no* relationships between two variables can be a significant finding. If, for example, we found no relationship between race and IQ scores, this would be an important finding in itself.

Often, however, the discovery of a two-variable relationship is not sufficient to deal with the research question at hand. There are three reasons for going beyond two-variable relationships to more complicated analyses: first, we need to be sure that an observed statistical association actually represents a meaningful relationship; second, if we're interested in the causes of a dependent variable (as we almost always are), we usually want to understand the causal mechanism in more detail, thus necessitating the introduction of additional variables into the explanation; third, even if we're satisfied with a two-variable relationship by itself, we often want to know if it exists among different kinds of people (such as men and women, white-collar workers and blue-collar workers, or blacks and whites).

There are two ways of going beyond two-variable relationships. First, we can introduce several independent variables and see how well they help us predict the dependent variable. This is called *multivariate analysis*, and we'll talk about it in some detail in Chap. 8. While related to multivariate analysis in many ways, the techniques we're going to describe in this section are unique and important enough to justify a separate discussion. In fact, they are a cornerstone of scientific research.

Second, we can achieve a deeper and more accurate understanding of two-variable relationships by *controlling* for one or more additional variables. It's easiest to grasp the idea of controlling if we imagine a relationship between two variables, controlling for a third variable that has distinct categories (such as a nominal- or ordinal-scale variable). Suppose we find a relationship between education and income: the more education one has, the higher one's income is likely to be. If we then control for sex, we examine the relationship between education and income *within* each sex group. We're holding sex constant by seeing how education relates to income within a sample of people who are alike on the variable "sex." We do this for the same reason that a chemist tries to control the physical conditions surrounding a chemical reaction (including dirt in his test tube): he wants to be sure that only certain variables are contributing to (and thus are responsible for) his results. Since sex certainly has something to do with education, income, and the relationship between the two, controlling for this variable is important for a fuller, more precise understanding of the original relationship.

There are special terms that describe relationships with and without controls, and you should be familiar with them. A relationship between two variables (i.e., with no controls) is called a *zero-order relationship*. The *order* of a relationship indicates the number of variables being controlled for. In our example above, we proposed controlling for one variable, sex. This would be a *first-order relationship*. If we controlled for sex, race, and occupation, we would have a *third-order relationship*.

In the rest of this chapter, we'll consider each of the possible reasons for controlling and give examples so that you can deepen your understanding of what controlling means and become more aware of its uses.

Spuriousness:
Is the Relationship Real?

When we gather data on two variables, cross-tabulate them, and find a statistical relationship, the first question we have to ask is: "Is this more than a statistical relationship? Does this relationship really tell us some-

Table 7-1 Fertility by Altitude, South America
(Hypothetical Data)

Altitude	FERTILITY		Total	N
	High	**Low**		
High	62.5%	37.5	100.0%	800
Low	33.3%	66.7	100.0%	1,200
Total	45.0%	55.0	100.0%	2,000
	$Q = +.54$			

thing true and valid about what's going on?" For example, it's been found that birthrates among people living at high altitudes in certain Latin American countries are higher than those of people living at low altitudes—a positive relationship between altitude and fertility. Should we then try to lower birthrates by moving people to lower altitudes? Well, believe it or not, there were a few people who thought they had discovered a fascinating causal factor in fertility rates, until someone pointed out that those living at high altitudes tend to be Indians and that Indians, for a host of reasons having nothing to do with altitude, tend to have very high rates of fertility. Thus, the original relationship was a nonsensical one having nothing to do with cause. In social science, we call such a relationship *spurious*.

Let's look at some hypothetical data to see how an interpretation of spuriousness might be statistically supported in this example. We begin with the relationship between altitude and fertility, which might look like that shown in Table 7-1.

In Table 7-1, $Q = +.54$, indicating a substantial tendency for people living at high altitudes to have higher fertility than those living at low altitudes. Given that the idea of altitude causing high fertility is a bit bizarre at best, we might then ask, "Are people who live at high altitudes different from those living at low altitudes, and might those differences lead to differences in fertility?"

Since it's often been found that Indian populations have higher fertil-

Table 7-2 Altitude by Race, South America
(Hypothetical Data)

Race	ALTITUDE		Total	N
	High	**Low**		
Indian	75.0%	25.0	100.0%	800
Non-Indian	16.7%	83.3	100.0%	1,200
Total	40.0%	60.0	100.0%	2,000
	$Q = +.87$			

Table 7-3 Fertility by Race, South America
(Hypothetical Data)

| Race | FERTILITY | | Total | N |
	High	Low		
Indian	75.0%	25.0	100.0%	800
Non-Indian	25.0%	75.0	100.0%	1,200
Total	45.0%	55.0	100.0%	2,000
	$Q = +.80$			

ity than non-Indian populations, we would then check to see if Indians tend to live at high altitudes more than non-Indians. In Table 7-2 we see that this is, indeed, the case. There's a positive relationship between being an Indian and living at high altitudes ($Q = +.87$). Do the Indians in this population have higher fertility than non-Indians? Table 7-3 shows that they do: there's a positive relationship between being an Indian and having high fertility ($Q = +.80$).

We've now found relationships among all three variables, a condition that must be met for controlling to make any sense. If, in fact, altitude is related to fertility only because of its relationship with race, then controlling for race should produce two subtables showing independence between altitude and fertility. Table 7-4 shows the relationship between altitude and fertility, controlling for race.

First notice that if we convert back to frequencies and add the comparable cells of the two subtables in Table 7-4, we get Table 7-1 (try it). Second, notice that in both subgroups (Indians and non-Indians) there's no relationship between altitude and fertility. Once we hold race constant, the relationship disappears. This is what we'd expect in the case of spuriousness, and these statistical findings support our theoretical reasoning. It's most important to keep the distinction between empirical findings and theoretical interpretations clear. The data don't carry their

Table 7-4 Fertility by Altitude, Controlling for Race, South America
(Hypothetical Data)

| | INDIANS | | | | NON-INDIANS | | | |
| | FERTILITY | | | | FERTILITY | | | |
Altitude	High	Low	Total	N	High	Low	Total	N
High	75.0%	25.0	100.0%	600	25.0%	75.0	100.0%	200
Low	75.0%	25.0	100.0%	200	25.0%	75.0	100.0%	1,000
Total	75.0%	25.0	100.0%	800	25.0%	75.0	100.0%	1,200
	$Q = 0.00$				$Q = 0.00$			

own interpretation with them. For example, you'll soon see that there are situations in which we control for a third variable, find that the relationships disappear within the control groups, and conclude something *other* than spuriousness. This is where sound theoretical reasoning comes in. We must decide in advance what interpretation we'll place on the possible results; which is to say, we have to think the problem through in substantive terms before consulting our data.

You might be wondering at this point how we know that the relationship between race and fertility is "real" and the relationship between altitude and fertility is spurious. Maybe it's the other way around. Perhaps altitude really does have a causal impact on fertility (perhaps by affecting the physiology of conception) and race is related to fertility only because it's related to altitude. Well, we can test this alternate model by rearranging the data in Table 7-4. Let's examine the relationship between race and fertility, *controlling for altitude*.

Table 7-5 shows the relationship between race and fertility within each altitude group (you should go to Table 7-4 and satisfy yourself that Table 7-5 is simply a rearrangement of the cells). If altitude is the cause of higher fertility, and if the relationship of race to fertility is spurious, when we control for altitude, the relationship between race and fertility within groups alike on altitude should go to zero. As you can see, this is not the case: the race-fertility association is as strong as it was before ($Q = +.80$). Controlling for altitude makes no difference whatsoever. Therefore, the second model does not hold. The interpretation of the relationship between altitude and fertility as spurious is supported and the alternative is decidedly not supported.

We detected spuriousness in the above example by *controlling* for race. In this case, race is called an *extraneous variable*. We examined the relationship between altitude and fertility among Indians and among non-Indians. Upon doing so, we found that among Indians, alti-

Table 7-5 Fertility by Race, Controlling for Altitude, South America (Hypothetical Data)

	HIGH ALTITUDE				LOW ALTITUDE			
	FERTILITY				FERTILITY			
Race	High	Low	Total	N	High	Low	Total	N
Indian	75.0%	25.0	100.0%	600	75.0%	25.0	100.0%	200
Non-Indian	25.0%	75.0	100.0%	200	25.0%	75.0	100.0%	1,000
Total	62.5%	37.5	100.0%	800	33.3%	67.7	100.0%	1,200
	$Q = +.80$				$Q = +.80$			

SOURCE Table 7-4.

tude had no relationship with fertility, and the same was true among non-Indians. Each of these controlled relationships is called a *partial relationship*. Thus, when we controlled for the third variable, the original relationship "disappeared." In order for this to happen, there had to be a relationship between race and altitude and a relationship between race and fertility. Indians tend to have higher fertility than non-Indians: this is the real relationship. Since Indians just happen to live at higher altitudes, altitude appears to have an effect which is, in fact, spurious.

In the social sciences, relationships involving more than two variables are often presented in diagrams such as the following:

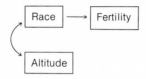

A straight arrow suggests a causal (nonspurious) connection between two variables, with the dependent variable being at the head of the arrow. A curved arrow indicates that no causal relationship is being suggested (i.e., altitude doesn't cause race and vice versa). The above diagram reflects the spurious nature of the relationship between altitude and fertility (as shown by the absence of a straight arrow between the two variables). We'll use more of these diagrams, and it's to your advantage to gain some ability to read and understand them.

There are many silly examples of spuriousness (such as the fact that fire damage is positively related to the number of firemen fighting the fire; does this mean that firemen cause the damage and, if we sent no firemen, there would be no damage?), but there are serious ones, as well. For example, many studies have documented a positive relationship between liberal racial attitudes and educational attainment. Reinforced by a popular belief in the enlightening effects of education, this might lead us to believe that a partial answer to the problem of racial prejudice is a greater investment in education (especially college) for all citizens. Before placing our confidence in such a solution, we should first consider the possible spuriousness of the relationship between education and racial attitudes.

An alternate (and somewhat disturbing) explanation of the observed statistical relationship between education and prejudice is that while educated people are more likely to give liberal responses in an interview situation, they are, in fact, just as prejudiced as everyone else. In other words, educated people are more likely to give a *socially acceptable response* to an interviewer, even though that response does not reflect their true feelings. If we could somehow control for the variable, "tendency to give honest answers in an interview setting, even when those answers are not perceived by the respondent as being socially acceptable," then we could go a long way toward deciding whether or not the observed relationship between educational attainment and racial attitudes is real or spurious. Again, in order to control, there must be three relationships: a positive one between education and expressed racial tolerance, a positive one between expressed racial tolerance and the tendency to give socially acceptable answers rather than the truth (assuming that racial tolerance is perceived by most people as being the socially acceptable response), and a positive relationship between educational attainment and the tendency to give socially acceptable responses rather than the truth.

If the relationship is in fact spurious, then we'd expect to find that among people who tell their true feelings in interview situations, there is no relationship between education and prejudice. This would indicate that the original relationship appeared in our data not because of some meaningful causal relationship, but because of the way people with different educations handle themselves in interviews. If, on the other hand, the relationship between education and prejudice *persisted* among people who tell the truth, this would support the assertion that education's relationship with prejudice is real and worthy of further study, if not action on a public policy level. Unfortunately, measuring the tendency to tell the truth in interviews is very difficult.

The idea of spuriousness is one of the most important in the social sciences. The establishment of the nonspuriousness of an observed relationship is the first and most important step in any analysis of data.

Understanding Causal Relationships: Intervening Variables

Suppose we have a relationship and we're confident that it's not spurious, such as that between sex and heart-attack rates. For most of this century men have been more likely than women to suffer heart attacks. If we score "being a man" with a plus and "being a woman" with a minus, we can say there's a positive relationship between sex and heart attacks.

The obvious questions are: "Why is this so? What is it about being born a man that leads to a greater propensity to have a heart attack?" There's considerable evidence that stress plays a role in heart attacks. Is it possible that men find themselves in situations that are more stressful than those women encounter? If men are subject to greater and more protracted stress than women, and if stress is a cause of heart attack, then this might help explain the observed statistical relationship between sex and heart attacks. Diagrammatically, the problem looks like this:

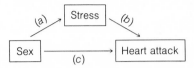

We know that sex and heart attack are related (arrow c). In order to understand this relationship more fully, we've hypothesized that differences in stress levels may play a role. For this to be true, stress must be related to both heart attack (arrow b) and sex (arrow a). If either of these latter relationships doesn't exist, then our hypothesis is untenable.

We might design a study in which we gathered data on the stressfulness of heart-attack victims' situations before their attacks occurred, with a carefully matched control group of people who had not had attacks. To test our idea, we'd then group people together according to stress level and *within each level* note the existence of a relationship between sex and heart attack. If men and women differ in heart-attack rates because of sex differences in stress, then, once we confine ourselves to people with the same level of stress, there should be no sex differences in heart-attack rates, since they're alike on the variable that we think really causes heart attacks directly. If stress fully explains the relationship between sex and heart attack, then *the partial relationships, controlling for stress, should be zero.*

Be careful to note that although the partial relationship is zero, we don't conclude that the zero-order relationship was spurious. *Statistically*, we have the same kind of result above as we did when we examined the relationship between altitude and fertility, controlling for race. The interpretation of results, however, depends on sound reasoning. In the fertility example we considered two alternatives: either altitude had some mysterious effect on fertility, or some factor (e.g., race) was related to both fertility and altitude in a *plausible* way and thereby explained the zero-order relationship as spurious. In the case of sex and heart attacks we have more than a statistical accident; it makes sense that being a man will lead to other roles and life situations than a woman encounters, and that those differences may result in higher levels of stress which in turn lead to higher rates of heart attack for men. The only way we can tell the difference is by using our heads.

In terms of the time ordering of variables, the control variable is an intervening variable only when it occurs between the independent and dependent variables; this is never the case with spuriousness.

Although you may find, as I do, the above explanation to be "reasonable" and "plausible," you should always remember that there are many reasonable and plausible explanations for any phenomenon. As you read articles that offer explanations, you should try to think of alternative logical explanations the author may have overlooked.

In our example, there's a time order to the variables: one's sex is determined at birth, stressful experiences intervene, and one's state of health is the last piece of data gathered. In this case, the variable "stress" is called an *intervening variable* because it intervenes between the two variables in the zero-order relationship. One could argue, of course, that the causal chain works in the opposite direction, that being sick raises the level of stress. In our design, however, we've measured stress in individuals who haven't contracted coronary heart disease and are in good health. This should establish the direction of causality in this case. If we take stress measurements after the contraction of disease, however, the direction of causality becomes difficult to determine.

When we control for stress, two things are likely to happen to the partial relationship between sex and heart attack: either it will go down to zero, or it will go down, but not to zero. If it goes to zero, then we have statistically explained the zero-order relationship and we can erase arrow *c*. Does this then mean that sex has nothing to do with heart attacks? No, not at all. Insofar as sex has some direct effect on stress (through sex roles, for example), then it has *indirect effects* on heart attack through the intervening variable "stress." If we wanted to combat heart attacks, we could work directly to reduce the stress experienced by people; we could also work farther back in the causal chain and try to change those forces which lead men to experience inordinate amounts of stress.

It's more likely that the partial relationship between sex and heart attacks will go down when we control for stress, but not all the way to zero. This means that some of the relationship is due to the intervening effects of stress and some is not. At this point there are two possibilities: first, there may be genetic differences between men and women that directly affect the likelihood of heart attack; second, there may be other intervening variables (e.g., personality variables such as masculinity) that may be responsible for sex differentials in heart attack. If we want to explain fully the zero-order relationship, we must continue our search for theoretically sound intervening variables to control for. I can't emphasize too strongly that the selection of control variables must be governed by sound theoretical reasoning; we can't just go out and control for every variable we can measure. We could control for every variable known and the partial relationships between *any* two variables would disappear, but we wouldn't understand what was going on.

The use of intervening variables allows us to understand mechanisms by which an independent variable affects a dependent variable. In our previous example we found that being a man was a liability. The use of intervening variables helps us discover just how being born a man ultimately results in higher heart-attack rates, which variables form

Table 7-6 Income by Education
(Hypothetical Data)

Education	INCOME		Total	N
	High	**Low**		
High	90%	10	100%	1,000
Low	10%	90	100%	1,000
Total	50%	50	100%	2,000
	$Q = +.98$			

which parts of the causal chain, and how much importance is attached to each part of the chain. Such analysis is invaluable in picking apart causal relationships.

Let's take a look at an example with some tables. First consider the relationship between education and income in Table 7-6. In this group the relationship is almost perfect ($Q = +.98$) and positive: the greater the educational level, the higher the income. Suppose we now ask, "Why do people with high educations have high incomes?" The most obvious possibility is that higher education leads to better jobs, which in turn lead to higher incomes. To explore this, we first examine the relationship between education and occupational level as well as that between occupational level and income.

Table 7-7 says that the higher one's education is, the higher one's occupation tends to be; Table 7-8 says that the higher one's occupation is, the higher one's income tends to be. This completes a causal chain:

$$\text{Education} \longrightarrow \text{Occupation} \longrightarrow \text{Income}$$

To see if occupation is an intervening variable between education and income, we examine the education-income relationship within the two categories of occupation, as in Table 7-9. The partial associations reflect a large drop from the zero-order association in Table 7-6 ($Q = +.18$ versus $Q = +.98$). Thus, when we control for occupational level, the association between education and income all but disappears. Notice that we're *not* concluding spuriousness here, even though the statistical

Table 7-7 Occupation by Education
(Hypothetical Data)

Education	OCCUPATION		Total	N
	High	**Low**		
High	80%	20	100%	1,000
Low	20%	80	100%	1,000
Total	50%	50	100%	2,000
	$Q = +.88$			

Table 7-8 Income by Occupation
(Hypothetical Data)

| | INCOME | | | |
Occupation	**High**	**Low**	**Total**	*N*
High	88%	12	100%	1,000
Low	12%	88	100%	1,000
Total	50%	50	100%	2,000
	$Q = +.96$			

Table 7-9 Income by Education, Controlling for Occupation
(Hypothetical Data)

| | HIGH OCCUPATION | | | | LOW OCCUPATION | | | |
| | INCOME | | | | INCOME | | | |
Education	**High**	**Low**	**Total**	*N*	**High**	**Low**	**Total**	*N*
High	89%	11	100%	800	15%	85	100%	200
Low	85%	15	100%	200	11%	89	100%	800
Total	88%	12	100%	1,000	12%	88	100%	1,000
	$Q = +.18$				$Q = +.18$			

results are the same as in the case of spuriousness. The difference lies in our theoretical understanding of the variables. Education does affect income in these data, but indirectly, through higher occupational levels. The fact that the partials aren't zero shows that education does have a small direct effect on income.[1] The partial associations obtained by controlling for occupation help us identify the mechanisms through which education affects income levels.

Component and Antecedent Variables

So far we've talked about two kinds of control variables, extraneous variables (used in the detection of spuriousness) and intervening variables (used to break down and explain causal mechanisms). We can illustrate a third type of control variable by considering the relationship between education and fertility; in many countries there's a negative relationship between years of schooling completed and the number of

---

[1] For example, two people with exactly the same jobs may have different incomes if their educational levels differ.

children born in a lifetime. We then might ask, "What is it about education that leads to lower fertility? What happens in college, and how does this affect the number of babies people have?" In this case we're searching for a fuller and more detailed understanding of the meaning of education. We want to understand what it is about education that produces this effect. Education reflects many different variables, such as objective knowledge, the ability to reason, values, aspirations, and time spent "out of circulation" (which results in older ages at marriage). None of these variables are intervening variables, since they are a part of education. If we imagine school as a black box, we know that people who've been in college boxes are different from those who've stopped after emerging from high school boxes. We want to know what goes on in those boxes. Until we do, we won't know what education means and we won't understand how it affects fertility or anything else.

To delineate the meaning of educational attainment, we might control for those variables that are part of education, such as those cited above. This type of control variable is called a *component variable*, because we regard it as a piece of another variable (education). For example, if we assume that having a baby is a rational decision (not a very good assumption, but bear with me), we might test people's ability to reason, and control for that variable. If the partial relationship between education and fertility went down, we might then reasonably conclude that to be more educated *means* to be more rational, which leads to lower fertility (assuming that having smaller families is a rational thing to do).

In another example, social class is positively related to the educational aspirations of parents for their children. Lower-class parents tend to have lower aspirations for their children than middle- and upper-class parents do. In this case, the independent variable (social class) is a general characteristic that includes many component characteristics such as income level, educational attainment, cultural and ethnic background, and occupation. In controlling for such variables, we're trying to answer the question: "What is it about a particular social class that makes people have certain aspirations for their children?" Or "What are the characteristics that make someone consider himself a member of a particular social class, and how do *those* characteristics affect aspirations?" In both cases we're trying to understand more fully the meaning of a particular characteristic in terms of more specific characteristics and causal factors.

A fourth type of control variable is the *antecedent variable*. In the previous section, we started with the zero-order relationship between education and income and sought intervening variables. What if we had started with the relationship between occupation and income (Table 7-8)? Noting that higher-level occupations bring higher incomes with them, we might then ask, "What causes occupation? Why do some people have higher-level jobs than others?" In picture form, this is what we've got:

$$? \longrightarrow \text{Occupation} \longrightarrow \text{Income}$$

The variables represented by the question mark are those which precede occupation and cause variation in job level. Again, an obvious possibility is education. If, in fact, education is a cause of occupation, then we have

$$\text{Education} \longrightarrow \text{Occupation} \longrightarrow \text{Income}$$

which should look familiar to you. If this model holds, then if we control for *occupation*, the relationship between education and income should go to zero (as it almost does in Table 7-9). In addition, however, if we control for *education*, the relationship between occupation and income should *not* go down. Table 7-10 shows the relationship between occupation and income, controlling for education. You can see that the partial associations are every bit as strong as they were before (the increase from .96 to .98 isn't meaningful).

Education is called an *antecedent variable* in the above model, because it comes before the original independent variable. At this point you might feel confused about the use of the terms *antecedent* and *intervening*. In this model,

$$\text{Education} \longrightarrow \text{Occupation} \longrightarrow \text{Income}$$

education is an antecedent variable to occupation. We start with the two-variable relationship between occupation and income and then add education to the model. If we start with the two-variable relationship between education and income and then add occupation to the model, occupation is an intervening variable, education is the original independent variable, and income is the dependent variable. The application of *antecedent* and *intervening* depends on what zero-order relationship you start with and what kind of variables you add to the model.

Table 7-10 Income by Occupation, Controlling or Education (Hypothetical Data)

| | HIGH EDUCATION | | | | LOW EDUCATION | | | |
| | INCOME | | | | INCOME | | | |
Occupation	High	Low	Total	N	High	Low	Total	N
High	99%	1	100%	800	45%	55	100%	200
Low	55%	45	100%	200	1%	99	100%	800
Total	90%	10	100%	1,000	10%	90	100%	1,000
	$Q = +.98$				$Q = +.98$			

Since controlling for occupation fails to reduce the relationship between education and income completely to zero, the most faithful representation of this three-variable model is as follows:

This tells us that some of education's impact on income is direct and that some of it is indirectly exerted through occupational levels.

We might then ask, "How do differences in education arise?" Some possible answers are family background, intelligence, and aspirations. We can propose these as antecedent variables only if they are all related to education, occupation, and income. If we control for both education and occupation, and examine the partial relationships between family background, intelligence, and aspirations and find that they have disappeared, then we can conclude that these factors play an antecedent role. Remember, however, that controlling for these last variables in the causal chain should not destroy the relationship between education and income, occupation and income, or education and occupation. The causal chain would now look like this:

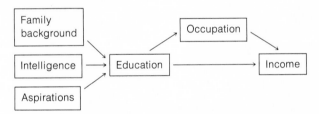

The introduction of antecedent variables enables us to trace back from the dependent variable to root causes and thus gives us a fuller understanding of what's going on.

Distorter and Suppressor Variables

In the case of extraneous, intervening, component, and antecedent variables, we started with a zero-order relationship and controlled for variables to verify the existence of a relationship (nonspurious) or to explain a relationship by filling out the causal mechanism or tracing back the causal chain. Sometimes we find *no* relationship where we expect there to be one. For example, suppose we gathered data on social class and racial prejudice.[1] We'd expect to find a negative relationship between

---

[1] Adapted from an example in Morris Rosenberg, *The Logic of Survey Analysis* (New York: Basic Books, 1968), pp. 94 ff.

social class and prejudice. Suppose we find no relationship. Does this mean that lower-class people are as liberal toward blacks as middle- and upper-class people? Or is there in fact a negative relationship that is being hidden by something?

In our search for clues, let's look at the cross tabulation of this relationship (with letters instead of percentages in the cells) (See Table 7-11.)

If the relationship were negative, then the percentages in the first column would get higher as we went from upper- to lower-class people, and the percentages in the second column would get *smaller* as we went from upper- to lower-class people (be sure you see this before going on). However, we found no relationship, which means that $a = c = e$ and $b = d = f$ (be sure you see this, too). This means that either too many upper-class people are prejudiced (making percentage a too large) or too many lower-class people are not prejudiced (making percentage f too large), or some combination of the two.

At this point, the solution to the puzzle may have already occurred to you. What would happen if our sample were taken in an area with a large percentage of blacks? Blacks tend to be members of the lower class much more than whites; they also are quite unlikely to be prejudiced against blacks! If there are a lot of blacks in the sample, and if they fall disproportionately in the lower class, then the lower class is going to have an inflated percentage "not prejudiced." If we remove the blacks from the sample, then the percentage in cell f is going to fall; the more lower-class blacks there are in the sample, the more the percentage will fall. As f falls, of course, e is going to increase (since together they add to 100 percent in the marginals). Then the relationship will emerge as negative.

We controlled for race, and by doing so, the relationship between social class and racial prejudice "emerged." In this case, race is called a *suppressor variable*, because the failure to control for it "suppresses" the zero-order relationship, making it *appear* to be weaker than it is.

The variable "race" is able to mask the relationship between social class and racial prejudice because of the way in which it is related to the latter variables. Being black tends to mean "lower-class"; but (and this is the crucial point) being lower-class is *positively* related to prejudice among whites, but *not* related to prejudice among blacks. Including blacks in the sample—lumping them in with lower-class whites—covers

Table 7-11 Racial Prejudice by Social Class

Social class	Prejudiced	Not prejudiced	Total
Upper	a	b	100%
Middle	c	d	100%
Lower	e	f	100%

up the tendency of lower-class whites to be relatively likely to be racially prejudiced in comparison with middle- and upper-class whites. The only way to allow the relationship between class and prejudice to emerge is to remove the blacks from the sample by statistically controlling for race.

If we'd taken our sample in a city where the population is mostly black, the relationship between class and prejudice might have appeared to be *positive*, since the lower class would then be so loaded with blacks that as a group lower-class people might look less prejudiced than middle- and upper-class people. In this case, controlling for race would make the relationship actually change direction, from positive to negative. Here we would call the variable "race" a *distorter variable* because its presence (uncontrolled) actually makes the relationship between the independent and dependent variables appear to be in the wrong direction.

To summarize, the presence of a suppressor variable makes a relationship appear weaker than it actually is; the presence of a distorter variable makes the relationship appear to be in the wrong direction. Controlling for such variables enables the true relationship to emerge.

We use controls to understand two-variable relationships more fully. In many cases we try to include several variables in a causal model (as in the discussion of antecedent variables and the explanation of income differences). You'll notice, however, that most causal models consider only a handful of variables, and you might feel that the effort is not worthwhile since so many variables are left out. By necessity we must set practical limits on the number of variables that are considered in the analysis of any problem. Even so, by delineating causal chains and the often complex interrelations among variables in even a limited causal model, we can make substantial progress toward understanding a theoretical problem through empirical research.

Specification

You'll recall that in Chap. 6 we looked at the negative relationship between occupation (scoring white-collar as plus) and favoring racial segregation, for a sample of American adults. We measured the strength of association with Yule's Q, which equaled $-.45$, a moderate negative association. We might be tempted to leave it at that and conclude that there's a "moderate" occupational difference in racial attitudes among American adults.

The problem with "leaving it at that" stems from the fact that the data in Table 7-12 represent an enormous variety of people who've been lumped together. There exists the danger of wrongly concluding that the relationship found among all Americans lumped together exists within all subgroups of Americans as well. Table 7-12 is the "sum" of an infinite

Table 7-12 Support for Racial Segregation by Occupation, United States, 1968

| | SUPPORT FOR RACIAL SEGREGATION | | | |
Occupation	Favors	Doesn't favor	Total	N
White-collar	11.1%	88.9	100.0%	422
Blue-collar	25.0%	75.0	100.0%	332
Total	17.2%	82.8	100.0%	754

number of subtables: we could construct a table for blacks, whites, men, women, college graduates, illiterates, married, widowed, single, and divorced people *ad infinitum*. If we made an exhaustive and mutually exclusive set of tables, one for each minute subgroup of Americans, and literally added those tables up (adding comparable marginals and cells), we'd arrive at Table 7-12. The question we want to ask is this: "Does the relationship we've observed hold between all kinds of white- and blue-collar workers, regardless of their other characteristics?"

For example, is the relationship among people living in the south the same as that among those living outside the south? To answer this question, we control for region (defined as "south" and "nonsouth") and look at the relationship between occupation and favoring segregation *within* each of those subpopulations. This process is called *specification*, because we're looking at a relationship observed on a general level to see if it holds among specific subgroups of the population. This gives us two tables, one for southerners and one for nonsoutherners (Table 7-13).

Both the percentages and the Q's tell us that occupation makes a much larger difference in the south than in the nonsouth. In *neither* region is the relationship of the same strength as that we observed on the national level. If we want to talk about a relationship between two

Table 7-13 Support for Racial Segregation by Occupation, by Region, United States, 1968

| | SOUTH | | | | NONSOUTH | | | |
Occupation	Favors	Doesn't favor	Total	N	Favors	Doesn't favor	Total	N
White-collar	14.4%	85.6	100.0%	125	10.0%	90.0	100.0%	297
Blue-collar	43.9%	56.1	100.0%	107	16.0%	84.0	100.0%	225
Total	28.0%	72.0	100.0%	232	12.6%	87.4	100.0%	522
	$Q = -.65$				$Q = -.26$			

variables, we have to be very conscious of just what group our data refer to. If it's based on a national sample, for example, we know there are many different kinds of people involved and the relationship is likely to look quite different from group to group. If we're interested in understanding the relationship fully, at some point we have to explain why the association is low in the nonsouth and substantial in the south.

A second example illustrates how substantively important specification can be. In the United States there's a positive relationship between educational attainment and income. If we specify for race, however, we find that the relationship is stronger among whites than it is among blacks; if we specify for sex, we find that the relationship is stronger among men than among women. A positive relationship means that people with high educations tend to have high incomes. The weaker relationships among blacks and among women indicate that, relative to whites and men, these groups have higher percentages with high educations and relatively low incomes. By specifying for race or sex, we can see that education doesn't pay off equally for all groups. This tells us much more about the relationship between education and income than we could learn from a national sample alone.

Specification is thus a valuable tool in the search for a detailed description and understanding of two-variable relationships.

Controls and Small Samples: Running Out of Cases

If we're analyzing data from a small sample or population, we can run into problems when we try to control for one or more additional variables. For example, suppose our data consist of 100 respondents. We first examine the relationship between social class and support for racial segregation. Social class has, say, three categories (upper, middle, and lower) and support for racial segregation has two (favors, doesn't favor). This will make a 3×2 table with six cells. If the cases were distributed evenly, this would provide an average of $100/6 = 16.67$, or approximately seventeen cases per cell. What happens if we control for race? If race has two categories (white and nonwhite), we now have two 3×2 tables with a total of twelve cells and an average of $100/12 = 8.33$, or approximately eight cases per cell. If we had controlled for a variable with, say, eight categories, our controlled relationship would consist of eight 3×2 tables with a total of forty-eight cells and an average of just over two cases per cell.

The problem with small samples is that we tend to run out of cases as we control for additional variables. We encounter empty cells, even though we know there are people who possess those combinations of characteristics.

There are three ways of dealing with this problem. The first is to gather larger samples or to study larger populations. The second is to make the tables smaller by combining variable categories (e.g., dichotomizing). This can raise problems of its own, however, such as concealing the true pattern of a relationship. The third is to simply refrain from controlling for additional variables. The best solution is the first, which should be taken into account when selecting a population or sample for study. The remaining two, although certainly legitimate, are far from ideal and can often be avoided during the first stages of research.

Summary

The analysis of two-variable relationships by the introduction of control variables is one of the arts of the social sciences. The subtleties and complexities that can arise in the analysis of data are often beyond the most experienced researcher (and the best computer). In this chapter we've touched on the main ideas and procedures that you're most likely to encounter in the social science literature. The literature on the analysis of relationships is vast and deep, and if you'd like to dig deeper than we've been able to do here, consult the suggested readings at the end of the chapter.

I want to stress that the data themselves can't tell us what to do with them. The analysis of data depends on common sense, rational thinking, sound theoretical reasoning, a healthy dose of intuition, some luck, and the substantive knowledge the researcher brings to the problem. When you read articles that include the analysis of data, it's imperative that you keep in mind that the researcher's analysis is based on a series of decisions—which variables to control, what interpretations to place on the results—and that every decision means that alternatives have been rejected. You have a right to expect an author to tell you how and why judgments were made. Only then can you make up your mind about the meaning and significance of the findings. Your common sense, ability to reason, intuition, and substantive knowledge are vital ingredients for your success as a consumer, a person who can learn from the empirical research of others.

Problems

7-1 "People who are in hospitals are more likely to die than people who are not in hospitals. There is thus a positive relationship between hospitalization and death." Researcher A suggests that there is something about hospitals that makes people die.

a. How would you use controls to test this idea?

b. What kind of variable (intervening, antecedent, etc.) would you control for?

c. What idea would you be testing?

d. What kinds of statistical results might you get, and what would they tell you about the idea you're testing?

7-2 "Young men (18 to 24) are far more likely than young women to die in automobile accidents." Suppose we wanted to understand why this relationship exists.

a. How could you use controls to deal with this problem?

b. What kind of variable (extraneous, antecedent, intervening, etc.) would you control for?

c. What kinds of statistical results might you get, and what would they tell you about the problem at hand?

7-3 Suppose we find a negative relationship between social class and sexist attitudes. We're interested in discovering what it is about social class that influences sexist attitudes.

a. How could you use controls to deal with this problem?

b. What kind of variable would you control for?

c. What kinds of statistical results might you get, and what would they tell you about the problem?

7-4 We find a positive relationship between alienation and the propensity to commit crimes. We're interested in discovering the sources of the alienation that leads to crime.

a. How could you use controls to deal with this problem?

b. What kind of variable would you control for?

c. What kinds of statistical results might you get, and what would they tell you about the problem?

7-5 We find a relationship between two variables X and Y, and the strength of the association is much lower than we expected it to be (close to zero).

a. What might be going on here?

b. How could you use controls to deal with the problem?

c. What kind of variable would you control for?

d. What kinds of statistical results might you get, and what would they tell you about the original relationship?

7-6 We find a relationship between two variables Z and Y, and the relationship is in a *direction* opposite to the one we expected (i.e., we thought it would be positive, but it's negative)

a. What might be going on here?

b. How could you use controls to deal with the problem?

c. What kind of variable would you control for?

d. What kinds of statistical results might you get, and what would they tell you about the original relationship?

Suggested Readings

1 Blalock, Hubert M., Jr.: *Causal Inferences in Nonexperimental Research.* Chapel Hill: University of North Carolina Press, 1964.
2 _____: "Theory Building and Causal Inferences," in Hubert M. Blalock, Jr., and Ann B. Blalock (eds.), *Methodology in Social Research*, pp. 155–198. New York: McGraw-Hill Book Company, 1968.
3 Cole, Stephen: *The Sociological Method*, 2d ed., chap. 4. Chicago: Markham, 1976.
4 Davis, James A.: *Elementary Survey Analysis.* Englewood Cliffs, N.J.: Prentice-Hall, 1971.
5 Hyman, Herbert: *Survey Design and Analysis.* Glencoe, Ill.: The Free Press, 1955.
6 Lazarsfeld, Paul F., and Morris Rosenberg (eds.): *The Language of Social Research*, sec. II, parts A and B. New York: The Free Press, 1955.
7 Loether, Herman J., and Donald G. McTavish: *Descriptive Statistics for Sociologists*, chap. 8. Boston: Allyn and Bacon, 1974.
8 Rosenberg, Morris: *The Logic of Survey Analysis*, especially appendix B, "The Arithmetic of Controls." New York: Basic Books, 1968.
9 Zeisel, Hans: *Say It with Figures*, 5th ed., chaps. 7–11. New York: Harper & Row, 1968.

8

multivariate
analysis

When we include more than one independent variable in trying to predict or explain variation in a dependent variable, we're using *multivariate analysis*. Technically, the material in Chap. 7 deals with multivariate analysis, since controlling involves the addition of one or more variables to an original zero-order relationship. While Chaps. 7 and 8 have a great deal in common, the material here is enough of an extension beyond the previous chapter to call for a separate treatment.

In this chapter we'll discuss several sets of techniques that allow us to deal with complex causal models. For the most part, we'll confine ourselves to techniques applicable to interval- and ratio-scale variables only. The mathematics in this chapter is the most advanced thus far, but even here I've tried to include only that which is necessary to understand the logic behind and the results of multivariate analytic techniques. This is the kind of chapter you should first read through quickly and then go back through for a careful study.

We use multivariate analysis to accomplish several kinds of tasks. First, it allows us to use several independent variables to explain variation in a dependent variable. Second, it allows us to use many independent variables to predict the value of a dependent variable. Third, it allows us to determine which independent variables have the greatest impact on a dependent variable (e.g., which is the most important factor in getting a job—skill, intelligence, race, sex, age, or educational degrees?). Fourth, it allows us to specify the relationships among the *independent* variables in order to discover the mechanisms by which they relate causally to the dependent variable. In short, multivariate analysis represents the most sophisticated empirical approach to the problems of scientific explanation and prediction.

Multiple Regression and Correlation

In Chap. 6 we discussed simple linear regression (one independent and one dependent variable). Multiple regression is an extension of two-variable regression. The underlying logic is the same with some embellishments. You might want to return to the discussion in Chap. 6 and refresh yourself before proceeding with multiple regression.

It's often the case that we want to see how well a set of independent variables can jointly predict or explain a dependent variable. For example, we might want to see how well we can explain income by using education, occupational status,[1] race, family background, and intelligence-test scores, *all working together*. What this means is that knowing people's educational attainment helps us predict their income; if, in addition, we know their occupation, this improves our accuracy of prediction because we know more about characteristics that are related to income.

However, if education, all by itself, explains 25 percent of the variation in income (that is, $r^2 = .25$) and occupation explains 20 percent, this does *not* mean that knowing educational attainment *and* occupation will explain 45 percent (that is, $25\% + 20\%$) of the variation in income. Why? Remember that the independent variables provide us with information that helps us predict the dependent variable. If I know your education, I *automatically* know something about your occupation as well, and vice versa. For example, if you have a Ph.D., you are most likely not a garbage collector, and if you have only a grade school education, you are certainly not a nuclear physicist. In other words, the two independent variables are related *to each other*. This "overlap" means that the information given by knowing both is less than the *sum* of the information conveyed by each alone.

The general formula for a multiple regression is

$$Y = a + b_1X_1 + b_2X_2 + b_3X_3 + b_4X_4 + \cdots$$

where each X represents an independent variable.

---

[1] There are many scales used to convert nominal and ordinal variables into a ratio form. One might be to ask people to rank occupations from low to high in terms of status. We could then calculate the average rank for each occupation and use this numerical score to measure how high one's occupational status is.

The slopes associated with each independent variable are somewhat different from those in linear regression. In multiple regression, each slope represents the impact of the independent variable *while all other variables in the equation are held constant*. It's as if we looked at the two-variable relationship between, say, X_1 and Y among people who are identical on all the other independent variables. This tells us the impact that each independent variable has *over and above the effects of the remaining independent variables*. In our above example, the partial slope for occupation tells us what information about income we get from knowing occupation *in addition* to what education has already told us. These slopes are in the units of the independent and dependent variables (e.g., change in dollar income per year of additional schooling) and are called *partial slopes* (or *partial-regression coefficients*).

As with slopes, we can also compute partial-correlation coefficients. These tell us how accurately we can predict Y from knowing the value of an independent variable (say, X_1) while holding the other variables in the equation constant. We can also compute a *multiple-correlation coefficient (R)*, which indicates how accurately we can predict Y by using all the independent variables at once. R^2 has the same interpretation as r^2, except that it applies to the explanation of Y by more than one independent variable.

Both partial slopes and correlations are used in testing models such as the simple one we mentioned in Chap. 7. We looked at the relationship between income and education. Our question was: "Does education directly affect how much money one makes, or does it indirectly affect income through its effects on occupation?" In other words, once we *control* for occupation (i.e., examine the relationship between income and education among those who have similar jobs), does education still have a relationship with income? To answer this question, we perform a multiple-regression analysis with income as the dependent variable and with education and occupational status as the independent variables:

$$\hat{Y} = a + b_1 X_1 + b_2 X_2$$

where X_1 is years of school completed and X_2 is an occupational status score.

If education's effects on income are indirect, than once we hold occupation constant, education's impact should be zero (or close to zero). This means that b_1 should be zero in the above equation. On the other hand, if education has effects on income *independent* of those of occupation, b_1 will not be zero. We can perform the same kind of analysis using partial correlation coefficients, although, as we've mentioned, the interpretation is in terms of prediction accuracy, not impact.

Multiple regression can be used also for prediction and estimation.

For example, the U.S. Bureau of the Census tries to estimate the population of states and countries during years that fall between decennial censuses. One of the methods used is a multiple-regression equation which estimates population (the dependent variable Y) with four independent variables (X_1 to X_4). The equation for New York State counties. and metropolitan areas for the 1970s is[1]

$$\hat{Y} = .0203 + .1847X_1 + .2283X_2 + .1528X_3 + .4406X_4$$

where X_1 = elementary school enrollment for grades 1 through 8 plus elementary special and elementary ungraded
X_2 = the 2-year average of resident births
X_3 = the 2-year average of resident deaths
X_4 = the number of registered automobiles

Note that in this case the substantive or causal connection between the dependent and independent variables is irrelevant to the task, and there's no interest in determining which independent variables have the greatest effects on population; the sole purpose is to predict population size accurately.

Where do such equations come from? When the Census Bureau conducts a census, there's a population count for each county in the state of New York (in 1970, for example), as well as records on births, deaths, school enrollments, and automobile registrations during the census year. Using the county as a unit of analysis, they perform a multiple-regression analysis, yielding the above equation. To use it throughout the 1970s, they must assume that the pattern of relationships among those variables remains the same throughout the decade.

Standardized Slopes

A problem arises in comparing the slopes of independent variables in a multiple-regression analysis. In one of the examples above, we predicted income with education and occupational status. Suppose X_1 is education and X_2 is the occupational status score, and the partial slope for education is greater than for status. Our first impulse might be to conclude that education has a greater independent impact on income than occupational status has, but what do the results really tell us?

The partial slope for education (b_1) tells us how many dollars are associated with an increase of 1 year of schooling; the comparable slope for occupation tells us how many dollars are associated with each increase of one point on the occupational-status scale. However, it isn't fair to compare the impact of 1 year of schooling with that of one point

[1] U.S. Bureau of the Census, *Current Population Reports: Estimates of the Population of New York Counties and Metropolitan Areas: July 1, 1972 and 1973*, ser. P-25, no. 527, 1974.

on a rating scale; since the units are different, the slopes cannot be compared. How many status points equal 1 year of schooling? It's like translating apples into oranges.

We've encountered this problem in a variety of forms already. In frequency distributions we found that we couldn't make comparisons if the totals weren't the same; the same was true of means and variances. In each case we converted the data to some common denominator. By making the units *standard*, we made meaningful comparisons possible.

In the case of partial slopes, we make the following kind of conversion. If 1 year of schooling (independent of occupation) means \$500 in additional income, the *unstandardized* slope is $b_1 = \$500/\text{year}$. If we divide \$500 by the size of the standard deviation for income (s_Y) and 1 year by the standard deviation of years of schooling (s_{X_1}), we have the change in income expressed in standard deviations associated with each increase of one standard deviation of years of schooling.

$$\frac{\$500/s_Y}{1 \text{ year}/s_{X_1}} = \beta_1 = b_1 \left(\frac{s_{X_1}}{s_Y}\right)$$

We've converted both numerator and denominator of the partial slope from the original units (dollars and years of schooling) to numbers of standard deviations, by dividing each variable in the equation by *its own* standard deviation. The symbol for the *standardized partial slope* is the Greek letter beta (β).

For example, if the standard deviation of income is \$6,000, then the numerator of the partial slope is $500/6,000 = 1/12$. If the standard deviation of years of schooling is 4 years, then the denominator becomes $1/4$. The *standardized* partial slope is then

$$\frac{\dfrac{1}{12}}{\dfrac{1}{4}} = \frac{1}{3} = .33$$

This tells us that, with occupational status held constant, for every increase of one standard deviation in educational attainment there is an increase of .33 standard deviation of income. If we do the same thing for occupational status, and get a partial slope of, say, .44, then we know that occupational status produces a greater change in income than educational attainment does. When we translate the partial slopes into this form, we can compare them without worrying about the fact that education scores may run from 0 through 16 and occupational status may run from 1 through 100.

These special partial slopes go by several names: *standardized slopes, standardized regression coefficients,* or *beta weights.* All three terms refer to the same thing.

An Example of Multiple-Regression Analysis in Action

The combination of interesting and important problems with sophisticated, properly used statistical techniques is a social scientist's dream, and not encountered as often as one would like. Otis Dudley Duncan has produced a small masterpiece, "Inheritance of Poverty or Inheritance of Race?"[1] in which he uses multiple-regression analysis to study the problem of income differences between American blacks and whites. In 1962 the differences between black and white mean incomes amounted to $3,790. He's concerned with the commonly held position among those interested in racial problems, that poverty breeds poverty, that blacks are poor because their parents were poor and disadvantaged, and passed on their poverty to their sons via poor educations, occupations, and mental abilities.[2] Duncan suggests that the inheritance of disadvantaged backgrounds does not tell the whole story, that the inheritance of race is very important as well. In other words, if blacks had the same backgrounds as whites, they would still make less money because they're black.

Duncan uses data from the 1962 study of Occupational Changes in a Generation. The respondents used by Duncan are restricted to native-born men 25 to 64 years old with nonfarm backgrounds. The study is based on a national probability sample.

Duncan performs a multiple-regression analysis using the respondent's income as the dependent variable and five background characteristics as independent variables (shown below with the symbols we'll use later in the actual regression equations):

E_f = respondent's father's education[3]
O_f = respondent's father's occupation[4]
S = number of siblings in respondent's family of origin
E_r = respondent's education[3]
O_r = respondent's occupation[4]
I = respondent's income for 1961[5]

---

[1] Otis Dudley Duncan, "Inheritance of Poverty or Inheritance of Race?" in Daniel P. Moynihan (ed.), *On Understanding Poverty* (New York: Basic Books, 1969).

[2] See, for example, Michael Harrington, *The Other America: Poverty in the United States* (Baltimore: Penguin, 1963), p. 21; *1964 Economic Report of the President* (Washington, D.C.: Government Printing Office, 1964), pp. 69–70; *The War on Poverty*, Committee Print, Select Committee on Poverty of the Committee on Labor and Public Welfare, United States Senate (Washington, D.C.: Government Printing Office, 1964), pp. 2 and 35.

[3] Education is measured on a scale that reads as follows: 0 = no years completed; 1 = elementary 1 to 4; 2 = elementary 5 to 7; 3 = elementary 8; 4 = high school 1 to 3; 5 = high school 4; 6 = college 1 to 3 years; 7 = college 4 years; 8 = college 5 years or more.

[4] Occupation is measured with the Duncan socioeconomic index of occupational status.

[5] Income is measured in thousands of dollars.

Now, before you go on, familiarize yourself with the variables involved and their representative symbols. Read the footnoted descriptions of the variables and be sure you understand what they mean (we won't describe Duncan's occupational-status scale). We're going to use these symbols in a pair of multiple-regression equations which are intimidating enough without your being thrown by the meaning of the variable symbols. Take your time.

Duncan performs the analysis separately for blacks and whites (the white group includes the trivial number of nonwhites who are not blacks). The form of the two equations is as follows:[1]

$$\text{Whites: } \hat{I} = a + b_1 E_f + b_2 O_f + b_3 S + b_4 E_r + b_5 O_r$$
$$\text{Blacks: } \hat{I} = a + b_1 E_f + b_2 O_f + b_3 S + b_4 E_r + b_5 O_r$$

Before we go on, let's look at these equations and make sure you understand them. Both equations include the same variables, but for two different groups of people (whites and blacks). Income ($\hat{I}$) is the dependent variable (i.e., the one caused by the other variables in the model). The a is the regression constant: when all the independent variables have a value of zero, income equals the value of a.

The b's (b_1 through b_5) are the partial-regression coefficients (slopes) for each independent variable. These tell us what the impact of each independent variable is on income *independent of the effects of the other independent variables.* We've used small b's instead of Greek β's because these coefficients are *unstandardized.* If we'd wanted to see which variables had the greatest independent effects on income, we'd have used standardized regression coefficients, and the equations would look like this:

$$\text{Whites: } \hat{I} = a + \beta_1 E_f + \beta_2 O_f + \beta_3 S + \beta_4 E_r + \beta_5 O_r$$
$$\text{Blacks: } \hat{I} = a + \beta_1 E_f + \beta_2 O_f + \beta_3 S + \beta_4 E_r + \beta_5 O_r$$

All these equations represent the same story; the respondent's income is seen as the product of five factors: his father's education and occupation, the size of his family of origin (number of siblings), and the respondent's own education and occupational status. The equations allow us to deal with several kinds of problems, but before you go on, be sure you feel comfortable with them. Be sure you can start at the income end of the equation and work your way through, explaining each term's meaning as well as that of the equation as a whole.

---

[1] As before, the "hat" (^) over the symbol for income (I) signifies that the values of I generated by the equation are *predictions.*

When Duncan computed the actual values of the partial-regression coefficients (*unstandardized*), he got the following results:

Whites: $\hat{I} = 1.90 - .008E_f + .022O_f - .016S + .299E_r + .071O_r$
Blacks: $\hat{I} = 2.08 + .043E_f - .005O_f - .025S + .249E_r + .021O_r$

If you study these equations (please do), something should seem strange. The impact of the number of siblings is negative for both whites and nonwhites (−.016 and −.025), as it should be, since the larger a family is, the harder it is for children to get ahead in the world. However, the partial slope for the respondent's father's education is *negative* for whites (−.008), which says that the higher the father's education is, the lower the son's income is; this doesn't make any sense. The catch to this will be explained in material we haven't covered yet, but crudely put, this partial-regression coefficient *isn't statistically significant from zero*. This means that the slope of −.008 represents random error that comes from the fact that we're drawing a sample and not performing a census. It could just as well have been +.008 in another sample. Don't worry about this just now. You might want to return to this after studying Chap. 12.

In most research reports that use regression analysis, the partial-regression coefficients are presented in a form such as Table 8-1. Note the footnote in the table, which tells us we *cannot* be confident that the starred partial slopes are *not* zero in the population. Thus, Duncan's first finding is that a number of factors thought to have direct effects on in-

Table 8-1 Partial-Regression Coefficients for the Regression of Respondent's Income on a Series of Stratification Variables, for Native Men 25 to 64 Years Old, with Nonfarm Background and in the Experienced Civilian Labor Force, by Race, March 1962

Independent variable	PARTIAL-REGRESSION COEFFICIENTS	
	Blacks	Whites
Father's education (E_f)	.043*	−.008*
Father's occupation (O_f)	−.005*	.022
Number of siblings (S)	−.025*	−.016*
Respondent's education (E_r)	.249	.299
Respondent's occupation (O_r)	.021	.071
Regression constant	2.08	1.90

* Coefficient less than its estimated standard error in absolute value.

come apparently do not: among blacks, father's education and occupation as well as the size of the family do not have significant *direct* effects on the son's income; among whites, the same is true for the father's education and the size of the family. Remember that these coefficients refer to *direct* effects (i.e., not through an intervening variable), which is not to say that these variables have nothing to do with income. We'll see more about this later on.

Duncan approaches the problem of "inheritance of poverty or inheritance of race" by using the entire regression equations in an ingenious and revealing way. You'll remember that the perspective of regression analysis is one of prediction: if we plug in the values for the five independent variables for a respondent, the resulting value of income is the best available prediction of what his income actually is. If we plug in the *means* for each of the five independent variables (for whites, say), we get the mean income for that group. Thus, the mean income for whites is a direct function of the means for these five variables multiplied by the appropriate regression coefficients. The same is true for the black equation.

The inheritance-of-poverty (versus inheritance-of-race) argument suggests that the gap between white and black incomes is a function of background differences. In other words, blacks make less money because their fathers had inferior educations and occupations, they came from larger families, and they themselves have inferior educations and occupations. To test this idea, Duncan formulates the problem in terms of the question: "What if blacks had the same background characteristics as whites? Would they then have the same incomes?" If, in fact, the income gap is caused by inferior backgrounds (as the inheritance-of-poverty argument suggests), then equalizing backgrounds should equalize incomes.

Duncan tests this idea by plugging the *white* means for the five independent variables into the equation for *blacks*. Be careful to note his intention: he's keeping the white means as they are, but subjecting whites to the same set of partial-regression coefficients as apply to blacks. Remember what the regression coefficients tell us: How much impact does a variable have on income? How much of a payoff is associated with each additional year of school, each additional point of occupational status, etc.? Thus, the whites still have the same level of attainment (both of fathers and of respondents), but now they must, in Duncan's words, play the same game as blacks.

Keep in mind that a regression equation has two basic kinds of numbers: scores on variables and a set of regression coefficients. In this case, the scores tell us how privileged one's background is; the set of regression coefficients tell us how effectively that background is converted into income. The inheritance-of-poverty argument suggests that the income gap between whites and blacks is a function of the former; the inheritance-of-race argument suggests that the latter set of factors is involved; it's not enough for a black man to have a socioeconomic background equal to that of whites, because being black is a liability in itself. In blunter terms, blacks with high qualifications are discriminated against because of their race.

When Duncan inserted the white means into the black regression equation, the resulting predicted mean income for whites was lowered by $2,360, closing the gap between blacks and whites by that amount. This leaves $1,430 still unaccounted for. Thus, if blacks and whites were identical on these five important background characteristics, there would still be a gap of $1,430 in mean incomes. In Duncan's own words:

> . . . there remains the sum of $1,430 not yet accounted for. This is about three-eighths of the total gap of $3,790. Unless and until we can find other explanations for it, it must stand as an estimate of income discrimination. . . . Specifically, it is the difference between Negro and white incomes that cannot be attributed to differential occupational levels, differential educational attainment . . . differences in size of family of origin, or differences in the socio-economic status thereof.[1] . . .

Duncan has succeeded in applying sophisticated techniques to a problem of more than academic interest. It's of interest to those in government who make policy decisions vital to the socioeconomic advancement of blacks. Duncan's findings strongly suggest that the elimination of disadvantaged backgrounds is not a sufficient cure for poverty, that race (discrimination) plays a powerful role in the transfer of poverty from generation to generation. He suggests that

> if there were remedies for all these forms of discrimination, so that only the handicap of family background remained, that handicap would be materially diminished in the next generation. It would be further attenuated in successive generations under these ideal conditions, and while some persisting differential in achievement due solely to initial background handicaps would be observed for several decades, it would tend to disappear of its own accord.[2]

This is a model application of sophisticated analysis performed on sample data.

Duncan draws an additional picture with the results of his multiple-regression analysis, which we should look at both for its substantive interest and the practice it will give you in understanding the results of such analyses. He examines several regressions in order to pick apart the transfer of background advantages (and disadvantages) from generation to generation.

---

[1] Duncan, *op. cit.*, p. 100.
[2] *Ibid.*, p. 102.

He starts by examining the effects of the respondent's family characteristics on the respondent's own educational achievement, both for blacks and for whites. Figure 8-1 is a picture of two regression equations, one for blacks and one for whites, using *standardized* regression coefficients (beta weights). The straight arrows indicate a causal link with the head of the arrow at the dependent variable. The curved arrows show that there is a correlation between the two connected variables, but no causal link is being asserted in this analysis. If we put these diagrams in the form of equations, they'd look like this:

$$\text{Whites: } \hat{E}_r = 4.04 + .181E_f + .091O_f - .117S$$
$$\text{Blacks: } \hat{E}_r = 3.07 + .336E_f + .006O_f - .071S$$

where E_r is the respondent's education (the dependent variable), E_f is the respondent's father's education, O_f is the father's occupational status, and S is the number of siblings. (Compare these equations with Fig. 8-1 and be sure you see that they describe the same thing.) The important thing to notice is that the impact of father's education on son's education is stronger for blacks than for whites (.336 versus .181), as reflected in the standardized regression coefficients. Thus, the regression analysis tells

Figure 8-1 Regression of respondent's education on selected background characteristics, by race.

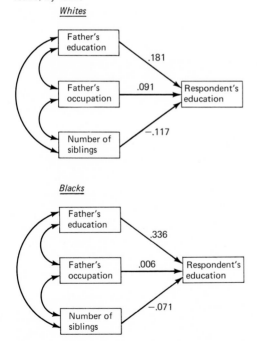

Whites

Blacks

us that blacks are more successful than whites in passing on educational achievement to their sons. This of course means that *low* achievement levels are passed on more consistently, too; nonetheless, if a black father gets a lot of schooling, he is more successful than a comparable white father in passing it on to his son.

This might startle you, since this seems inconsistent with the disadvantaged position blacks find themselves in. You will be less startled when you examine the results of a second set of regression analyses performed by Duncan.

In the second step, Duncan uses the son's occupational status as the dependent variable and all his family's characteristics plus the son's educational attainment as the independent variables. The equations, for blacks and whites, look like this:

Whites: $\hat{O}_r = .73 + .256E_f + .138O_f - .365S + 7.964E_r$
Blacks: $\hat{O}_r = 4.72 + .811E_f + .005O_f - .105S + 3.653E_r$

Again, go through these equations, starting with the dependent variable, and be sure you understand the parts and the whole before going on.

Take a look at the regression coefficients for the respondent's education. Clearly, the impact of additional years of schooling on occupational status is much greater for whites than for blacks (7.964 versus 3.653). If we now look at Table 8-1 once again (please do so), we see that the son's occupational status has a much greater independent impact on income for whites than for blacks (.071 versus .021). The story is now complete. While black fathers have more success in passing their educational achievements on to their sons, the sons of white fathers are more able to convert the educational advantage into an occupational advantage and, in turn, the occupational advantage into a higher income. Thus, blacks are in a frustrating position: their educations don't pay off for them in better jobs to the extent that they do for whites; and better jobs don't pay off in money terms as much as they do for whites. In each case, comparing the regression coefficients of blacks and whites allows us to compare the impacts of different advantages on such things as occupational prestige and income.

We've spent considerable space on this series of examples, but I hope you begin to see how much we can learn by carefully examining the results of complicated and sophisticated statistical analysis. It allows us to address questions that are often fascinating and of considerable practical importance.

Path Analysis

Path analysis is a technique for evaluating entire causal models. It utilizes multiple-regression techniques, but the results are presented in a way different from that discussed earlier in this chapter. Duncan, in his article discussed earlier as an example of multiple-regression analysis, also uses path analysis. Recall that he was interested in the effects that fathers' educations and occupations, the number of siblings in the respondent's family, and the respondent's education and occupation had on the respondent's income. You'll also recall that Duncan performed several multiple regressions using these factors as independent variables, and that he performed separate analyses for blacks and for whites. If we drew a picture of the black regression equations, we'd have the information shown in Fig. 8-2. Let's go through this diagram and see just what it tells us.

First, path analysis imposes a number of requirements on the relationships between the included variables. (1) All the causal relationships work in one direction only (e.g., father's education causes son's education, but son's education doesn't cause father's education), which is symbolized by a one-way arrow going from the cause to the effect; another way of putting this is that all relationships must be asymmetrical or "simple recursive."[1] (2) All the variables must have a definite time ordering. (3) All variables that are not affected by other variables in the model (i.e., father's education and father's occupation) are called ex-

Figure 8-2 Path diagram representing a model of the socioeconomic life cycle in the Negro population, with path coefficients estimated for native men 25 to 64 years old with nonfarm backgrounds and in the experienced civilian labor force (March 1962). (*Source:* Otis Dudley Duncan, "Inheritance of Poverty or Inheritance of Race?" in Daniel P. Moynihan (ed.), *On Understanding Poverty*, New York: Basic Books, 1969, p. 90.)

Blacks

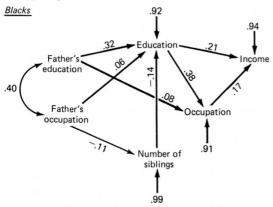

---

[1] Strictly speaking, path analysis does permit causation to run in both directions at once (e.g., racist attitudes cause racist behavior which in turn reinforces racist attitudes), but the calculation of the coefficients is messy enough to justify sticking to simple recursive path analysis here.

ogenous variables and are joined by a curved arrow; we encountered the use of the curved arrow in the discussion of multiple regression, and the meaning here is the same; it represents a relationship that is not considered causal. In fact, the causal nature of the relationship isn't considered relevant to the task at hand.

There are two kinds of numbers represented in a path-analysis diagram. First, there are the numbers associated with the connecting arrows. These numbers are standardized regression coefficients (beta weights) and tell us how great an impact each variable has on another variable *independent of the other variables in the model.* Since the coefficients are standardized, we can compare their magnitudes: for example, among blacks, son's education has a greater impact on son's income (.21) than son's occupation (.17) has. These standardized regression coefficients, when used in a path analysis, are called *path coefficients.* (Be sure to look at the diagram and find the above numbers.)

You'll also notice that for four of the variables (all but father's education and father's occupation), there are arrows coming out of nowhere, with numbers attached. These numbers are coefficients of alienation (go back to Chap. 6 and refresh your memory if you need to) and reflect the amount of variation in these variables left *unexplained* by the variables in the model (it's the square root of the unexplained variance). For example, the coefficient of alienation for income is .94. If we square this number, we get the proportion of the variation in income that is *not* explained by the variables in the model, or $(.94)^2 = .88$. Thus, the model explains 12 percent of the variation in income.

The path coefficients are calculated through a *series* of multiple regressions. We begin with the independent variables that are closest to the dependent variable and work backwards. For example, we first do the regression of income on son's occupation and get the path coefficient (.17). We then perform a multiple regression of income on both son's occupation and son's education. This tells us how much of the effects of education is direct and how much is indirect.

What are path diagrams good for? What do they tell us that a single multiple-regression equation doesn't? First, multiple regression determines the direct (independent) effects of each independent variable on the dependent variable, as measured by the beta weights. Path analysis, however, allows us to determine the magnitude of the *indirect* effects as well. We do this by simply multiplying paths together. For example, education's direct effect on income is .21. In addition, education affects income indirectly through occupation. The path from education to occupation has a coefficient of .38, and that from occupation to income has a coefficient of .17. The indirect effect of education through occupation on income is measured by the *product* of these two paths, or $(.38)(.17) = .06$.

The effects of father's education on son's income provide a second example. Father's education has no direct impact on son's income (reflected by the absence of an arrow connecting the two), but this doesn't mean that father's education is unimportant. It *indirectly* affects son's income in three ways: through the son's education, (.32)(.21); through the son's education and then the son's occupation, (.32)(.38)(.17); and through the son's occupation, (.08)(.17). The sum of these compound paths is .10. Using path diagrams, we can see that while father's education has no direct effects on son's income (something that multiple-regression equations would have told us — the beta weight would have been close to zero), it certainly plays an indirect role in determining the son's income (a finding that a multiple-regression equation wouldn't have told us).

Path analysis also allows us to spell out the relationships among the independent variables, something we can't accomplish with a single multiple-regression equation. For example, in Fig. 8-2, we see that most of the impact of father's education on the son's income is exerted through the son's education [compound path of (.32)(.21) = .07], and then the son's occupation [compound path of (.32)(.38)(.17) = .02]; very little influence is exerted directly through the son's occupation [compound path of (.08)(.17) = .01]. Interestingly, father's occupation does not work directly through the son's occupation (there is no arrow between father's and son's occupation) but only through the son's education and *then* through the son's occupation [compound paths of (.06)(.21) = .01 and (.06)(.38)(.17) = .004] as well as a minor series of complex routings through number of siblings, son's education, and son's occupation. (You should go through the above paragraph, referring to the path diagram in Fig. 8-2, and satisfy yourself that you understand where the compound paths come from and what they stand for.)

Path analysis is an important theoretical tool because it forces the researcher to specify explicitly *all* the relationships in a causal model. Multiple-regression analysis by itself would tell us only the relationships between the independent variables and the dependent variable. By working through the model with a series of multiple regressions, we see not only direct effects of independent variables on the dependent variable, but indirect effects and the patterns of interrelationships among all variables in the model as well. Path analysis is experiencing growing popularity in the social science literature as social scientists move toward more comprehensive explanatory models.

Conclusion

Although we've only scratched the surface of path, regression, and correlation analysis, there's enough here to enable you to make sense of most of the literature you'll encounter. There are a number of ideas that you should be sure you understand. You should be able to explain to someone the logic of multiple regression and correlation, the meaning of partial slopes and partial-correlation coefficients. You should be familiar enough with standardized coefficients not to be confused by their use.

As with all the topics we've encountered, the most important thing is to keep your head, take your time, persevere, and think about what the methods are trying to accomplish and what the results mean. If you haven't discovered it already, as you encounter data, you'll find that a surprising amount of understanding is based on common sense. Don't slight your own ability to reason and to learn from data, and pay attention to those internal signals that tell you that something isn't quite right.

This chapter concludes Part One of this book. In Part One we've tried to outline the basic empirical tasks of social research and the major statistical approaches in use today. In Part Two we'll again be talking about description and explanation, but with a twist. In Part One we made little mention of the sources of our data, or whom they represented. In Part Two we'll address the problem of going about the tasks of description and explanation without gathering information from all members of a population. If we find a positive relationship between X and Y in a sample, what can we say about the direction and strength of the relationship in the population? How confident can we be that our sample information represents the population from which it was drawn? Questions like these reflect the task of *inferential statistics*, which we now turn to.

Before going on, you might want to spend some time going through the glossary, Appendix A.

Problems

8-1 Suppose we examine the multiple relationship between academic achievement (based on achievement tests scored from 0 to 100) and two independent variables, father's educational attainment and the amount of money spent by the school per student, and get the following results:

$$\hat{Y} = 10 + .30X_1 + .05X_2 \qquad R = +.54$$

where $\hat{Y}$ is the predicted achievement-test score, X_1 is the years of school completed by the father, and X_2 is the school's expenditures per student per year. The partial-regression coefficients are standardized. What story does this equation tell?

8-2 Given a multiple regression and the following standardized and unstandardized regression coefficients (partial slopes):

Independent variable	Unstandardized coefficient	Standardized coefficient
X_1	$b_1 = 2.1$	$\beta_1 = 1.6$
X_2	$b_2 = 3.0$	$\beta_2 = 1.9$
X_3	$b_3 = 1.5$	$\beta_3 = 2.2$

a. Compare the effects of independent variables X_2 and X_3. Which has the greater independent impact on Y?

b. Briefly explain where you got your answer and why it's correct.

8-3 In what ways is path analysis an improvement over multiple-regression analysis?

8-4 Consider the path diagram shown in Fig. 8-3.

a. In terms of explained variance, which variable in the model is best explained by the other variables in the model?

b. Which variable has the greatest independent impact on son's income?

c. Does number of siblings have a direct impact on son's income?

d. How would you go about measuring the *indirect* effects of number of siblings on son's occupation? Do it.

Figure 8-3 Path diagram representing a model of the socioeconomic life cycle in the white population, with path coefficients estimated for native men 25 to 64 years old with nonfarm backgrounds and in the experienced civilian labor force (March 1962). (*Source:* Otis Dudley Duncan, "Inheritance of Poverty or Inheritance of Race?" in Daniel P. Moynihan (ed.), *On Understanding Poverty,* New York: Basic Books, 1969, p. 90.)

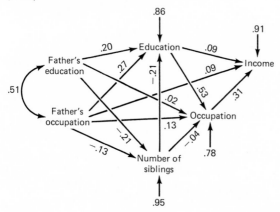

e. How would you go about measuring the *indirect* effects of number of siblings in income? Do it.

f. How much of the variance in son's income is explained by this model?

g. What does the curved arrow connecting father's education and father's occupation mean?

Suggested Readings

1 Blalock, Hubert M., Jr.: *Social Statistics*, 2d ed., chap. 19. New York: McGraw-Hill Book Company, 1972.

2 Cohen, Jacob: "Multiple Regression as a General Data-analytic System," in Lieberman, Bernhardt (ed.), *Contemporary Problems in Statistics*. New York: Oxford University Press, 1971.

3 Darlington, Richard B.: "Multiple Regression in Psychological Research and Practice," in Lieberman, Bernhardt (ed.), *Contemporary Problems in Statistics*. New York: Oxford University Press, 1971.

4 Duncan, Otis Dudley: "Inheritance of Poverty or Inheritance of Race?" in Daniel P. Moynihan (ed.), *On Understanding Poverty*, pp. 85–110. New York: Basic Books, 1969.

5 Ezekiel, Mordecai, and Karl A. Fox: *Methods of Correlation and Regression Analysis*, 3d ed., chaps. 10, 11, 13, 25, and 26. New York: John Wiley & Sons, 1967.

6 Hays, William L.: *Statistics for the Social Sciences*, 2d ed., secs. 16.15, 16.16, 16.18, 16.20. New York: Holt, Rinehart and Winston, 1973.

7 See the collection of articles on multivariate analysis in Lazarsfeld, Paul F., and Morris Rosenberg (eds.): *The Language of Social Research*, sec. II. New York: The Free Press, 1955.

8 Loether, Herman J., and Donald G. McTavish: *Descriptive Statistics for Sociologists*, chap. 9. Boston: Allyn and Bacon, 1974.

9 A series of articles on path analysis has appeared in *Sociological Methodology, 1969*, edited by Edgar F. Borgatta. San Francisco: Jossey, Bass, 1969. These include Kenneth C. Land, "Principles of Path Analysis"; David R. Heise, "Problems in Path Analysis and Causal Inference"; and in the 1970 volume of the same name, see Otis Dudley Duncan, "Partials, Partitions and Paths."

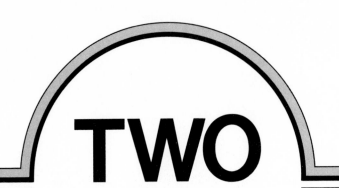

TWO

If we were interested in studying a particular population (e.g., textile workers in the United States) and could take a census of them, the descriptive and explanatory tasks of the social sciences could be well handled with the techniques discussed in Part One. Usually, however, we aren't in a position to take censuses of large populations, because it requires more time and money than we have. Even if we had a lot of time and money, some populations are infinite (tossing coins is an example) and in others the process of gathering data is destructive. (To test the breaking point of pieces of steel, taking a census would require us to destroy everything we make!)

We want to describe and explain phenom-

STATISTICAL
INFERENCE

ena at a population level of analysis, and yet we don't have the means to carry out studies of entire populations. Necessity forces us to select samples from populations of interest, and we're left with the task of using sample data to describe and explain relationships within whole populations. The set of procedures and principles that we use to study populations without conducting censuses is called *inferential statistics*, and it's the subject of Part Two.

The descriptive and analytical techniques described earlier in this book are as appropriate to sample data as they are to population data. The task of inferential statistics is to help us generalize from sample results to the parent population.

9

taking samples

Although we're usually not aware of it, we take samples all the time. We constantly select information from populations, form impressions, and make decisions from them. When we vote for a political candidate, we rely on only a small fraction of the total information. When we meet someone, our impressions are based on limited perceptions. The problem with such samples is that there's no way to know how representative they are. Politicians release only favorable information; all of us try to put our best foot forward when we interact with others. In short, we're unable to consider the entire population of information when we select our samples. The purpose of scientific sampling is to identify and exhaustively consider all members of a population and make selections in such a way as to ensure a representative sample.

If you could ask any group of people a question, whom would you ask and what would you ask them? I'd like to know, for example, how assembly-line workers feel about their jobs. How would we go about doing such a study? How would we know that our results accurately represented the population without taking a census?

First, we have to precisely define the population we're studying. It might be "all people classified by the management as assembly-line workers at the John P. Blup Company in St. Petersburg, Florida." Now, if the number of workers is pretty small (100 to 200, say) then we could gather information on all of them (i.e., take a *census*) without too much trouble. On the other hand, if we're talking about all assembly-line workers who work for Ford at Detroit area plants,[1] then we've got a very large number of people, probably too large to census without spending an enormous amount of money. In such a case, we'd like to be able to ask our questions of only *some* workers and be able to use their answers to represent accurately the feelings of *all* the workers. In other words, we want to select a *representative sample*. This chapter is about how it's done and how you as a reader can evaluate sampling procedures to tell bad samples from good ones.

Keep in mind that we're rarely able to evaluate a specific sample; we usually can't say, "This or that sample is or is not representative." Most of the time we can evaluate only the procedure used to select a sample. If we have confidence in the *procedure*, then we *infer* that the resulting sample is a good one.

Sampling the Assembly Line: A "Simple" Sample

First we have to decide how large a sample to select. The general rule is to take as many people in your sample as you can afford. The typical cost of gathering and processing information on one person in such a study is around $60. Suppose we have $30,000 to spend; this would allow us to select around 500 workers for our sample.

You may be asking at this point, "Does it matter what *proportion* of the population we select?" Believe it or not, in most cases where the population is large enough to force us to take a sample, the proportion we take doesn't significantly affect our accuracy. The important thing is the *absolute size of the sample*. For now, take this on faith, we'll explore it in more detail in later chapters when we talk about statistical inference.

We've defined our population already: "all workers classified by management as 'assembly-line,' working in Ford plants located in the Detroit area." We get a map, draw a line enclosing the city and the selected contiguous communities, and make a list of the factories included. From each factory manager we obtain a list of all assembly-line workers. This list, which contains all members of the population, is called the *frame* of the sample.

Notice that in this case we actually obtained a list of the entire population. Sometimes (as with national studies) this isn't possible. In such cases (as you'll see in the discussion of complex samples) we can still draw a representative sample if we precisely define the population. Populations can thus be sampled if they are either enumerated or precisely defined.

---

[1] "Detroit area" would have to be precisely defined, perhaps as the city proper plus selected contiguous communities.

There are three basic conditions that any representative sampling procedure *must* satisfy. First, all members of the population must have a chance to get in the sample, which means that the frame must be complete.

Second, the "chance to get in the sample" must be *known;* in other words, we have to be able to state precisely what the *probability* was that any member of the population would be picked. It's desirable to have the chances be equal, but it's not necessary, because we can make corrections for unequal chances after we've gathered the data.

Third, the sample selections must be independent of each other. What this means is that the selection of one member should not increase or decrease the overall chance of selection for any other member. For example, if we select a representative sample of 300 San Francisco male residents and interview both them and their wives, we can use the male sample to represent husbands and the female sample to represent wives. We *cannot* lump both groups together and try to use the entire sample of 600 to represent all San Franciscan married people. Why not? The selection of wives depended on the selection of husbands. Since husbands and wives tend to resemble each other on many characteristics, our sample will tend to be more homogeneous than the population, and thus not representative. We could use our sample to represent all married *couples* in the city, with a sample size of 300 couples.

A second example may clarify this important point. If we wanted to expose animal tissues to treatment to see if they subsequently developed cancer, we might take pieces of tissue from many animals, expose them to the treatment, and compare the effects with those of animal tissues not exposed. Suppose we use 100 animals, taking one piece of tissue from each. The sample size is 100. We could, however, select two animals and take 50 pieces of tissue from each. We would still have 100 pieces of tissue, but would the results be as valid as before? No. Because each set of 50 tissues is drawn from one animal, each piece is not an independent example of animal tissues in general. Coming from the same host, they will most likely have important similarities that would occur less frequently if drawn from many different hosts. The situation is the same with couples: a sample of 300 couples should not be used as a sample of 600 individuals.

How do we go about satisfying these conditions? By having a complete list we've satisfied the first. There are several ways we can satisfy the other two. The most widely known is the *simple random sample* (or *random sample* for short). This is how it's done. We assign a number to each person on our list. Let's say there are 25,000 assembly-line workers in our population; that means we'll number our names from 1 through 25,000 (no small task). Then, we use a *random-number table* to make our selections.

What's a random-number table? As we said earlier, the word *random* has a precise meaning: every possible outcome is equally likely. We could make a random-number table ourselves by placing 10 balls numbered 0 to 9 in a pot, shuffling them, and picking one ball. We write down its number, throw it back, mix them up, and repeat the process. If our mixing and picking were thorough and unbiased, the resulting list would consist of random numbers (digits). On each draw each digit has an equal chance of being drawn regardless of what happened on previous draws. Now, to generate a table large enough to do us any good would take a lot of mixing and picking; so, we have a computer do it for us, substituting a random electronic process for the physical process of selecting numbered balls. (Although computer-generated random numbers are in fact only pseudo-random, they work effectively in most sampling problems.) There are books published that contain nothing but row upon row of *truly* random digits, sometimes as many as 1 million.[1]

Now, we've decided to take a sample of 500 names, and so we systematically go through the table looking for numbers between 1 and 25,000. Each time we find one we go down the list to that numbered person and check him off. We keep doing this until we've selected 500 different people. Every one had an equal chance of being picked, because in a random-number table no one number is more likely to come up than another.

We should note here that the techniques of statistical inference assume that sampling was done *with replacement*, which means that each person could theoretically be selected more than once. In practice this is rarely done, and sampling is done *without replacement:* once a case is selected, it's removed from consideration on subsequent draws. This can have serious effects on the accuracy of results if the sample size is a substantial proportion of the total population. The exploration of these effects and corrections for them is beyond the scope of a book such as this, but you should be aware that field researchers are often driven by the demands of practicality to violate the theoretical assumptions that underlie inference techniques.

With our list of 500 sampled names, we're ready to go into the field and get our data.

This is the simplest kind of sampling procedure, but it's used infrequently because assigning those 25,000 numbers and selecting the 500 numbers from the random-number table is a lot of work. So, to save time, energy, and money, researchers usually resort to a technique called *systematic* sampling whenever they have a list of the population. There are 25,000 people in the population and we want a sample of 500. This means we could take every 50th (that is, 25,000/500, called a *skip in-*

---

[1] See The Rand Corporation, *A Million Random Digits* (Glencoe, Ill.: The Free Press, 1955).

terval) name on the list to draw a sample of 500. All we have to do is decide where on the list to start. To do this, we take a random number between 1 and 50. If the random number were 25, we would select people with numbers, 25, 75, 125, 175, 225, etc. through 24,975. For each possible starting point we would have a unique sample. Each person on the list can be in only one sample. Since each starting point is equally likely, each possible sample is equally likely and each person has an equal chance of having his sample selected and thereby being included in the study.

In a simple random sample, not only do all individuals have an equal chance of selection, but all combinations of individuals are equally likely as well. In systematic sampling, however, not all combinations are possible once the list is finalized. In our example above, workers with numbers 125 and 126 cannot appear in the same sample. Only people with numbers that are separated by 50 names can appear together. If we assume, however, that the list itself is "well shuffled" (i.e., essentially random), then all combinations are equally probable.

Usually, this is not a terribly risky assumption to make. It's dangerous, however, when the list is arranged in order from high to low (or low to high) on an important characteristic. For example, if the list were arranged from high to low status, choosing a starting point at the top of the list would generate a sample with higher average status than would be the case if the starting point were farther down the list Another problem arises if the list is characterized by *periodicity*. For example, suppose we were sampling apartments from a list of apartments in a housing project. If the skip interval were 10 and if every 10th apartment happened to be a corner apartment, we might get very biased results when studying social interaction in housing projects, because people in corner apartments are likely to be more socially isolated than those in interior apartments. For these reasons it's important to check lists beforehand to ensure they are well shuffled.

Does selecting a sample randomly or systematically *guarantee* that our sample is representative? No. Our ideal sample would be a group of people that matches the population on every characteristic except size. We're very unlikely to draw such a sample, however; there will be variation from sample to sample simply by chance. The larger our sample, however, the more confidence we can have in our results. We'll talk about sample sizes and accuracy later on.

Sampling Error

In Chap. 2 we talked about two kinds of error, random error and bias. There are comparable errors in sampling. As we've already said, samples will vary around the truly accurate sample, and this random variation results in sampling error. Stratifying (next section) and using large samples help to reduce the chance of such error considerably.

As in the case of measurement, bias poses more of a problem. For example, in telephone polls people who don't own a telephone (poor people, for example) are excluded. If poor people have important characteristics in common (such as voting Democratic), this can have disastrous effects on the accuracy of results.

It's sometimes possible to detect bias in a sample. If we take a sample of American families, for example, we can compare the sample with the population on several key characteristics measured by the census, such as income, age, education, race, and sex. This kind of checking can at least give us clues to possible bias. Beyond this, the only way we can evaluate the possibility of bias is to inspect the sampling frame and procedures carefully for any systematic exclusion of members of the population.

Stratification:
Avoiding Bizarre Samples

In our study of assembly-line workers, would it be possible to get a sample that overrepresented men and underrepresented women? Or that overrepresented blacks and underrepresented whites? Yes, it's possible by chance alone even if we select the sample properly. Random-number tables are truly random only in the long run. So, what can we do?

If we have information on a characteristic such as sex *before* we draw our sample, we can guarantee that the sample will match the sex distribution of the population. All we have to do is separate men and women in our lists and draw separate samples within the two groups. If there are three men for every woman in the population, then we draw three men for every woman in our sample until we have 500 (i.e., 375 men and 125 women). This process of dividing up the population into important groups (such as by sex, race, education, occupation, or age) and then drawing samples within each group to ensure proper representation in the final sample is called *stratification*. Each of the groups (e.g., men and women) is called a *stratum* (the plural is *strata*).

If we stratify a sample, and do it well, we've narrowed down the possible outcomes by eliminating samples that are greatly in error. Thus, a sample of 200 people drawn with effective stratification will be less likely to be in error than a sample of 200 people drawn without stratifying. The stratified sample is of the same size as the unstratified sample, but because of the sample design, it's more likely to be accurate. When one sample of a given size has a greater likelihood of accuracy than a second sample of the same size, we say the first sample has greater *efficiency*. In most cases, stratification improves the efficiency of a sample design. At the very worst a stratified sample will yield the same level of accuracy relative to sample size as a simple random sample will. In other words, stratification can't hurt the sample: it can only help it or have no effect at all.

Whether we stratify or not, however, it's important to remember an important rule: If we draw a sample that represents a group, then that sample represents *all* subgroups as well (provided the sample is large enough). If we draw a representative sample of Americans, then we also have a representative sample of all Protestants, children, schoolteachers, southerners, and assembly-line workers. As long as our selection procedures follow the rules, our sample will go wrong only by chance; and by drawing a sufficiently large sample, we can make those chances of error very, very small.

Oversampling

Suppose we wanted to conduct a survey of students at a particular college, and could afford to select and interview only 200 students. Suppose there are 10,000 students enrolled, 90 percent of whom are white and 10 percent of whom are nonwhite. If we drew a sample that faithfully reflected the racial composition of the student body, we'd draw 180 whites (90 percent of 200) and 20 nonwhites (10 percent of 200). As we saw in Chap. 7, however, 20 cases are probably too few to examine relationships between variables in any detail, a 3×4 table, controlling for a two-category control variable, would entail a total of 24 cells, more than the total number of nonwhite cases. This means we'd have a number of empty cells, and the analysis would be of little value.

If we select more than 20 nonwhites, their proportion in the sample will exceed their proportion in the population, and the sample won't be representative of the entire student body. In such situations, this is, in fact, just what we do. We might, for example, select a sample of 100 whites and 100 nonwhites. This would greatly improve our ability to analyze relationships among whites and nonwhites separately. This is called *oversampling*.

What happens when we perform an analysis on the entire sample? The sample would then be 50 percent nonwhite, which certainly overrepresents them. Suppose we're interested in the mean number of children that people expect to have, and further suppose that nonwhite college students, on the average, expect to have more children than white college students. Remember that the mean number of children expected is the sum of the answers of individuals divided by the number of individuals. By stratifying the sample by race and oversampling nonwhites, we've inflated the total number of children expected (by including a disproportionate number of nonwhites who as a group expect slightly more children than whites) without changing the total number of individuals at all. Therefore, if we calculate a mean for the entire sample (whites plus nonwhites), it will be too large.

We've included five times the number of nonwhites and just over half the whites who, given their proportional representation in the population, should have been in the sample. If we multiply each nonwhite score by .20, the total number of expected children contributed by the nonwhite group to the overall mean will be what we'd expect to get if we'd selected only 20 nonwhites instead of 100 (100 × .20 = 20). If we then multiply each white score by 1.8, the total number of children contributed by the whites to the overall mean will be what we'd expect to get if we'd selected 180 whites instead of 100 (100 × 1.8 = 180). In calculating the mean for the entire sample, we use these multipliers to force the sample to be representative of the population. These multipliers (.20 and 1.8) are called *weights*, or *sampling weights*.

Sampling weights are used in situations other than the deliberate oversampling above. In general, they allow us to correct for unequal probabilities in the selection process. Of course, in order to determine the value of sampling weights, we must know what the true probabilities of selection are, a piece of information that isn't always available.

In the above example we stratified by race, a rather easy characteristic to observe, and oversampled for nonwhites. Suppose we wanted to do a study of people with suicidal tendencies. Since there'd be little way of identifying suicidal members of a large population before we drew the sample, and since they amount to a very small proportion of the population, we couldn't use oversampling to ensure a subsample of people with suicidal tendencies that would be large enough for detailed analysis. In such circumstances, one solution is to draw an enormous sample. For example, suppose people with suicidal tendencies amount to 1 percent of a population. If we wanted 100 such cases for statistical analysis, we'd have to draw a sample of 10,000 people in order to get an expected value of 100 people with suicidal tendencies, hardly an ideal situation.

In practice, we send interviewers to a large sample of people and conduct very short interviews (perhaps 5 minutes long) designed to find out whether or not they possess the rare characteristic we're interested in. These interviewers are called *screeners*. The design of such short interview schedules is difficult and the process is still very expensive. It's for this reason that it's very difficult to conduct studies of people with rare characteristics.

Response Rates

We select a sample of 500 assembly-line workers, and we send out our interviewers. What do we do if 50 of the people don't want to be interviewed? We now have a 90-percent *response rate* (450/500 × 100). Most people would probably say that a loss of only one in ten isn't very serious, and they'd probably be right; but what if we'd received refusals from 100 workers, or from 200? What then? Can we argue that the remaining workers represent the population?

If everyone in the sample is equally likely to refuse our interviewers, then there's no problem: we'd be left with a smaller but unbiased sample. The problem is that some people are more likely than others to refuse to cooperate, and such people often have other characteristics in common as well (such as political attitudes). As the response rate goes down, the danger of getting biased data goes up. The frustration is that we rarely know exactly what the bias is, not to mention how great it is. All we know is that the likelihood of bias gets higher. This can't help but shake our confidence in the data.

To make matters worse, sometimes a specific question within a survey will have less than a 100-percent response rate. Suppose we conduct a survey and get a response rate of 80 percent. Further suppose that one of the questions is somewhat controversial and 40 percent of the respondents refuse to answer. The sample itself has an 80-percent response rate, and, of those respondents, only 60 percent answered the question. In terms of representing the population, the response rate for this question is only (60%) (80%) = 48%, which is dismally low. Therefore, when you read research reports, you must notice two kinds of response rates, one for the study as a whole and one for each question.

As a general guideline, a response rate of 85 percent or more is quite good; 70 to 84 percent isn't bad but it isn't good, either; below 70 percent there's a serious chance of bias; and below 50 percent is downright disaster. I don't mean to suggest that information on 250 people (out of 500) isn't interesting or informative; it simply can't be trusted as a representative sample of a population. One way to see how disastrous low response rates can be is to consider preelection polls. Suppose 30 percent favor candidate A, 40 percent favor candidate B, and 30 percent are undecided. Should candidate B feel confident? The only way to be sure (and fair) is to assume the worst, that all the undecided votes are against him. In this case, candidate B would lose 60 to 40 percent, a landslide by political standards. If candidate B remains in the lead even when the undecided votes are hypothetically cast against him, only then can he be sure he's on safe ground.

This problem was important in the public-opinion polls that preceded the 1948 United States presidential elections. There was a large group of people who were undecided, and the pollsters assumed they would eventually vote in the same proportions as those who had made a decision at the time of the poll. The pollsters thus predicted that Dewey would defeat Truman by a landslide. In fact, the undecideds voted overwhelmingly for Truman and he won the election.

The pollsters assumed the undecideds would favor Dewey. Truman's expression says it all.

I've seen reports with response rates of 10 percent (typical of mail surveys, for example) in which the authors seriously used the sample to make inferences about the population. Data based on a 10-percent response are virtually worthless as far as representing the population is concerned. And yet researchers are reluctant to give up, especially after spending a lot of time and money in the effort. Unfortunately, one solution for them is to omit reporting the response rate. It's rare to find published response rates; at best the omission is inexcusable.

Complex Samples

When you're interested in a population as large as a state (or even a small town), you're not likely to have a list of everyone's name and address. What then? Populations need not be listed, only precisely defined. In these circumstances sampling can get pretty complicated, but let's pick a manageable example to show you what happens.

Let's say we want to take a sample of households in a town. First we get a map of the town, one which shows accurately each block. Then we might divide the town into socioeconomic strata, based on any information we might have about the living conditions throughout the area. Within each geographic stratum, we number each block (with a ball-point pen we put a little number on each block). Within each stratum we use random numbers to choose a sample of *blocks*. Then we take a piece of paper and walk around each block we've selected and make a list of everything on the block, in order. At this point we have a list of all the households on our selected blocks. We could line the lists up within each stratum and treat them like one big list. Then we could draw a systematic sample of houses from the stratum lists.

In such a design every household has an equal chance of being selected because every block has an equal chance and every house on the selected blocks has an equal chance. As you can see, samples of this kind are drawn in *stages* (and are often called *multistage samples*). The important thing is that in each stage we *know* what the chances of selection are.

Cluster Sampling

Suppose we have a city with 100,000 dwelling units (DU's), from which we want to take a sample of 1,000 DU's (or 1 percent). We stratify the population into several geographical areas. For purposes of illustration, we'll talk about just one area, area 1.

Suppose area 1 has 5,000 DU's. We want to take 1 percent of them in our sample, or $(.01)(5,000) = 50$ DU's from area 1. Since area 1 is spread out over many city blocks, to send interviewers to isolated houses will require substantial time and money. Because of the economic constraints of large survey research projects, especially those done on a national level, we usually select bunches of houses (*clusters*) from selected blocks. This makes things easier and quicker for the interviewer: instead of going to five houses on five separate blocks, the interviewer now gets five interviews from one block. Let's see how it's done.

Suppose we decide to select clusters of five households once we've selected a sample of blocks. This means we'll select $50/5 = 10$ blocks from area 1. Note that because some blocks may be very small and some very large, we may wind up selecting *no* clusters from some blocks and more than one cluster from the larger ones. Keep this in mind as you read.

Suppose area 1 has 500 blocks. We number the blocks in a pseudorandom fashion and select 10 of them. We send our listers out to record every DU on the 10 selected blocks, getting the results shown on p. 172.

Column 1 gives the block number. Column 2 tells us how many DU's are on each block. If we think of the ten lists as one big list, with the DU's numbered consecutively from 1 to 100, column 3 tells us which DU's are located in which blocks (for example, DU's 1 to 20 are in block 1 and DU 43 is in block 4). For the moment, ignore the final two columns.

We want to select 50 DU's from the 100 DU's in our 10 selected blocks.

Block number	Number of DU's	DU number	Selected number of clusters	Selected number of DU's
1	20	1–20	2	10
2	6	21–26	0	0
3	15	27–41	2	10
4	9	42–50	1	5
5	9	51–59	1	5
6	6	60–65	0	0
7	5	66–70	1	5
8	8	71–78	1	5
9	10	79–88	1	5
10	12	89–100	1	5
Total	100		10	50

Fifty DU's is equivalent to $50/5 = 10$ *clusters* of five households each. The next step is to determine how many clusters to take from each of the 10 blocks. We use systematic sampling with a skip interval of $100/10 = 10$. Suppose the random starting point is 8. Our selections will then be DU's 8, 18, 28, 38, 48, 58, 68, 78, 88, and 98.

The 8th DU is in block 1; the 18th is also in block 1. Therefore, we'll select two clusters from block 1, or 10 DU's. Notice that this doesn't necessarily mean that we'll wind up including DU 8 in our sample. At this stage of the sampling, we're "hopping" through the blocks and each of our "steps" is 10 DU's long. Every time we "land" in a block, we select one cluster of 5 DU's from that block. The actual selection of DU's must wait for the next stage of sampling.

The 28th DU is in block 3; so is the 38th. Therefore, we'll select two clusters from block 3. Notice that we didn't "land" in block 2, because it was so small. The chances of one's block being selected are directly proportional to the block's size (in terms of the number of DU's), as it should be.

The 48th DU is in block 4. The 58th is in block 5; the 68th is in block 7; the 78th is in block 8; the 88th is in block 9; and the 98th is in block 10. We'll select one cluster from blocks 5, 7, 8, 9, and 10. (See column 4 of the table for summary.)

Now block 1 has 20 DU's, of which we're going to select two clusters of five each, or 10 DU's. We can use systematic sampling within the list for block 1. We use the same procedure to select the correct number of clusters from each of the blocks chosen in the last stage.

In the first stage (selecting the original 10 blocks), each person's block had an equal chance of being selected. In the second stage, everyone still had an equal chance of being chosen. If we had taken the same number of people from each block, it wouldn't have been fair to those on large blocks, since they would be up against more "competition" than those on small blocks. So, we took a larger number from the larger blocks than from the smaller. Two blocks were actually skipped altogether. In this way, we keep the chances of being selected equal throughout all stages of the sampling process.

There are some sample designs in which the chances are not equal. In the case of oversampling, we do this deliberately and correct later with the use of weights. In some cases, we don't know how many DU's there are in area 1 and therefore may give people in that area a disproportionately large (or small) chance of selection in comparison with people in other areas. If the sampling is done carefully, however (i.e., if we keep accurate records and know something about the mathematics of sampling), we can use sampling weights to correct for these unequal probabilities after the sampling is finished.

Cluster sampling is designed to save time and money, but it does so at some costs in accuracy. People who live near each other tend to be more alike on a variety of characteristics than people who live far away from each other. For this reason, cluster samples tend to be more homogeneous than a simple random sample of the same population would be. In other words, they tend to underestimate the variance.

Cluster sampling is an example of the kinds of compromise one must often make in social science research; the ideal techniques dictated by statistical theory are often impractical, and we must make a compromise in accuracy. In most cases the compromise that accompanies cluster sampling is not serious, and researchers can make some corrections for its effects on estimates of variances of the study variables.

Some Samples to Stay Away From

Your roving reporter collaring people on the street is not taking a representative sample of any group we can define (i.e., of any population). They often acknowledge that the samples "aren't random" but then proceed to act as if they represented everyone in the world. Turn off the TV, laugh hysterically, or go get something to eat, but whatever you do, try not to take such samples *seriously at all*.

Big circulation magazines love to send out 100,000 questionnaires and print stories based on 10,000 replies. The sample sounds so big (and it is) that readers ignore the 10-percent response rate. But, you know better, so don't take those seriously either.

Never trust the results of mailed questionnaires unless the authors give the response rate and it's acceptable. Usually they won't publish the response rate and that's an immediate tip-off.

Samples that consist of "all members of the introductory psychology class" represent that particular class and no one else.

When pharmaceutical companies test new drugs, they often use inmates of prisons. In this case they're trying to represent the population of all potential users of the drug without taking a scientific sample from that population. This works only if prisoners represent the range of physiologies in human populations, a condition that does not necessarily hold. Drug companies, however, are faced with an enormous problem: they can hardly take a representative sample of people and be confident of talking a large proportion of them into being guinea pigs. They must compromise.

Beware the misuse of the word *random*, as in "shoppers selected at random." This rarely means what it says.

Many commercial pollsters use *quota samples*. This means that the interviewer is instructed to obtain respondents who have specified characteristics. For example, if an interviewer is to interview 100 respondents, he might be instructed to find 90 whites, 10 blacks, 5 upper-class people, 70 middle-class, and 25 lower-class (defined perhaps by income levels), and so on. The problem with this methodology is that the interviewers can select anyone they want by any means as long as the final sample has the proper number of people with the specified characteristics. While the sample may reflect the population on those characteristics, there is no way of knowing that it reflects characteristics (such as attitudes) for which there was no quota.

In practice, quota samples have a fairly good "track record"; many research organizations have used quota samples, and various checks have shown them to be surprisingly accurate. The problem is that *there is no theoretical reason to expect this to happen*. The fact that some number of quota samples in the past have been reasonably accurate doesn't mean that future quota samples will be accurate. Studies that use samples drawn with the techniques described in this chapter not only work well in practice, but are *theoretically sound*. As you'll see in the chapters to come, we can estimate the probability that sample estimates of population characteristics are in error; we cannot do this with quota samples.

Whether or not to accept the results of quota samples is a difficult issue. If past performance is used as a criterion, then accepting the results of a quota sample is not terribly risky. If, however, we apply more stringent criteria (as this author does), then quota samples should be regarded with a somewhat jaundiced eye and considerable critical reservation.

Use your head, especially in making evaluations of possible bias. You'd be amazed at what you can uncover just by using common sense. In a recent poll of women in Connecticut, there was one black woman in a sample of 110. You *know* something's wrong here. You have to ask yourself the question: "Does this make sense?" Develop some confidence in your own sense of what's reasonable and what's silly.

Parting Shots

After all is said and done, you're sitting with an article in front of you and chances are that the author hasn't told you how he drew the sample or what his response rate was ("We drew a representative sample of 100 wives . . ." or "These conclusions are based on a scientifically selected sample of . . ."). The temptation is awfully great to say, "The sample is probably a good one" when the results agree with your ideas, and to say, "How can I take this research seriously without a full description of the sample?" when the results rub you the wrong way. Until researchers (and reporters) start giving more details, a lot of people are going to give in to this temptation; some might do so even with the details.

There are some research outfits that have high standards and can probably be trusted (such as the Institute for Social Research at the University of Michigan and the National Opinion Research Center at the University of Chicago). But they generate only a fraction of the published data. You must keep in mind that while commercial pollsters do some quality work, they must often cut corners in order to keep their costs at a level attractive to customers. Unfortunately, the corners are often cut in the sampling stage as well as in fieldwork (e.g., substituting a neighbor for a respondent who isn't home). If you want to learn something about the world instead of getting your own ideas supported, you have to consume information critically. You now have some knowledge that will help you ask some fairly critical questions, and I hope you know enough to tell a reasonable answer when you see one. Ultimately, I think, how much valid information you acquire from sample data and how much junk you get will depend on your willingness to combine what you know with good sense and patience. If you care about the truth, it's well worth it.

There are a number of new terms in this chapter, and you should think about what they mean in your own words. We've talked about *simple random*, *systematic*, and *multistage* sampling procedures, about *bias*, *random error*, *efficiency*, and *stratification*, about *response rates*, about the three conditions all samples must satisfy, and about a number of samples to be wary of. Try to explain these to someone else.

Problems

9-1 Consider the following statements about samples. For each, if you see nothing disturbing, circle "OK"; if you think there's something wrong (i.e., the statement is false *or* it describes an improperly drawn sample), circle "Not OK" and *briefly* describe the problem.
   a. A sample of 1,000 respondents can represent a population of 1

million people with much more accuracy than a sample of 1,000 can represent a population of 1 billion.

OK   Not OK

b. "We drew a random sample of all American adults."

OK   Not OK

c. "Our study of attitudes of American youth is based on a systematic sample of 500 students enrolled in Wesleyan University for the spring semester, 1975."

OK   Not OK

d. Cluster samples are economical, but the resulting samples usually overestimate the homogeneity of the population.

OK   Not OK

e. Stratification can never hurt a sample. At worst, it will be as accurate as a simple random sample.

OK   Not OK

9-2 We want to do a study of inmates at a state prison. We want to use a sample of the 10,000 inmates. The sample size will be 500. In terms of this study:
a. Define the population.
b. What would the sampling frame most likely be?
c. Would you use a systematic or a simple random sampling procedure? How would they differ?
d. What would be the difference between sampling with and without replacement? What would be the probable effect of using one instead of the other?
e. How and why might you stratify this sample?
f. How and why might you deliberately oversample some groups?
g. When describing results for the whole sample, how would you correct for oversampling?

9-3 What three conditions must all samples satisfy in order to justify the use of inductive statistics? Have you satisfied them in Prob. 9-2? Where and how?

9-4 How might you draw a sample of households in your hometown? Would clusters be appropriate? How might the use of clusters help you? Hurt you?

9-5 "We drew a scientific sample of state residents from telephone directories. We were unable to contact 20 percent of the respondents and an additional 20 percent refused to be interviewed. We feel we have a representative sample of state citizenry."

a. Do the procedures and results indicate that the sample is probably representative of state citizens? Why or why not?

b. How could we try to verify the sample's representativeness?

9-6 "In reviewing our measures, we're confident that there's little or no bias involved. The only measurement error will be random. The same will be true of any sampling error. As everyone knows, random error does not distort most statistical results."

a. Do you agree? Why or why not?

9-7 "Our sample consists of all members of Introductory Sociology, 250 in all. While the sample is not large, it's large enough for most statistical purposes."

a. Is the sample "large enough"? For what?

b. Whom does the sample represent?

9-8 "We obtained a complete list of all members of the Army (active and retired) living at Fort Sam Houston on June 1, 1969. We stratified the list by rank, branch of service, and sex. Within strata we selected a systematic sample. The resulting sample contained 1,600 persons. We obtained a response rate of 87 percent. (10 percent were unavailable for interview and 3 percent refused to be interviewed.)"

a. Is the sample "large enough"? For what?

b. Is the sample a good one? Why or why not?

c. Do you have any reason to suspect sampling bias? Why or why not?

Suggested Readings

1 Blalock, Hubert M., Jr.: *Social Statistics*, 2d ed., chap. 21. New York: McGraw-Hill Book Company, 1972.

2 Davis, James A.: "Great Books and Small Groups: An Informal History of a National Survey," in Phillip E. Hammond, *Sociologists at Work*. New York, Basic Books, Inc., Publishers, 1964.

3 Kish, Leslie: *Survey Sampling*. New York: John Wiley & Sons, 1965.

4 Likert, Rensis: "Public Opinion Polls," in Ronald Freedman et al., *Principles of Sociology*, rev. ed., pp. 52–62. New York: Holt, Rinehart and Winston, 1956.

5 Loether, Herman J., and Donald G. McTavish: *Inferential Statistics for Sociologists*, chap. 3. Boston: Allyn and Bacon, 1974.

6 Moser, C. A.: *Survey Methods in Social Investigation*, chaps. IV–VII. London: Heinemann, 1958.

7 Mueller, John H., Karl F. Schuessler, and Herbert L. Costner: *Statistical Reasoning in Sociology*, 2d ed., chap. 12. Boston: Houghton Mifflin Company, 1970.

8 Selltiz, Claire, et al.: *Research Methods in Social Relations*, 3rd ed., appendix A. New York: Holt, Rinehart and Winston, 1976.

9 Warwick, Donald P., and Charles A. Lininger: *The Sample Survey: Theory and Practice*. New York: McGraw-Hill Book Company, 1975.

10 Stephan, Frederick F., and Philip J. McCarthy: *Sampling Opinions: An Analysis of Survey Procedure*. New York: John Wiley & Sons, 1958.

10

statistical inference and some new kinds of distributions

In this chapter we're going to introduce a number of new ideas and ways of looking at distributions without showing you how they're used right away because there's too much to explain in one bite.

In order to understand how statistical inferences are made from sample data, you first need to understand some of the technical tools and language that go along with them. We're going to talk about *probability* and *sampling distributions, standard errors,* and *normal curves* without telling you how they're used until we're through all of them. They all fit together and need each other; you can't fully understand their application until you understand them all individually.

So, to read this chapter, pick a time when you're relaxed and uninterrupted. Concentrate on understanding what's here and have faith that before too long you'll see how it all hangs together and enables us to use sample data to make inferences about populations. I think you'll find it worth your patience.

New Ways of Looking at Distributions

A distribution is a picture portraying how often events or characteristics occur. If we have a variable (such as daily cigarette smoking) with a set of possible scores, then a frequency distribution of the variable for a group of people consists of the number of people giving each type of response. A percentage or proportional distribution gives the relative number of people giving each type of response. Suppose we gathered data that look like those given in Table 10-1.

To simplify the example, we've assumed that no one smokes more than three packs per day. For each level of cigarette smoking we have both the absolute frequency (the *f* column) and the relative frequency (the "percentage" and "proportion" columns). What I want you to do now is to make the leap between thinking of distributions in terms of frequencies, percentages, and proportions to thinking of them in terms of *probabilities*. To review, the probability of someone having a given characteristic is the number of people with that characteristic relative to (i.e., divided by) the total number of people being considered. In Table 10-1, for example, the probability of choosing someone who smokes 6 to 10 cigarettes per day is 52/303 = .172. Now notice that Table 10-1 lists the probabilities for each possible smoking level. A distribution such as this, one that lists all possible outcomes (for example, 1 to 5, 6 to 10, 11 to 20, etc.) and their probabilities, is called a *probability distribution*.

Every time we have a proportional distribution, we have a probability distribution. This means, of course, that we can turn any frequency or percentage distribution into a probability distribution.

Now, for a second leap in your thinking about distributions. So far we've looked at presenting distributions in terms of tables (e.g., Table 10-1) and to some extent graphs. In graphs, the height of the curve (or bar or whatever) has been used to indicate the proportion of cases with a particular score. As a bar graph, Table 10-1 would look something like Fig. 10-1.

If we round off the corners and represent the bar graph with a curved line, then we get something like the line graph shown superimposed on the bar graph. The line graph indicates that most smokers are concentrated around one pack a day with a peak in the half- to full-pack group. The distribution is unimodal (one hump) and slightly skewed to the right (look at the graph and make sure you see this).

Table 10-1 Cigarettes Smoked per Day, by People Who Smoke (Hypothetical)

Cigarettes smoked	*f*	Percentage	Proportion
1–5	39	12.8%	.128
6–10	52	17.2	.172
11–20	91	30.0	.300
21–40	76	25.1	.251
41–60	45	14.9	.149
Total	303	100.0%	1.000

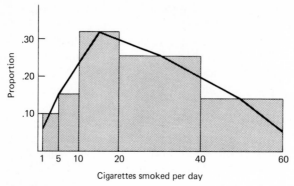

Figure 10-1 Bar graph representation of Table 10-1.

This isn't the only way we can draw a picture of this distribution. Instead of talking about the height of a curve, think instead of the *area underneath a curve*. We'd have to use calculus to figure it out (which we won't do because we don't have to), but we could measure the area enclosed by the curve and the horizontal axis in terms of square inches, for example. Let's say that Table 10-1 pictured in these terms looks something like Fig. 10-2.

The vertical axis no longer represents proportions. In this curve it's the area that's important. For example, in Fig. 10-1 we found the proportion of smokers who smoked 11 to 20 cigarettes a day by seeing how high the third bar was. It rose to the .30 level (30 percent). In Fig. 10-2, the proportion of smokers in the 11 to 20 category would be equivalent to the proportion of the total area under the curve that's contained between the two lines rising vertically from the 11 and 20 points on the horizontal axis. We've made a direct translation here from proportion of cases to

Figure 10-2 Representation of Table 10-1 in terms of the area underneath the curve.

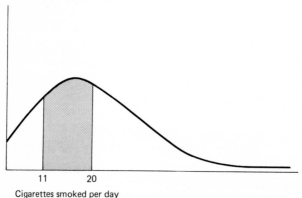

proportion of area. If we've drawn the curve correctly, the proportion of the total area that's between the lines should be .300.

There's nothing magical going on here; this is simply a different way of visually describing a distribution.

Figure 10-2 is thus a probability distribution (called a *probability density function*) which tells us the probability of any *range* of scores (e.g., between 5 and 25 or greater than 30 or less than 15, etc.).

We've made three leaps, then: first, from frequency, percentage, and proportional distributions to probability distributions; second, from probabilities of exact scores to probabilities of ranges of scores; third, from the height of a curve to indicate probabilities to the proportion of the area contained between two scores.

It's fair to ask at this point, "Why probabilities? Why areas instead of heights?" Statistical inference is the process of making probability statements about sample findings. By "probability statements" I mean things such as "We're 99-percent sure (i.e., the probability is .99) that in the long run our research procedures will give accurate results, and in this case the proportion of people who would vote for Ms. X if the election were held today is somewhere between .52 and .56." We're using our sample result (in this case the proportion in the sample is .54) to make an estimate of the population (the estimate being "somewhere between .52 and .56") and we're attaching a probability (level of confidence) to our procedures ("we're 99-percent sure"). Probabilities are what statistical inference is all about.

Second, in order to make these probability statements, we have to use some special probability distributions. These distributions aren't based on observations of the world (i.e., they aren't empirical); they're derived mathematically. They're theoretical. These distributions are represented as curves, and the probabilities are measured by areas. If we want to understand and use these special distributions, we have to understand curves that use areas.

If you feel you understand the idea of a probability distribution (i.e., you can explain it intelligibly to someone else), and if you feel comfortable thinking of curves that use proportions of total area to represent distributions and probabilities, then you're ready to go on.

Theoretical Probability Distributions: Sampling Distributions

Suppose we're interested in the proportion of people who define themselves as "happy." First we could go out and ask everyone in the population (say all people over 10 years old in the United States) if they consider themselves happy. The *population distribution* would consist of the

Table 10-2 Proportional
Distribution of Replies to the
Question: "Do you consider
yourself to be happy?" for All
Americans 10 Years Old and
Older (Hypothetical)

Reply	Proportion
Yes	.60
No	.40
Total	1.00 ($N = 167,000,000$)

proportional distribution of those millions of replies. (See Table 10-2.)

If we pick someone at random from this population, the above distribution tells us that the probability of that person considering himself happy is .60, or, in the long run, six out of ten will say yes.

Now, instead of asking everyone, we could, of course, take a sample. The *sample distribution* might look something like that given in Table 10-3. Whereas Table 10-2 is the probability distribution for the population, Table 10-3 is the probability distribution for a single sample. Eventually we'll use the sample result to estimate the population proportion.

Now it's time to introduce a third and most important kind of distribution. In our example, we've drawn a single sample of 10,000 people, and for that single sample we've computed the proportion who consider themselves to be happy (.58). Notice that the sample proportion is off by .02 (the difference between .60 and .58). Although we'd never do it in practice, suppose we drew a second sample of 10,000 people and computed the proportion who consider themselves to be happy. What might we get then? We might get something like .59 or .56 or .62 or even .60. We know we'd find chance variation from sample to sample.

Table 10-3 Proportional
Distribution of Replies to
the Question: "Do you
consider yourself to be
happy?" for a
Hypothetical Sample of
All Americans 10 Years
Old or Older

Reply	Proportion
Yes	.58
No	.42
Total	1.00 ($N = 10,000$)

Now imagine that we selected an enormous number of samples of 10,000 people, say a billion samples. For each sample we compute the proportion who consider themselves happy. We now have a billion scores, each of which is a proportion computed from an independently drawn sample of 10,000 people. We could then construct a frequency distribution showing how many *samples* had proportions of .58, how many of .59, how many of .60 and so on. (See Table 10-4.)

It's important to get ourselves oriented here so we know just what we've got. We've got a population of 167 million people from which it's possible to draw an infinitely large number of samples of 10,000 people. We're imagining that our super computer actually drew 1 billion such samples and for each computed the proportion of people considering themselves happy. Table 10-4 shows the possible outcomes (which I've arbitrarily limited to .57 through .63, just to keep things simple), the number of *samples* with each outcome (e.g., in 50,000,000 of those billion samples the proportion happy was .57), and the percentage and proportional distributions that come from that frequency distribution. We now have a distribution of *sample results* with the probability associated with each result. This should ring a bell; we've got a *probability distribution of sample results*. Such a distribution is called a *sampling distribution*. (Notice the "ing" at the end, differentiating it from a sample distribution. Don't confuse the two.) Each of the billion "cases" in this distribution is a sample result (like a proportion or a mean).

I've said there are an infinite number of samples that could be drawn with replacement from any population (see Chap. 9 if you need refreshing), and that sampling distributions are theoretical. One billion samples is a very large number, but it does not exactly represent the theoretical sampling distribution because the latter is based on an *infinite* number of samples. No matter how many samples we drew, the resulting distribution of sample results would only approximate the

Table 10-4 Distribution of Sample Proportions

Sample proportions*	f	Percentage	Proportion
.57	50,000,000	5%	.05
.58	100,000,000	10	.10
.59	200,000,000	20	.20
.60	300,000,000	30	.30
.61	200,000,000	20	.20
.62	100,000,000	10	.10
.63	50,000,000	5	.05
Total	1,000,000,000	100%	1.00

* Rounded to the nearest hundredth.

sampling distribution. I've used the 1 billion samples to help you grasp the idea of a probability distribution of sample results, but you should be aware of the fact that sampling distributions are theoretical, based on an infinite number of samples, and incapable of being derived empirically (no matter how large a computer we use).

Like all distributions that involve numbers as scores, sampling distributions have means and standard deviations. They also have shapes. For example, the sampling distribution in Table 10-4 has a mean of .60 and a standard deviation of 0.014. It's unimodal and symmetrical. (See Fig. 10-3a.)

The standard deviation of a *sampling* distribution has a special name, the *standard error*.[1] The name makes sense when you consider what sampling distributions represent. Notice that the mean of the sampling distribution is .60, which is the same as the proportion in the population, the number we're trying to estimate with our sample result. Of those billion samples, however, only 30 percent are within rounding error of the true value. The rest are off by some amount. A large standard error means that the samples are widely spread out, which means a relatively large proportion of the samples you could draw would be off by a wide margin. On the other hand, if the standard error is small, the samples are tightly clustered around the population proportion (the number we're after), making any one sample (and we draw only one) a pretty accurate estimate. It comes down to the difference between Figs. 10-3b and c.

So, the larger the standard deviation of a sampling distribution is, the more likely it is that a single random sample is in error as an estimate of the population value. Hence the special name, standard error.

The language can be confusing when you talk about sampling distributions. For example, a sampling distribution is a probability distribution in which the cases are samples and the scores are sample characteristics such as means or proportions. Since the sampling distribution

Figure 10-3a Graph of Table 10-4.

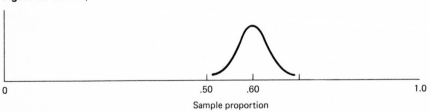

Sample proportion

---

[1] Standard errors are symbolized by the Greek letter sigma (σ) with a subscript telling us which statistic the sampling distribution represents. For example, the standard error for sample proportions is symbolized by σ_{P_s}, the standard error for sample means by $\sigma_{\bar{x}}$, etc.

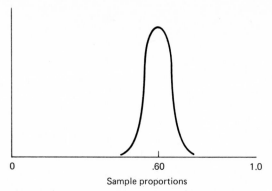

0   .60   1.0
Sample proportions

Figure 10-3b Hypothetical sampling distribution of
sample proportions, with relatively small standard
error.

has a mean, we can find ourselves talking about the mean of the
sample means or the mean of sample proportions (the average proportion). Keep in mind just what's in the distribution (means, proportions,
etc.) and then remember that the mean of the distribution refers to whatever characteristic the distribution describes.

The sampling distribution has a standard deviation too. In this case
we're talking about the variation in sample means (or proportions), and
the variation is relative to the population mean (or proportion). The
meaning of the numbers is the same, we've just shifted from looking at
individuals to looking at samples of individuals.

Now, there are some loose ends lying around, and although we can't
tie them up completely right now, it might help to identify them and
make some promises to get to them soon. First of all, as we hinted

Figure 10-3c Hypothetical sampling distribution of
sample proportions, with relatively large standard
error.

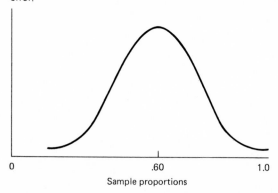

0   .60   1.0
Sample proportions

above, the mean of a sampling distribution is always equal to the population mean (or proportion). If we're measuring income, for example, the mean of the sampling distribution (the probability distribution of sample mean incomes) will always equal the mean income in the population.[1] However, we don't know what that mean is (if we did, why do a study?), so at first you might react with a "big deal, so what?" For the moment I ask your indulgence. You'll see soon enough how we make use of this.

Second, we know the sampling distribution has a standard deviation (standard error), but since we never actually draw an infinite number of samples, how can we calculate it? The answer to this is that we estimate it from the sample standard deviation. In general, the standard error of the mean is the population standard deviation divided by the square root of the sample size. However, since we don't know what the population standard deviation is, we estimate it by using the sample standard deviation. With reasonably large samples (100 or more cases) this is a good estimate. For example, if the sample standard deviation of cigarettes smoked per day is seven cigarettes, and our sample has 100 people in it, the estimated standard error of the sampling distribution of the mean number of cigarettes smoked per day is

$$\frac{s}{\sqrt{n}} = \frac{7}{\sqrt{100}} = \frac{7}{10} = .7 = \sigma_{\bar{x}}$$

We'll talk about other standard errors (e.g., for sample proportions) in Chap. 11.

Third, in order to use a distribution, we have to know not only its mean and standard deviation, but its shape as well. If we knew that, too, we'd know everything we'd need to know to calculate the probabilities that allow us to make statistical inferences. Again, since we don't actually draw all possible samples, how do we know the shape of the sampling distribution?

We're aided here by a mathematical theorem called the *central-limit theorem*. According to this theorem, the more cases we include in our sample, the more closely the sampling distribution approximates one particular shape, called the *normal curve*. This holds *regardless* of the shape of the population distribution.

The normal curve is symmetrical and unimodal, and looks like Fig. 10-4. If the size of our particular sample is large enough, we know by the central-limit theorem that the comparable sampling distribution (the probability distribution of the infinite number of samples of that size that could be drawn from the population) will be "normally" shaped.

---

[1] This doesn't hold for all population characteristics we might want to estimate, but it does hold for those we discuss in this book.

The normal curve

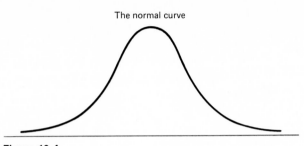

Figure 10-4

Let's take an example to demonstrate the central-limit theorem. Instead of studying people, we'll focus on dice. Imagine the population of all dice in existence.[1] If we could locate them all and record the numbers on their upturned faces, the population distribution would look like that shown in Fig. 10-5. Each number on a die has an equal chance of being face up. Since there are six possible numbers, one-sixth of all dice should have a 1, one-sixth should have a 2, etc. The distribution in Fig. 10-5 is rectangular, which is a far cry from normal. The average die face value is $(1 + 2 + 3 + 4 + 5 + 6)/6 = 21/6 = 3.5$. Suppose we wanted to draw random samples from the population of all die faces and estimate the population mean. What would the sampling distribution look like, depending on the sample size?

Let's start with a very small sample, $n = 2$. We roll two dice, add up the faces, and divide by 2 to get the sample mean. Depending on what we roll, there are 11 possible outcomes, each of which has an associated probability. (See Table 10-5.)

If you want to see more clearly where the probabilities in Table 10-5 come from, examine Table 10-6. The row variable is the face value for the first die, the column variable is the face value of the second die, and the cells are the averages of each row-column combination. For ex-

Figure 10-5 Proportional distribution of the face values of the population of all existing dice.

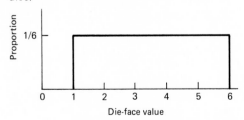

---

[1] This example has been adapted from Hubert M. Blalock, Jr., *Social Statistics*, 2d ed. (New York: McGraw-Hill Book Company, 1972), pp. 181–184.

Table 10-5 Sampling
Distribution for Dice,
Sample of Size 2,
Mean Values

Mean	Probability
1.0	1/36
1.5	2/36
2.0	3/36
2.5	4/36
3.0	5/36
3.5	6/36
4.0	5/36
4.5	4/36
5.0	3/36
5.5	2/36
6.0	1/36
Total	36/36 = 1.00

ample, in the first row, second column, we see that if we roll a 1 on the first die and a 2 on the second die, the average face value is $(1 + 2)/2 = 1.5$. Notice that there are 36 cells (the denominator of the probabilities in Table 10-5).

Since there are 36 possible outcomes, to get the probabilities in Table 10-5, all you have to do is count up the number of outcomes that have an average of 1.0, for example, and divide by 36.

If we were to draw a picture of Table 10-5, it would look like Fig. 10-6. Notice that this graph indicates the probability of a particular outcome by the height of the curve, not the area. For the purposes of this example, this is of no consequence. Also notice that the peak of the curve is above the point 3.5, which is the population mean. The mean of the sampling distribution is exactly equal to the population mean.

Table 10-6 Mean Face Values for Two Dice

First die	SECOND DIE 1	2	3	4	5	6
1	1.0	1.5	2.0	2.5	3.0	3.5
2	1.5	2.0	2.5	3.0	3.5	4.0
3	2.0	2.5	3.0	3.5	4.0	4.5
4	2.5	3.0	3.5	4.0	4.5	5.0
5	3.0	3.5	4.0	4.5	5.0	5.5
6	3.5	4.0	4.5	5.0	5.5	6.0

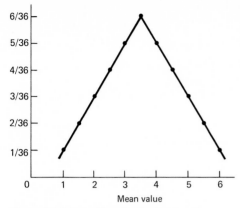

Figure 10-6 Sampling distribution for dice, sample of size 2 (mean values).

The most important thing to notice is that even though the sample size is extremely small, the sampling distribution is symmetrical and is a lot closer to a normal curve than the rectangular population distribution is.

Now let's try a sample of size 3. In tabular form, the sampling distribution looks like that shown in Table 10-7. If we drew a picture of this sampling distribution, it would look like Fig. 10-7.

If you compare Fig. 10-7 with Fig. 10-4, you can see that the sampling distribution of die means is approaching a normal shape, even with a sample of only three cases. While this example doesn't *prove* the central-limit theorem, it does serve to dramatize how sampling distributions rapidly approach a normal shape even when the population distribution is decidedly nonnormal. You should notice once again that the mean of the sampling distribution is equal to the population mean. For practical purposes, the sampling distribution approaches a normal

Table 10-7 Sampling Distribution for Dice, Sample of Size 3, Mean Values

Mean	Probability	Mean	Probability
1.00	1/216	3.67	27/216
1.33	3/216	4.00	25/216
1.67	6/216	4.33	21/216
2.00	10/216	4.67	15/216
2.33	15/216	5.00	10/216
2.67	21/216	5.33	6/216
3.00	25/216	5.67	3/216
3.33	27/216	6.00	1/216
		Total	216/216 = 1.00

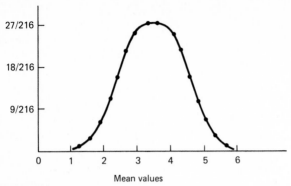

Figure 10-7 Sampling distribution for dice, sample of size 3 (mean values).

shape very quickly as sample size increases. Even with samples of only 30 cases, the sampling distribution is so close to a normal shape that the error involved is trivial.

Technically, the central-limit theorem holds only for samples that are drawn randomly, with replacement. Practically, samples are rarely simple random and are very rarely drawn with replacement. However, as long as cases are selected independently and with known probabilities, the violation of the theorem's assumptions does not have serious consequences, and there are correction factors that can be used with small samples. There is error involved, of course, but not so great as to undermine the usefulness of most practical applications.

Perspectives

When we do a study, we focus on a population, a well-defined group of people or things of interest to us. Each variable we study is distributed within that population in some way. What we usually do is to draw a sample of the population in a way that, given our resources, maximizes the likelihood that it represents the parent population with enough accuracy to justify settling for a sample instead of a census.

When our data have been gathered, we have only one sample of a given size, drawn by one set of sampling techniques. Behind that single sample, however, there lies a theoretical distribution — a probability distribution — of the outcomes of the infinite number of samples as large as ours that could have been drawn from the population. If our sample is even moderately large, we know what the sampling distribution will look like (approximately normal), we can estimate how much variation there is in the sampling distribution (with the estimated standard error), and we know that the mean of the sampling distribution exactly equals the mean in the population. With this in hand, we can use our sample mean or proportion to make estimates of the population mean or proportion, and use some special tables to attach levels of confidence (in terms of probabilities) to our estimating procedures. To do this, we need to know how to use the tables associated with the normal-curve distribution. In Chap. 11, we'll put it all together and see what we can do with statistical inference.

Before you continue, you should be able to explain to someone the meaning of a probability distribution, how you use areas under curves to represent one, and most important, what a sampling distribution is. You should be able to take a variable like income and, in terms of it, describe the meaning of the following: the population distribution, a sample distribution, a *sampling* distribution, the population mean, the sample mean, the mean of the *sampling* distribution, the population standard deviation, the sample standard deviation, and the *sampling* distribution's standard deviation (the standard error). You should be able to explain what the central-limit theorem means. Understanding these now will really pay off later on.

The Normal-Curve Distribution

We've seen that we need to know three characteristics of a sampling distribution in order to use it to calculate probabilities: the mean, the standard error, and the shape. While we don't know the actual value of the sampling distribution's mean (the average sample mean or proportion), we do know that it equals the population mean (or proportion). We can use the sample standard deviation and the sample size to estimate the standard error. The central-limit theorem allows us to assume a "normally" shaped sampling distribution for even moderately large samples. To use all this to make statistical inferences, we must first understand how to use sampling distributions and, in particular, the normal-curve distribution.

The normal curve is perhaps the most useful probability distribution in statistics as used by social scientists. It is bell-shaped, as in Fig. 10-8. The upper and lower ends of the curve are called *tails*. Half the cases lie above the mean, half lie below. In order for a distribution to be normal, it must be more than bell-shaped; it must conform to a rather complicated mathematical formula. Some normal curves are flatter or more peaked than others; they don't all look exactly the same.

There are many curves which, although bell-shaped, aren't normal. They differ from normality by being either too flat or too peaked. The degree of peakedness (as a deviation from normality) is called *kurtosis*. If a curve is flatter than a normal curve, it's *platykurtic*; if it's more peaked than a normal curve, it's *leptokurtic*. You'll rarely see these terms

The normal curve

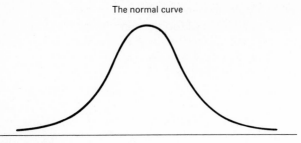

Figure 10-8

used (although economists do refer to them), but it's worthwhile to be familiar with them.

In inferential statistics, the normal distribution is used to describe a sampling distribution. The height of the curve (as we've pointed out earlier) is not important to us; we're interested in areas. The mean of the sampling distribution lies at the peak of the curve. To use the normal curve in inference, the *units* of the horizontal axis must be in terms of standard deviations (*standard errors* in a sampling distribution), and this fact is crucial for our use of the curve. If we're dealing with income with a standard deviation of, say, $6,000, then instead of having a distance of $9,000 on the horizontal axis, we have a distance of 1.5 standard deviations (9,000/6,000).

This is simply a translation process from one set of units to another (such as converting Fahrenheit to Celsius or dollars to pesos). If the standard deviation is $6,000, then each distance of $6,000 on the horizontal axis is equivalent to one standard deviation (each 8 cents of American currency is equivalent to one Mexican peso), and vice versa. Suppose we have a distribution of college-board scores which is normal, with a mean of 500 and a standard deviation of 100 (see Fig. 10-9).

In this distribution we can express distance along the horizontal axis in two ways. On the upper line, distance is expressed in terms of test-

Figure 10-9 Distribution of college-board scores for high school seniors.

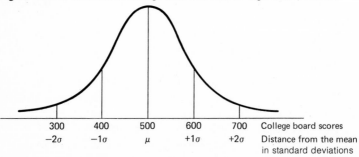

| 300 | 400 | 500 | 600 | 700 | College board scores |
| -2σ | -1σ | μ | $+1\sigma$ | $+2\sigma$ | Distance from the mean in standard deviations |

score points, with the first line to the right of the mean being 100 points above the mean. Since each 100 points is equivalent to one standard deviation in the distribution, then a score of 600 is one standard deviation above the mean (second line of numbers in Fig. 10-9). Similarly, a score of 300 is 200 test-score points below the mean, or two standard deviations below the mean (200/100).

Distance from the mean, when expressed in terms of standard deviations, is called a Z score. Thus, for a score of 400, the comparable Z score is -1 [or $(400 - 500)/100$]. The minus sign tells us that the point is below (less than) the mean, and the number tells us how many standard deviations below the mean the point is. A score of 700 is two standard deviations above the mean; the location could be described as Z score of $+2$. Z scores are also known as *standard scores*.

Mathematicians have computed a table, called the normal-curve table, which tells us what proportion of cases lie between the mean of any normal distribution and any specified number of standard deviations above (or below) the mean. (See Table 10-8.) We use this table by first expressing the number of standard deviations to the nearest hundredth (for example, 1.00, 2.33, etc.). If we want the proportion of cases that lie between the mean and 2.03 standard errors above the mean, we go down the left-hand column to the number 2.0 and then go across until we're under the column headed by .03. The four-digit number found there (.4788) is the proportion of cases that lie between the mean and 2.03 standard deviations above the mean. Since the curve is symmetrical, by doubling .4788 we get the proportion of cases that lie *within* 2.03 standard deviations of the mean (.9576). By subtracting .4788 from .5000 (since half the cases lie above the mean and half lie below), we find the proportion of cases that will be *at least* 2.03 standard deviations above the mean (or below the mean), or .0212. Double this number and we get the proportion of cases that will be at least 2.03 standard deviations away from the mean (either above or below), or .0424. This example is illustrated in Fig. 10-10.

Figure 10-10 Sampling distribution for sample means.

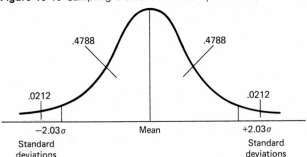

.4788   .4788

.0212   .0212

-2.03σ Mean $+2.03\sigma$
Standard   Standard
deviations   deviations

Table 10-8 Areas under the Normal Curve

Fractional parts of the total area (10,000) under the normal curve, corresponding to distances between the mean and ordinates which are Z standard-deviation units from the mean

Z	.00	.01	.02	.03	.04	.05	.06	.07	.08	.09
0.0	0000	0040	0080	0120	0159	0199	0239	0279	0319	0359
0.1	0398	0438	0478	0517	0557	0596	0636	0675	0714	0753
0.2	0793	0832	0871	0910	0948	0987	1026	1064	1103	1141
0.3	1179	1217	1255	1293	1331	1368	1406	1443	1480	1517
0.4	1554	1591	1628	1664	1700	1736	1772	1808	1844	1879
0.5	1915	1950	1985	2019	2054	2088	2123	2157	2190	2224
0.6	2257	2291	2324	2357	2389	2422	2454	2486	2518	2549
0.7	2580	2612	2642	2673	2704	2734	2764	2794	2823	2852
0.8	2881	2910	2939	2967	2995	3023	3051	3078	3106	3133
0.9	3159	3186	3212	3238	3264	3289	3315	3340	3365	3389
1.0	3413	3438	3461	3485	3508	3531	3554	3577	3599	3621
1.1	3643	3665	3686	3718	3729	3749	3770	3790	3810	3830
1.2	3849	3869	3888	3907	3925	3944	3962	3980	3997	4015
1.3	4032	4049	4066	4083	4099	4115	4131	4147	4162	4177
1.4	4192	4207	4222	4236	4251	4265	4279	4292	4306	4319
1.5	4332	4345	4357	4370	4382	4394	4406	4418	4430	4441
1.6	4452	4463	4474	4485	4495	4505	4515	4525	4535	4545
1.7	4554	4564	4573	4582	4591	4599	4608	4616	4625	4633
1.8	4641	4649	4656	4664	4671	4678	4686	4693	4699	4706
1.9	4713	4719	4726	4732	4738	4744	4750	4758	4702	4767
2.0	4773	4778	4783	4788	4793	4798	4903	4808	4812	4817
2.1	4821	4826	4830	4834	4838	4842	4846	4850	4854	4857
2.2	4861	4865	4868	4871	4875	4878	4881	4884	4887	4890
2.3	4893	4896	4898	4901	4904	4906	4909	4911	4913	4916
2.4	4918	4920	4922	4925	4927	4929	4931	4932	4934	4936
2.5	4938	4940	4941	4943	4945	4946	4948	4949	4951	4952
2.6	4953	4955	4956	4957	4959	4960	4961	4962	4963	4964
2.7	4965	4966	4967	4968	4969	4970	4971	4972	4973	4974
2.8	4974	4975	4976	4977	4977	4978	4979	4980	4980	4981
2.9	4981	4982	4983	4984	4984	4984	4985	4985	4986	4986
3.0	4986.5	4987	4987	4988	4988	4988	4989	4989	4989	4990
3.1	4990.0	4991	4991	4991	4992	4992	4992	4992	4993	4993
3.2	4993.129									
3.3	4995.166									
3.4	4996.631									
3.5	4997.674									
3.6	4998.409									
3.7	4998.922									
3.8	4999.277									
3.9	4999.519									
4.0	4999.683									
4.5	4999.966									
5.0	4999.997133									

SOURCE Harold O. Rugg, *Statistical Methods Applied to Education* (Boston: Houghton Mifflin Company, 1917), appendix table III, pp. 389–390, reprinted by permission of the publisher.

Using the normal-curve table, we find that in *any* normal distribution, roughly two-thirds of the cases will lie within one standard deviation of the mean, and just over 95 percent will lie within two standard deviations of the mean.

Being able to assume a normal *sampling distribution* is of enormous value. When we think of proportions of area as probabilities, we can see that even though we don't know what the population mean is, we do know the probability of our chosen sample falling within (or beyond) any given distance from the population mean. In Chap. 11, we'll make great use of this key fact.

So far, we've talked about distances from the mean as measured in standard-deviation (or standard-error) units. Most of us find it hard to think in terms of standard deviations. For example, suppose we're trying to estimate the average income in a population. If we can assume a normal-shaped sampling distribution, we know that there is only a 4.24 percent chance (2.12×2) of drawing a sample that will be off (high or low) by more than 2.03 standard errors (see Fig. 10-10). It's hard to visualize 2.03 standard errors; the statement would be far more meaningful if expressed in terms of dollars; i.e., "There's only a 4.24-percent chance of our sample mean being off by more than X."

We can translate from standard errors to dollars by recalling what a standard error is: it's the square root of the average squared deviation of sample means about the population mean, and its units are dollars. In other words, each standard error is equivalent to so many dollars. Let's say we gather a sample of income data on 400 people and the sample standard deviation is $6,000. The estimated *standard error* will be

$$\frac{\$6,000}{\sqrt{400}} = \$300$$

This means that each distance of one standard error on the horizontal axis of the sampling distribution is equivalent to $300. A distance of 2.03 standard errors from the population mean is therefore equivalent to $(2.03)(\$300) = \$609$. We can now say that with 400 cases and a normal sampling distribution, there is only a 4.24-percent chance of drawing a sample with a mean income that will be more than $609 above or below the population mean.

If we want to find the probability of being within a certain number of dollars of the population mean (say $450), we reverse what we've just done by first dividing the distance in dollars by the size of the standard error. This translates the dollar distance into standard errors:

$$\frac{\$450}{\$300} = 1.50 \text{ standard errors} = Z$$

We then go into the normal table and find the area that corresponds to 1.50 standard errors, or .4332. If the sample size is 400 and the sampling distribution is normal, then the probability of drawing a sample whose mean is within $450 of the population mean is (2)(.4332), or .8664. The probability of drawing a sample whose mean is off by *more* than $450 is $1.0000 - .8664 = .1336$.

If we want to translate a distance in standard errors into one in dollars, we multiply the number of standard errors times the number of dollars per standard error [for example, (1.50)($300) = $450]. You should think of some examples of your own and practice this back-and-forth translation between standard errors and raw scores.

Note that our example need not be in terms of dollars. The same process applies to numbers of children, years of schooling, the proportion of people voting yes on proposition A, or any other numerical variable.

There are several important ideas in this section that you should be sure of. You should be familiar with the normal curve and know that its units are in standard deviations (or standard errors) and that it expresses probabilities in terms of areas. You should be able to translate distances from the mean in raw scores (for example, IQ points) to Z scores and back again. Most important, you should be able to use the normal table to calculate the probability of getting sample results that are within a given distance of the mean or beyond that distance, whether that distance is expressed in raw scores or in Z scores.

I've found that playing around with actual problems helps immeasurably in understanding the normal curve and how it works. There are a number of problems at the end of this chapter, and I strongly suggest that you work through all of them. If you don't understand how the normal curve is used, it's most important that you find out now.

Problems

10-1 Assume it possible to measure the prestige of occupations on a numerical basis. You are given the following information: (1) *Blue-collar fathers* have sons whose occupational prestige scores are normally distributed with a mean of 80 and a standard deviation of 20. (2) *White-collar fathers* have sons whose occupational prestige scores are normally distributed with a mean of 100 and a standard deviation of 20.

    a. What proportion of the blue-collar fathers have sons with an occupational prestige score:

      (1) Above 95?

      (2) Between 72 and 87?

      (3) Between 90 and 105?

    (4) At least six points different from the mean?

    (5) Within one standard deviation of the *median?*

  b. An occupational Z score of +1.65 among sons of blue-collar fathers would correspond to what percentile among the sons of white-collar fathers?

10-2 Suppose we draw a representative sample of 400 people from a population and ask each respondent how many times he has changed residence in the past 5 years. The sample mean is 3.1 and the standard deviation is 2.0. The estimated standard error for the sampling distribution of sample means is

$$\frac{s}{\sqrt{N}} = \frac{2.0}{\sqrt{400}} = \frac{2.0}{20} = .10$$

Given this information, what is the probability that our sample mean is:

  a. *Within* one standard error of the unknown population mean?

  b. *At least* 2.25 standard errors above or below the unknown population mean?

  c. *Within* .20 residence change per 5 years of the unknown population mean?

  d. *At least* .25 residence change per 5 years from the unknown population mean?

Suggested Readings

1 Blalock, Hubert M., Jr.: *Social Statistics*, 2d ed., chap. 7. New York: McGraw-Hill Book Company, 1972.

2 Hays, William L.: *Statistics for the Social Sciences*, 2d ed., secs. 7.1–7.13, 7.16, 7.18, 7.21, 7.23, 8.1–8.4, 8.6, 8.7, 8.11, 8.13. New York: Holt, Rinehart and Winston, 1973.

3 Loether, Herman J., and Donald G. McTavish: *Inferential Statistics for Sociologists*, chap. 4. Boston: Allyn and Bacon, 1974.

4 Runyon, Richard P., and Audrey Haber: *Fundamentals of Behavioral Statistics*, 2d ed., chap. 7. Reading, Mass.: Addison-Wesley Publishing Company, 1972.

11

estimating population means and proportions with sample results

There are two basic uses of statistical inference. The first is the *estimation* of population characteristics using sample data. An example might be the estimation of the mean income in a population, using the mean income in a representative sample. The second use is in *hypothesis testing*. Although most of the literature emphasizes hypothesis testing, we're going to start with the estimation procedures for two reasons. First, I believe hypothesis tests are less useful, are often misinterpreted, and should receive less attention than they do. Second, I think statistical inference is easier to understand if we start with estimation. Hypothesis testing involves a reverse kind of logic that is often confusing if you don't already understand what's going on.

In this chapter we'll talk about the estimation of population proportions and means, as well as differences between populations. We'll take up hypothesis testing in Chap. 12.

To follow and understand this chapter, you'll need to understand means, proportions, sampling distributions, standard errors, and the use of the normal distribution.

Point Estimates

If we want to estimate a population proportion or mean (or any other population characteristic) using sample data, one obvious strategy is to use the comparable sample characteristic (proportion, mean, etc.). It's of course very unlikely that any sample mean will exactly equal the population mean, but if we want to use a specific value for our estimate, the sample mean constitutes the best information we have.

You'll recall that the mean of the sampling distribution of sample proportions equals the population proportion; you'll also recall that the mean of the sampling distribution of sample means equals the population mean. In both these cases, we call the sample characteristic an *unbiased estimate* because the average sample result exactly equals the population characteristic we're trying to estimate.

This is not the case with standard deviations. Suppose we're trying to estimate the mean income in a population. You'll recall from the last chapter that we often make use of the standard error of the sampling distribution, which equals the population standard deviation divided by the sample size:

$$\sigma_{\bar{x}} = \frac{\sigma}{\sqrt{N}}$$

You'll also recall that we used the sample standard deviation to estimate the unknown population standard deviation:

$$\text{Estimated } \sigma_{\bar{x}} = \frac{s}{\sqrt{N}}$$

Well, it turns out that *in the long run*, the sample standard deviation will tend to be a bit smaller than the population standard deviation; put another way, if we look at the sampling distribution for sample standard deviations, the average is a bit lower than the population standard deviation. The sample standard deviation is thus slightly biased downward.

To compensate for this, in estimating the standard error for means, we make the denominator smaller by one:

$$\text{Estimated } \sigma_{\bar{x}} = \frac{s}{\sqrt{N-1}}$$

By making the denominator slightly smaller, we make the estimated standard error slightly larger, compensating for the fact that sample standard deviations tend to slightly underestimate the population standard deviation.

In using sample characteristics to make estimates about populations, we usually want to have some idea of how accurate our estimate is. As we've said, it's very unlikely that *any* sample characteristic exactly reflects the population. We can, however, determine how likely it is that the population mean, for example, lies within a specified distance of the sample mean, and it's to such estimates that we now turn.

Estimating Population Means: Interval Estimates

Suppose we're interested in the number of children couples plan to have by the time they've finished having children. Because of the enormous cost involved in a census of a population as large as all married couples in the United States, we might take a sample of 400 couples. We send interviewers to each couple and ask each (among other things), "How many children do you plan to have by the time you're all finished having children?" We record and process their answers and get the distribution shown in Table 11-1.

As with every numerical distribution, this one has a mean and a standard deviation. In this case, the mean is 2.6 children and the standard deviation is 1.5 children. The estimated standard error of sample means is $1.5/\sqrt{400 - 1} = .075$ child.

Statistical inference is the process by which we make estimates of population characteristics (means, proportions, etc.) and attach probabilities (or levels of confidence) to them. Ideally, we might like to be able to say something like "I'm 99-percent sure that the mean number of children planned by American couples is 2.6." There are two problems with such a statement, however. First, the probability of any sample mean exactly equaling the population mean is incredibly small since there are an infinite number of possible sample results; we could never be at all

Table 11-1 Distribution of the Number of Children Planned by a Sample of American Married Couples, United States, 1974 (Fictitious but Reasonable Data)

Number of children planned	F	Percentage
0	40	10.0%
1	44	11.0
2	100	25.0
3	120	30.0
4	60	15.0
5	20	5.0
6	8	2.0
7	6	1.5
8	2	0.5
Total	400	100.0%

sure that our sample mean equaled the population mean. Second, even if this were not a problem, our sample result either equals the population mean or it doesn't (i.e., the probability is either 0 or 1); we can't legitimately attach the probability statement to our specific sample result.

The next best thing would be to estimate the population mean with a range of values (an *interval*) such as 2.4 to 2.8. This would solve the first problem raised above. The second problem requires us to express our confidence differently. While we can't express confidence in our specific interval (since the population mean is either in it or not), we can express our confidence in the procedures used to generate the data that lead to interval. The procedures consist of the sampling process; the confidence refers to the probability that such procedures lead to accurate results.

We have our sample mean, 2.6. We're going to construct an interval and use that as our estimate of the population mean. It makes sense to include our sample mean in that interval, since it's the best single estimate we have of the actual population value. Where in the interval should our sample mean be? Since our sample mean is as likely to be too high as too low, it's logical to put it at the center of the interval. We might, for example, add and subtract .6 to the sample mean and get an interval that runs from 2.0 to 3.2. That, however, might seem to be too broad; we might want to be more *precise*. The interval could be narrowed to, say, 2.5 to 2.7, a range of only .2 in contrast with the range of 1.2 in the first interval. Let's suppose that we'd like to be somewhat precise. We'd like to estimate that the population mean is between 2.5 and 2.7 children.

We've decided on an estimate (2.5 to 2.7) and are left with the job of calculating the probability that our procedures have resulted in an interval which covers the population mean. This is where we use the normal curve.

We've drawn our sample properly. We have a fairly large sample (400) which allows us (by the central-limit theorem) to assume that the sampling distribution of sample means is "normally" shaped. As we saw in Chap. 10, the normal-curve table is set up in terms of standard deviations (or in standard errors, when dealing with sampling distributions as we are here). So, before we can use the normal table to find the probability that our estimate covers the true mean, we have to convert our interval—2.5 to 2.7—into standard errors. Let's take a look at what this means.

Think of our interval as a straight horizontal line:

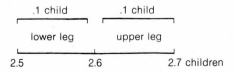

.1 child		.1 child	
lower leg		upper leg	
2.5	2.6	2.7 children

The interval has the sample mean (2.6 children) at its center and its length is .2 child (2.7 − 2.5). We obtained the interval by adding and subtracting the same quantity (.1 child) to the sample mean. We can convert the length of each leg from children to standard errors by dividing the number of children per leg (.1) by the number of children per standard error (.075 child). This gives us the number of standard errors per leg:

.10/.075 = 1.33 standard errors

Our interval is now expressed in standard errors and looks like this:

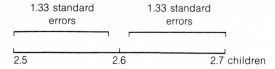

Instead of expressing our estimated interval as "the sample mean plus or minus .10 child," the interval now reads "the sample mean plus or minus 1.33 standard errors."

Figure 11-1 shows the sampling distribution for samples of size 400. Notice that we've assumed it to be "normally" shaped, and that the mean of the distribution (the average sample mean in this case) equals the population mean, the number we're trying to estimate. You'll remember from Chap. 10 that a puzzle of this curve is that one of its key features is a number we don't know (the population mean). We'll soon see why this doesn't stand in our way.

The length of the horizontal axis of the sampling distribution in Fig. 11-1 is measured in standard errors. The point marked with a $- 1\sigma_{\bar{x}}$, for example, represents a distance of one standard error below the population mean. You'll also recall that the normal table tells us what proportion of all possible samples will have means that fall within any given number of standard errors from the mean. For example, .6826 (just over two-thirds) of all possible samples will have means between one standard error below and one standard error above the population mean.

Our interval (2.5 to 2.7) is now also in terms of standard errors, and we could draw it below the sampling distribution in Fig. 11-1 as shown in Fig. 11-2. We've placed our interval at several possible places underneath the sampling distribution. In case a, our sample mean (2.6) equals the population mean exactly; in case b, our sample mean is higher than the population mean; in case c our sample mean is lower than the population mean. The point is that the interval we've proposed as an estimate of the population mean could sit in an infinite number of positions *depending on how much our sample mean (which is at the center of our interval) is in error.*

But since we don't know what the population mean is, how do we

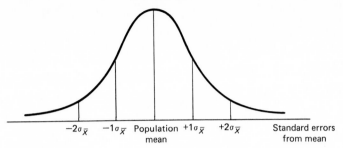

Figure 11-1 Sampling distribution for the mean number of children couples want.

know where our interval is and thus how accurate it is? Consider this question: "How far off does our sample mean have to be in order for the interval we constructed to *miss* the population mean?" See Fig. 11-3. In order for our interval to miss the population mean, the sample mean has to be so far above the population mean (as in *a*) that the lower boundary (2.5 in *a*) of the interval misses the population mean (the center of the sampling distribution); or the sample mean has to be so far below the population mean (as in *b*) that the upper boundary (2.7 in *b*) of the interval misses the population mean. In *a*, for example, how far is the sample mean from the population mean? The answer is that it's *just over the length of the lower leg away*. In *b*, the sample mean is just over the length of the upper leg away. As we know, the upper and lower legs are of equal length, .1 child or *1.33 standard errors*.

Figure 11-2 Sampling distribution of sample means with possible locations for a confidence interval constructed from a single sample.

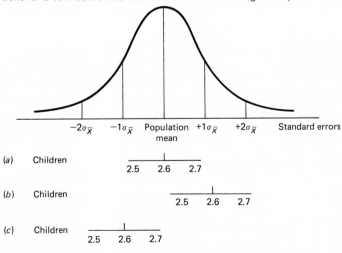

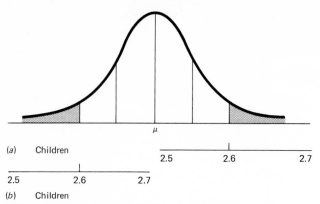

(a) Children

(b) Children

Figure 11-3 Sampling distribution for sample means, showing how much in error constructed confidence intervals must be in order to miss the actual population value.

Now, we're close to our answer. The interval we've constructed will miss the population mean if the sample mean is more than 1.33 standard errors from the population mean, either above or below.

From here on it's downhill. What's the probability of drawing a sample that is more than 1.33 standard errors from the mean? We're looking for the probability of drawing a sample result that will fall in either of the two shaded regions in Fig. 11-3. To do this we look in the normal table (Table 2 in Appendix C), down the left-hand column to the number 1.3 and over under the column headed by .03 to get the area contained between the mean and a point 1.33 standard errors from the mean: .4083 is the area (half of the *unshaded* portion of Fig. 11-3). What we want, however, is the proportion of samples that will lie *beyond* this area, and to get that, we have to subtract .4083 from .5000. We get .0917. Since we want the probability of getting a sample that falls in *either* of the two shaded regions, we double .0917 and get .1834.

We've calculated the probability of drawing a sample of 400 from the population and getting a mean more than 1.33 standard errors from the population mean. This probability (.1834) is also the long-run probability that an *interval* so selected (the sample mean plus or minus 1.33 standard errors) will *miss* the population mean.

Our estimate is: "The population mean lies somewhere between 2.5 and 2.7." There is a .1834 chance that we've drawn a sample with a mean that is so far from the population mean that the resulting confidence interval fails to include it. This means there is a $1.000 - .1834 = .8166$ chance that we've drawn a sample that resulted in an accurate confidence interval. Our level of confidence in our procedure is 82 percent. We've just used statistical inference to estimate a population mean.

There are an infinite number of possible samples that we could have drawn from the population; this means that there are an infinite number of possible sample means and an infinite number of possible confidence intervals with those means at their center. We've determined from the normal table that 82 percent of all possible sample means will fall within 1.33 standard errors of the true population mean. Therefore, 82 percent of all the possible confidence intervals (made by adding and subtracting 1.33 standard errors to a sample mean) will include the population mean. Our confidence level reflects our long-run chances of drawing such a sample result. As one author put it, "When we say that our confidence level is .95, we mean that we are using a crystal ball that is known to work 95 times out of 100, although on any given trial it either works or fails."[1]

Notice that we never needed to know the population mean. All we needed to know was that the sampling distribution was "normally" shaped. We could assume this because we properly drew a large sample.

The interval we've constructed is called a *confidence interval*. In this case we have an "82-percent confidence interval."

How Confidence Intervals Are Actually Constructed

In the previous section we started with an interval and then figured out probabilities. Usually, we start with an idea of how confident we want to be and then construct the interval. The procedure is the same, except in reverse. To be 82-percent sure means an 18-percent chance of error, which means a 9-percent chance of error in *either direction* (18%/2). This means we have to add and subtract to the sample mean a leg that's so long that our interval will miss the population mean only if the sample mean is among the upper or lower 9 percent of all possible sample means (see Fig. 11-4).

If our sample mean falls in either of the shaded areas in Fig. 11-4, the interval will miss the population mean. We've decided that we want this to happen only 18 percent of the time, that our sample mean (and thus our interval) will be too high only 9 percent of the time and too low only 9 percent of the time. How long must the legs on the confidence interval be in order for this to be true?

We answer this question by first rephrasing it: "How many standard errors do I have to go above or below the mean to cut off the upper and lower 9 percent of the possible sample means?" Back to the normal table, but this time instead of going from standard errors to probabilities

[1] James A. Davis, *Elementary Survey Analysis* (Englewood Cliffs, N.J.: Prentice-Hall, 1971), p. 57.

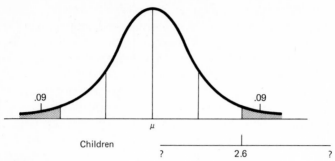

Figure 11-4

(as we did before), we go from probabilities to standard errors. We go into the body of the table and find the number that's closest to .4100 (or .5000 − .0900), which is .4099. This corresponds to 1.34 standard errors (slightly different from our previous figure of 1.33 because we rounded off our answers).

This tells us that if we add and subtract 1.34 standard errors from all possible sample means, only 18 percent of the resulting intervals will miss the population mean. To convert our interval from standard errors to number of children, we multiply 1.34 times the number of children in each standard error (.075), which equals .1. Adding and subtracting from the sample mean, this gives us our original interval of 2.5 to 2.7.

We've taken something known (our sample mean) and used a theoretical distribution to make an estimate of something unknown, and we've fixed in advance the probability that we're wrong. Not bad, when you think about it.

To illustrate some points and cement this procedure more firmly in your understanding, let's try a variation. Suppose an 18-percent chance of error is too much; suppose we stand to lose a lot by being wrong and want to be very sure that we're right. Suppose we want to be 99-percent sure of our crystal ball. What then? The procedures are the same, only the numbers are different (see Fig. 11-5).

Figure 11-5

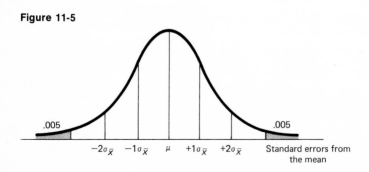

The interval will miss the population mean when the sample mean is in one of the shaded areas of Fig. 11-5. Each tail contains .5 percent (or 1%/2) of the possible sample means. We go to the normal table and find the number of standard errors that corresponds most closely to an area of .4950 (or .5000 − .0050) and get 2.575. If we go 2.575 standard errors above or below the population mean, we'll cut off the upper and lower .5 percent of the possible sample means (for a total of 1 percent of all possible samples). Intervals that consist of a sample mean plus or minus 2.575 standard errors will miss the population mean *only* when the sample mean is more than 2.575 standard errors above or below the population mean, and this can happen only 1 percent of the time. Our confidence interval is thus 2.6 plus or minus 2.575 standard errors, or, converting to numbers of children, 2.6 plus or minus .20 child. The interval now runs from 2.4 to 2.8.

Notice that our new interval is twice as wide as the old one (2.5 to 2.7), which means that our answer is less precise. This illustrates an important fact of statistical inference: the more *confident* we want to be, the less *precise* we can be. If we want to be very sure our interval includes the population mean, we'll have to make it broader than we would if we were willing to be less sure.

The *t* Distribution

In the preceding sections we've used Z scores to calculate the probability of drawing a sample mean a given distance from the population mean. For a variety of theoretical reasons, we cannot use the normal table to calculate probabilities for means when the sample size is small (approximately 100 or smaller). Instead, we use another sampling distribution, called the *t distribution*. The *meaning* of t is exactly that of Z. We use *t* to compensate for small samples and the random error involved in using the sample standard deviation to estimate the population standard deviation. There is a separate *t* distribution for each sample size. (See Table 3, Appendix C.)

With small samples, a value of *t* is larger than a comparable value of Z, thereby making the confidence interval wider. As the sample size increases, the *t* distribution approximates the normal table; for samples larger than 500 cases (approximately), using *t* and Z gives virtually identical results. It's necessary to use the *t* distribution only when dealing with means and only when the sample size is small.

I mention this so that should you encounter a *t* where you think there should be a Z, you'll know that the difference is a technical one and does not change the meaning of the probabilities involved.[1]

---

[1] If you'd like to pursue this, see Hubert M. Blalock, Jr., *Social Statistics*, 2d ed. (New York: McGraw-Hill Book Company, 1972), pp. 188–193.

Sample Size and Estimation

It makes sense that the larger the sample is, the more accurate our estimates are going to be. Confidence intervals demonstrate how true this is.

In our example we had a sample of 400 couples. What if we'd been able to afford to gather data from 3,600 couples: how would this affect our estimates? The difference is felt through the size of the standard error. Since we divide the sample standard deviation by the square root of the sample size, the bigger the sample, the larger the denominator is and thus the *smaller* the standard error is. With 3,600 couples the standard error is $1.5/\sqrt{3,600 - 1} = .025$ child instead of .075. Our second confidence interval (the one with only 1-percent chance of error) consisted of the sample mean plus or minus 2.575 standard errors. Since the standard error is now smaller than it was before, the two legs on the interval will be shorter: 2.6 plus or minus (2.575)(.025), or .06 child. Our interval with 3,600 couples is 2.54 to 2.66, which is considerably more precise than an interval of 2.4 to 2.8.

Notice that the level of confidence in our estimate is the same in both cases (99 percent) but our precision is greater with the larger sample. So, for any given chance of error, the larger the sample, the more precise we can be. Also notice that although the second sample is nine times as large, the standard error is reduced (and precision is increased) by the factor of only 3 (check this out for yourself).

Estimating
Population Proportions

To estimate a population proportion (e.g., the proportion of people that have seen at least one X-rated movie in a given year), we follow exactly the same procedures with only one change: the formula for the standard error changes since we're dealing with proportions instead of means. The standard error for sample proportions is

$$\sigma_{P_s} = \sqrt{\frac{PQ}{N}}$$

where P is the proportion of people in the population who have seen an X-rated movie and Q is the proportion who haven't (that is, $1 - P$). Since we don't know what P is (that's what we're after), we usually use a value of .5. Why? If we set P at .5, then Q is also .5, and the product (PQ) is .25. If we use any number higher or lower than .5 for the value of P, the product of P and Q will be lower than .25 (try some and you'll see that it's true). What we've done is to make the numerator of the standard error as large as it can possibly be. This tends to inflate the confidence interval, which increases the chance that it's accurate. By setting P at .5, we're being conservative and increasing our confidence in our estimate. If we're pretty sure that P is way below .5 (say .2), then we might want to use a lower figure. Keep in mind that the values we use are *estimates* of the population values.

Let's try an example. We're interested in the proportion of people who have seen an X-rated movie in the past year. In 1973 the National Opinion Research Center drew a sample of 1,504 Americans 18 years or older. In response to the question: "Have you seen an X-rated movie in the last year?" the distribution obtained was that shown in Table 11-2. We decide that we want our estimate to have only a 1-percent chance of error.

As we saw in the previous section, if we go 2.575 standard errors above or below the mean of the sampling distribution (in this case the mean of the sampling distribution is the population *proportion*), we'll draw an incorrect sample confidence interval only 1 percent of the time. This is true because from the normal distribution we know that only 1 percent of all possible sample proportions will be more than 2.575 standard errors from the population proportion.

To construct our interval, we add and subtract 2.575 standard errors from the sample proportion.

The standard error is[1]

$$\sigma_{P_s} = \sqrt{\frac{PQ}{N}} = \sqrt{\frac{(.3)(.7)}{1,504}} = .012$$

Table 11-2 Percentage Who Saw at Least One X-rated Movie during the Preceding Year, Americans, 18 and Over, 1973

Response	Percentage
Yes	25.1%
No	74.0
Don't know	0.6
No answer	0.3
Total	100.0% ($N = 1,504$)

SOURCE National Opinion Research Center, General Social Survey.

---

[1] Note that we used .3 for the estimate of P and .7 for the estimate of Q in the standard-error calculation. As we mentioned before, using .5 is appropriate whenever the sample value of P is not extremely large or small. In this case, the sample proportion is .25, which is quite a distance from .5. We've used .3 here to compensate for this. By using a value slightly above .25, we're being a bit conservative. Keep in mind that the selection of values in calculating the standard error is a matter of judgment; we could have used .25 or .27 or .35, for example. There is no one absolutely correct value.

The 99-percent confidence interval is the sample proportion plus or minus (2.575)(.012), or .25 plus or minus .031. The estimate is .22 to .28, and the degree of confidence is 99 percent. We're 99-percent sure that we've drawn an interval that covers the true proportion that saw at least one X-rated movie in the preceding year.

With larger samples, such tools are very powerful. If we drew a sample of 10,000 people from any population, we could construct 99-percent confidence intervals only two percentage points wide (for example, .61 to .63), *no matter how large the population was*. Most national surveys have sample sizes of 1,500 or so. There are several reasons for this figure. First, it's large enough to represent most subgroups of interest to social researchers. Second, and perhaps most important, it's a compromise between cost and precision. The smaller the standard error is, the narrower (and more precise) any given confidence interval will be. The larger the sample, the smaller the standard error. However, the standard error is decreased by the *square root* of any increase in sample size. In order to double our precision (or cut the confidence interval in half), we'd have to quadruple the sample size. With the costs of national surveys running at around $60 per respondent, there's a point of diminishing returns beyond which the additional cost of gathering data is not worth the relatively small absolute gains in precision for a given level of confidence. For these reasons, 1,500 has become a common sample size in national surveys.

At no point in these calculations did we ever need to consider population size. Unless the sample constitutes a considerable proportion of the population (say 10 percent), the relation of sample size to population is *irrelevant*. If the sample does constitute a substantial portion of the population, this *increases* our precision (the interval is narrower) for a given level of confidence.

Instant 99-Percent
Confidence Intervals for Proportions

When you're reading poll results and the article says that "less than half the people (46 percent) feel the Senator is doing a good job," you might like to see if it's possible that more than half approve of the Senator and the sample result of 46 percent is too low by chance. A handy way to do this is to construct a confidence interval and see if it goes above .50. If the 99-percent confidence interval, for example, runs from .40 to .52, then you can't rule out the possibility that more than half approve. If, on the other hand, the 99-percent confidence interval runs from .44 to .48, then you can be pretty sure that the population proportion is below .50.

For your use and entertainment, I've constructed a table that you can use to evaluate many of the poll results that use proportions or percentages.[1] For each sample size in the left column, the right-column figure completes the following statement: "The 99-percent confidence interval is the sample percentage plus or minus ____ percent."

So, if our sample size is 300 and the percentage of our sample in favor of the Senator is 46 percent, the 99-percent confidence interval is 46 percent plus or minus 7 percent — or 39 to 53 percent (if we are talking about proportions, the comparable figures are .46, .39, and .53).

Sample size	The 99-percent confidence interval is the sample percentage plus or minus
50	18%
100	13
300	7
500	6
800	5
1,000	4
1,500	3
2,000	3
3,000	2
5,000	2
10,000	1
50,000	1/2

Estimating Differences between Sample Proportions

As we've suggested before, our interest often extends beyond the characteristics of a single group to comparisons between groups. Are lower-class people more prejudiced than middle-class people? Do patients using a particular drug recover faster than patients using a placebo? Do women college professors make as much money as comparable men? Do blacks want more children than whites? Most empirical research hinges on such questions and depends on sample information to answer them.

In such cases, our interest centers on differences between group means and proportions. For example, suppose we're studying the relationship between sex and racial prejudices. Are men more likely than women to be racial segregationists?

The 1968 election survey conducted by the University of Michigan's Survey Research Center used a national probability sample of Americans 21 years and older and obtained the results shown in Table 11-3.

---

[1] As with all the inference techniques discussed in this book, they are applicable *only* to data from properly drawn samples. They cannot, for example, be used with quota samples or samples with low response rates.

Table 11-3 Whites in Favor of Racial Segregation by Sex and by Region, United States, 1968

	NONSOUTH				SOUTH			
Sex	**In favor**	**Not in favor**	**Total**	*N*	**In favor**	**Not in favor**	**Total**	*N*
Men	13%	87	100%	368	25%	75	100%	163
Women	13%	87	100%	458	34%	66	100%	202
Total	13%	87	100%	826	30%	70	100%	365

Clearly there are no differences between men and women in the nonsouth. There's a sex difference of 9 percent in the south, however (34% − 25%), with women appearing to be more in favor of segregation. Since we're estimating the difference between the populations of southern men and southern women, our observed difference of .09 will lie at the center of the confidence interval.

In order to use the normal table to compute the length of the confidence-interval legs and the associated probabilities, we need a "normally" shaped sampling distribution of *differences between sample proportions.*

Just what is such a distribution? With single samples we imagined drawing all possible samples and constructing a probability distribution of means or proportions. In this case we're drawing all possible *pairs* of samples (southern men and southern women), and for each pair we're calculating the *difference* between the two sample proportions in favor of racial segregation. The probability distribution of those *differences* is the sampling distribution.

The central-limit theorem also applies here: as the samples get larger, the sampling distribution closely approximates a normal shape. In addition, the mean of the sampling distribution (the average difference between samples of men and women) equals the actual difference between the populations of men and women.

Finally, as in all sampling distributions, there's a standard error. For proportions, the standard error for the sampling distribution of differences is

$$\sigma_{P_{s_1} - P_{s_2}} = \sqrt{\frac{P_1 Q_1}{N_1} + \frac{P_2 Q_2}{N_2}}$$

where P_1 is the proportion of all southern men (i.e., the population) who are segregationists, P_2 is the comparable proportion of southern women, and N_1 and N_2 are the respective sample sizes. In this case, the sample *p*'s are .25 and .34, and using .50 would unduly inflate the standard error. So, to allow for the small size of these proportions and yet be somewhat conservative, we'll use .30 and .35. We could also use the actual sample values without affecting the results greatly. Which you use is largely a matter of personal preference. The estimated standard error is

$$\sigma_{P_{s_1} - P_{s_2}} = \sqrt{\frac{(.30)(.70)}{163} + \frac{(.35)(.65)}{202}} = .049$$

To give you some idea of how the use of different values for P affects the size of the standard error, if we'd used .50 as the value for both P's, the standard error would have been .053; using the actual sample values of .25 and .34 would have yielded a standard error of .048. If we round the standard error to two significant places, the standard error is .05 regardless of which set of values we use.

We're now on familiar ground. We have a sample result (a difference of .09), a sampling distribution assumed to be normal, and an estimated standard error (.049). If we want to construct a 99-percent confidence interval, we need legs on the interval that are 2.575 standard errors long (from the normal table):

The 99-percent confidence interval is $(p_2 - p_1) \pm 2.575$ standard errors. We convert from standard errors to proportions by multiplying 2.575 times the value of a standard error (.049) and get .13. The interval runs from −.04 to +.22. We *cannot* be 99-percent confident that segregationist attitudes are more prevalent among women than men, since our interval includes zero.

How confident can we be that southern women are more likely than southern men to be segregationists? To answer this, we first find the confidence level for the interval of .09 ± .09 (or .0 to .18). Each leg in this interval is .09 long (in terms of proportions). To calculate probabilities, we convert the leg's length from proportions to standard errors: .09/.049 = 1.84. The area contained between the mean and 1.84 standard errors above the mean is .4671. We double this to get the confidence level of this interval, and get .9342.

Our estimate (.0 to .18) has a 93-percent confidence level. The probability of drawing a sample leading to an incorrect interval is 1 − .9342, or .0658. The probability of drawing a sample mean that is too low (i.e., that the difference is actually greater than .09) is .0658/2 = .0329. So, if we construct an *open-ended* interval consisting of two pieces (.0 to .18 and

.18 and above) the confidence level is $.9342 + .0329 = .9671$, or 97 percent. This is the confidence level for the estimate, "Segregationist attitudes are more prevalent among southern women than among southern men."

Estimating Differences between Sample Means

The procedures for estimating differences between sample means are the same as those for proportions, except for the difference in standard-error calculations. The standard error for differences between means is

$$\sigma_{\bar{x}_1 - \bar{x}_2} = \sqrt{\frac{s_1^2}{N_1 - 1} + \frac{s_2^2}{N_2 - 1}}$$

where s_1^2 and s_2^2 are the variances in the two samples and N_1 and N_2 are the two sample sizes.

Let's try an example. Suppose we're interested in the different numbers of children desired by white and nonwhite women. In 1961, data were gathered from a national sample of whites and nonwhites in answer to the question: "How many children would you have if you had your life to live over again?" The results are these:[1]

	Whites	Nonwhites
Mean	3.60	3.30
N	2,364	259
Variance	0.83	1.48

The standard error for the difference between two sample means is

$$\sigma_{\bar{x}_1 - \bar{x}_2} = \sqrt{\frac{s_1^2}{N_1 - 1} + \frac{s_2^2}{N_2 - 1}} = \sqrt{\frac{.83}{2,363} + \frac{1.48}{258}} = \sqrt{.0061} = .08$$

Suppose we want a 95-percent confidence interval. This means a 2.5-percent chance of error in either direction. We look in the normal table for the Z score that corresponds with the number closest to $.5000 - .0250 = .4750$, which is 1.96. (We can use the normal table because the number of cases is large.) Ninety-five percent of the possible sample differences are contained within 1.96 standard errors of the actual population difference. Each leg of the 95-percent confidence interval will be 1.96 standard errors long, or $(1.96)(.08) = .16$ child. The con-

---

[1] Pascal K. Whelpton, Arthur A. Campbell, and John E. Patterson, *Fertility and Family Planning in the United States* (Princeton, N.J.: Princeton University Press, 1966), table 19, p. 47.

fidence interval is thus the observed difference $(3.60 - 3.30 = .30)$ plus or minus .16, or from .14 to .46 child. Our estimate is that as a group, nonwhites report desiring from .14 to .46 more children than whites do; our confidence in our estimating procedures is 95 percent.

The Perpetual Trade-off: Confidence, Precision, and Sample Size

The leg of a confidence interval is equal to a number of standard errors multiplied by the size of the standard error in original variable units. For example, in the problem of the number of desired children in the last section, the leg's length was as follows:

$$\text{Length in children} = Z \text{ score} \times \text{standard error}$$

or

$$\text{Length in children} = Z \text{ score} \sqrt{\frac{s_1^{\,2}}{N-1} + \frac{s_2^{\,2}}{N-1}}$$

$$\qquad\qquad\qquad\qquad\qquad\quad\ \ precision \qquad confidence \qquad sample\ size$$

In this equation, the length of the interval indicates the *precision* of the estimate: the longer the interval, the less precise is the estimate. The Z score reflects the confidence level: the higher the confidence (and the *accuracy*), the farther out on the normal distribution we have to go to cut off the higher proportion of cases; hence the Z score is higher. The standard error can be raised or lowered by increasing or decreasing sample size. Keep in mind that the standard error is reduced by the reciprocal of the *square root* of sample size. Thus, taking four times as many cases reduces the standard error by a factor of 2 (or $\sqrt{4}$), not 4.

We can't increase our precision without lowered confidence or a larger sample; the only way to increase our confidence is to accept less precision or choose a larger sample. Once the data are gathered, confidence and precision can be increased *only* at each other's expense.

Some Concluding Notes

There are two important things you should keep in mind when reading articles that contain such estimates. First, what we've done here assumes there is only random measurement error (no bias). Statistical procedures can't do anything to make up for poor measurement or field work.

Second, all these techniques assume that the sample was properly drawn: i.e., that everyone in the population had a chance to get in the sample and that the actual probability can be calculated for each member of the population. Without this, we can't assume the sampling distribution is normal, and without that we might as well pack up and go home. This is why survey research is such an enormous job when properly done.

Keep in mind that all estimates based on samples have probabilities attached to them. As we'll see in the next chapter, it's a mistake to attribute definite decision-making powers to statistical inference processes. While we can use sample results to support a view of the world, they are never final and always carry with them a chance of error. While we may use sample results to help us make decisions, the decision-making process is not inherent in inferential statistics. It's a process involving subjective weighing of the meaning of differing probabilities of error.

Two basic topics have been introduced in this chapter. The first is the idea of confidence intervals, and you should understand where they come from and what they mean. The second is the relationship between precision, confidence, and sample size. See if you can explain both to someone else.

Problems

PRESIDENT SQUEAKS BY

11-1   Jock the Pollster (Special to the *New York Blot*)

"In the latest random sampling of American adults, 49 percent favored the impeachment of the President (based on a random sample of 900 adults, 18 years or older, living in the continental United States).

"These results indicate that if a referendum were held today, the President could be confident that less than a majority of Americans would vote for his impeachment. Although the margin is slim, the President could be confident of squeaking by."

a. Can the President be 99-percent sure that less than half of all Americans 18 years old and older favor his impeachment? Construct a 99-percent confidence interval and find out.

b. What is the probability that a majority favors impeachment?

11-2 "We drew a representative sample of voters and asked them the following question: 'In the upcoming bussing referendum, do you plan to vote in favor of bussing for racial-integration purposes or opposed?' Our sample consisted of 900 voters; our response rate was 83 percent. The sample proportion in favor was .55."

a. Predict the proportion voting in favor, with a 98-percent confidence level.

b. What is the probability that the referendum will pass?

11-3 "We drew a representative sample of night-shift and day-shift workers, 400 people in each group. Forty-four percent of the night-shift workers reported feeling alienated from their jobs while 35 percent of the day-shift workers reported feeling alienated. Clearly the night shift leads to greater feelings of alienation than the day shift."

    a. Do the data support this conclusion? Use any statistical technique you think is appropriate.

    b. How do you feel about the validity of the causal assertion in the final sentence?

11-4 "We used our sample data to estimate the difference between men's and women's incomes in the academic profession. Our 95-percent confidence interval is $1,000 to $2,000."

    a. Which of the following best summarizes these results?

        (1) "Ninety-five percent of the time, the actual difference between men's and women's means will be between $1,000 and $2,000."

        (2) "We're 95-percent sure our estimate includes the actual difference between the two populations."

    b. If we quadrupled the sample size, how would this affect the precision of our estimate?

    c. If we wanted a 99-percent level of confidence, would this increase or decrease our level of precision?

    d. If we wanted to increase our precision without changing the sample size, how would this affect our confidence level (accuracy)?

Suggested Readings

1 Blalock, Hubert M., Jr.: *Social Statistics*, 2d ed., chap. 12 and secs. 13.3, 18.1, 19.7. New York: McGraw-Hill Book Company, 1972.

2 Davis, James A.: *Elementary Survey Analysis*. Englewood Cliffs, N.J.: Prentice-Hall, 1971. For a discussion of confidence intervals for Yule's Q, see pp. 51–58.

3 Hays, William L.: *Statistics for the Social Sciences*, 2d ed., secs. 9.25–9.29. New York: Holt, Rinehart and Winston, 1973.

4 Loether, Herman J., and Donald G. McTavish: *Inferential Statistics for Sociologists*, chap. 5. Boston: Allyn and Bacon, 1974.

5 Mueller, John H., Karl F. Schuessler, and Herbert L. Costner: *Statistical Reasoning in Sociology*, 2d ed., chap. 13. Boston: Houghton Mifflin Company, 1970.

6 For an example of the use of confidence intervals, see Hansen, Morris H.: "How to Count Better: Using Statistics to Improve the Census," in Judith M. Tanur et al. (eds.), *Statistics: A Guide to the Unknown*, pp. 276–284. San Francisco: Holden-Day, 1972.

12

hypothesis testing

A *hypothesis* is an assertion about how things are or how things work. Hypothesis testing is decision making. We test hypotheses by assuming their *opposite* to be true and comparing our assumption with data. Support for the hypothesis comes from rejecting its opposite. As usual, one of our main goals is to attach a probability of error to our decision. This may all sound backwards (testing opposites), and it is. But it works, and in this chapter I hope to show you how.

Perhaps the most important thing to understand in this chapter is the meaning of hypothesis-test results. They are often misinterpreted, and because of their wide use, it's to your advantage to understand what they mean.

Hypothesis Testing Is Everywhere

Although you may not be aware of it, we all use a form of hypothesis testing in our everyday lives. Consider this situation. George has always acted like a friend to you. Today you have an appointment to meet him for lunch and he doesn't show up. Is this a reflection of George's feelings toward you? Can you still assume he's your friend? To make such a decision, you'd probably first talk to George and find out what happened. George says he forgot, pure and simple. Now what?

We want to test the hypothesis that George is not your friend. Why is this the hypothesis? Why isn't it "George *is* your friend"? The answer to this will make more sense as we go along, but in brief, it's this: if we make a specific hypothesis about the way things are, and reject that hypothesis, we can use sampling distributions to calculate the probability that we've made an error. If we cannot reject the hypothesis, we cannot calculate that probability. We suspect (on the basis of the behavior) that George is not your friend. In order to support this idea *with a known probability* of error, we must assume the opposite to be true and see if the data justify rejecting that assumption. In general, we test hypotheses by rejection of their opposites, since probabilities of error can be calculated *only* for *rejected* hypotheses. We therefore assume that George is your friend. If we can reject that hypothesis (called the *null hypothesis*), then the *substantive hypothesis* (George is not your friend) is supported (but never proved).

George and his behavior, like most people in the world, are complicated. His friendship is the sum of many attitudes and behaviors in many situations. We have only a sample of his behavior (he stood you up for lunch), and on the basis of that we want to make a decision about his friendship.

So, we assume for the moment that George *is* your friend. Most likely you would end up asking yourself, "Would a friend forget a lunch date?" The answer to that is: "It's possible," but it doesn't help us very much. We can phrase the question in a more precise way that allows us to make a decision: "How likely is it that a true friend would forget a lunch date?" When you see the word *likely*, the word *probability* should go off like a bell in your head. What's the probability that a true friend would stand you up?

Chances are you would conclude that although forgetting lunch isn't usual for friends, it isn't all that unusual, either. Lots of things can make the best of friends forget a social date. You probably wouldn't reject the assumption that George is your friend *because his behavior isn't very inconsistent with that assumption*. In this case you wouldn't reject the null hypothesis, and the substantive hypothesis (he isn't your friend) wouldn't be supported.

Now consider a more extreme example. George meets you for lunch, you eat, and he rather abruptly sticks you with the check. With a wave of his hand he walks off, saying, "It's all yours, pal." Not very friendly. The substantive hypothesis once again is "George isn't your friend." The null hypothesis is "George is your friend." How likely is his behavior given the assumption that he's your friend?

You might well conclude that the probability of a friend acting this way is very low, that his behavior is very inconsistent with the assumption of friendship. Somewhere in your head is a cutoff point: if his behavior is *too* inconsistent with the assumption that he's your friend, you might reject that assumption and conclude he's not.

Notice what we've done here. We had a suspicion. We assumed the opposite. We then measured the consistency between the assumption and the behavior by asking how likely the behavior was, *given* the assumption of friendship. The more *unlikely* the behavior (the lower the probability), the more likely we were to reject the assumption of friendship.

The decision you make depends on the cutoff point you use. No matter what you decide, there's always the chance you'll make a mistake. While a friend is unlikely to stick you with the check, it is possible. If you conclude he's not your friend, you might be rejecting a true friend (rejecting a true hypothesis is called a type 1 error). On the other hand, if you fail to reject the null hypothesis, you might be making the mistake of thinking George your friend when he isn't (failing to reject a false hypothesis is called a type 2 error). Unfortunately, in most cases there is no way of calculating the probability that this latter decision is a mistake.[1]

Imagine that you could actually calculate the probability that a friend would act this way; say the probability is .01, or, "one time out of a hundred a friend would stick you with the check." If you reject the null hypothesis and conclude he's not your friend, there's a 1-percent chance you've misjudged him and made a mistake. This is the key point in hypothesis testing: if we can calculate the probability that something would happen *given* the null hypothesis assumption, then we also know the probability that we've made a mistake when we reject it. In everyday life we can't calculate such probabilities, but with data (means, proportions, differences, etc.) we can.

Let's try a second example. You're shooting craps with Mary and she rolls two 7s in a row. Would you suspect loaded dice? You probably wouldn't, because although two 7s in a row is lucky, it's not all *that* lucky. Suppose she rolls five more 7s in a row, what then? Chances are you'd be getting quite suspicious, because the chances are *very* low that she'd roll seven 7s in a row with a fair pair of dice.

We've assumed that the dice are fair, and evaluated that assumption in light of our data (her seven rolls). If the data are very unlikely *given the assumption about the dice*, then we reject the null hypothesis that the dice are fair and conclude they aren't. Since we know that the probability of getting seven 7s with a fair pair of dice is very small, we reject the null hypothesis with a known probability that we've made a mistake. The only alternative is to assume that the dice are fair and a very "lucky" thing has happened.

---

[1] For some exceptions, see the discussion of the "power of the test" in, for example, Herman J. Loether and Donald G. McTavish, *Inferential Statistics for Sociologists* (Boston: Allyn and Bacon, 1974), pp. 148–151.

Suppose we assumed the dice were not fair. What's the probability of throwing seven 7s in a row with unfair dice? Since we don't know just how unfair the dice are, there's no way of calculating such a probability. The only kinds of hypotheses we can test are those that assume something specific about the world. When we assume the dice are fair, we assume that all six numbers are equally likely to come up (the probability is exactly 1/6 for each number). Having assumed this, we can calculate the probability of our outcome under that assumption. The assumption that the dice are not fair, however, doesn't tell us the exact chances of any one number coming up and thus doesn't allow us to calculate exact probabilities and thereby test a null hypothesis.

An Example of
Single-Sample Hypothesis Tests

You're a member of a city council, and a very important referendum is coming up for a public vote. You favor a *yes* vote. Next month the council will decide on the date for the referendum. You want to know how the public feels, because if you can't count on a majority of support, you'll try to delay the referendum until you can sway more votes to your side. You commission Jock the Pollster to find out if the public is on your side.

Your hope is that the proportion of people who'll vote yes is greater than .50 (or 50 percent). This is your substantive hypothesis. To test it, you assume the opposite, that the best you'll get is a tie (exactly .50). This is the null hypothesis. You might be wondering why the null hypothesis isn't that the population proportion is equal to or less than .50. As you'll see below, in order to test the null hypothesis, we have to assume a single value for the mean of the sampling distribution (which in this case is P). This means that the value in the null hypothesis has to be a single number rather than a range of numbers.

Jock goes out with his wizard team of interviewers and gathers opinions on a representative sample of 400 voters. The sample proportion indicating an intention to vote yes is .54.

As before we've drawn only one of many possible samples. The question is this: "If we assume that the proportion voting yes is actually .50 (i.e., that the null hypothesis is true), what's the probability of drawing a sample with a proportion on .54?" Or, phrased differently, "How inconsistent is our observation (the sample proportion) with our assumption about the population ($P = .50$)?" If the observation is *too* inconsistent with the assumption (i.e., the probability is very low), then, as before, we'd reject the null hypothesis and support the substantive hypothesis (P is greater than .50) with a *known probability* of error.

In making the decision about George, we relied on an imprecise cutoff point, a degree of inconsistency between behavior and the null hypothesis that would lead us to reject the null hypothesis. How inconsistent is "very inconsistent"? How low is a "very low" probability? It's a matter of judgment (as in the case of confidence intervals), and it comes down to deciding how large a probability of error is tolerable. In most of the literature, 5 percent is considered the largest acceptable chance of error. Let's suppose you're pretty anxious and don't want more than a 1-percent chance of error. Having set this probability *in advance*, we can proceed with the test.

We need to calculate the precise probability of drawing a sample proportion of .54 *given* the assumption that the population proportion is exactly .50. If the probability is .01 or less, then we'll conclude that the observation is so inconsistent with the assumption that we'll reject the assumption (the null hypothesis) in favor of the substantive hypothesis.

To calculate this probability, we need to go back to basics. There's a sampling distribution of all possible sample proportions. To use it to calculate probabilities, we have to do three things: (1) be able to assume it's "normally" shaped, (2) know something about the mean of the sampling distribution (the average sample proportion), and (3) calculate the standard error of the sampling distribution.

First, our sample has 400 cases, and we'll assume a normal sampling distribution. Second, with confidence intervals we never had an actual number for the mean of the sampling distribution (we just knew that it equaled the population value). In this case, however, *we've assumed that the population proportion (and hence the mean of the sampling distribution) has a value of exactly .50*. As you'll see, this makes things easier.

The third task (the standard error) is straightforward. The standard error of sample proportions is

$$\sigma_{P_s} = \sqrt{\frac{PQ}{N}}$$

If we set P at .50 (which makes sense since we've assumed P actually equals .50) and Q at $1 - P$, or .50, the standard error is

$$\sigma_{P_s} = \sqrt{\frac{(.5)(.5)}{400}} = \frac{.5}{20} = .025$$

It might help us see what we've got to work with if we draw a picture of the sampling distribution (see Fig. 12-1). We've assumed the sampling distribution to be normal; we've assumed P to be .50. Our sample result was .54. What, then, is the probability of drawing a sample proportion of .54 from a population with a population proportion of .50?

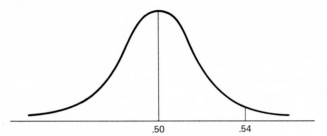

Figure 12-1 Hypothetical sampling distribution for sample proportions.

We can't use the normal table to calculate the probability of any one score (such as .54) because the table uses areas. We can, however, calculate the probability of getting a score of .54 or more: i.e., what's the probability of drawing a sample result at least as inconsistent with the assumption that $P = .50$ as our sample result? We first calculate the distance in proportions and then convert this distance to standard errors:

$$Z = \frac{.54 - .50}{.025} = 1.60$$

We're looking for the probability of getting a sample proportion that is *at least* .04 (or 1.60 standard errors) above the population proportion. We go to the normal table and look for 1.6 in the left-hand column and move to the right under the column marked 00. The area contained between the population proportion and 1.60 standard errors above is .4452. Since we want the probability of being *at least* 1.60 standard errors *above* the mean, we must subtract .4452 from .5000, getting .0548.

What does it all mean? We assumed that P was exactly .50. How inconsistent is our sample result (.54) with our assumption about P? The answer is that there's only a 5-percent chance of drawing a sample like ours from a population with a proportion of .50. Now we have to make a decision about our assumption, the null hypothesis. If our sample result is too inconsistent with the null hypothesis, we conclude that the null hypothesis is wrong. How inconsistent is "too inconsistent"? We decided that a probability of .01 or less meant the result was too inconsistent to allow us to support the null hypothesis. The probability we calculated, however, was .05, greater than .01. Therefore, we haven't satisfied our cutoff point and we can't reject the null hypothesis. It's directly comparable to our deciding that George's standing you up was unusual behavior for a friend, but not unusual enough to justify rejecting the assumption of friendship *without an intolerable probability* of error.

What does Jock tell you about the pending referendum? "If we reject the assumption that the best you'll get is a tie (and assume you'll win), there's a 5-percent chance we'll be wrong. If 5 percent is too large a chance of error for you, then you can't be confident of winning. You'd better put off the referendum and drum up more support."

Suppose you were willing to tolerate a 6-percent chance of error instead of 1 percent. Then the sample result would satisfy your cutoff point and you would reject the null hypothesis in favor of the substantive hypothesis. You'd say, "I'm 94.52-percent sure that I'm going to win." In this case we say the null hypothesis is rejected at the *.06 significance level*, which means that the probability of getting our sample result, given our assumption about P, was less then .06, which is also the probability of error associated with rejecting the null hypothesis.

Notice that we said earlier that the significance level must be established before calculating the actual probability. Why? The problem is that being human we may tend to allow our desire to reject a null hypothesis to influence our judgment about how much error to tolerate after the fact. To avoid a conflict of interest, we could decide beforehand what the significance level will be and then proceed. It's somewhat arbitrary, to be sure, but some researchers feel it's a necessary precaution against unnecessary subjectivity. As we'll see later on, this approach is in some ways problematic.

Notice also that had we made the null hypothesis, "You're going to win," we would not have been able to assume a specific value for the mean of the sampling distribution. Without this there would be no way to calculate the probability of getting our sample result. *The null hypothesis must assume a single value for the mean of the sampling distribution.*

You're going to encounter the word *significant* over and over again. For most people the word means "important" or "interesting," but in statistics it has a precise meaning that has nothing to do with importance. *Significant* in this case merely means that we're confident that P is greater than .50; it could be .5000000001 for all we know. To say P is "significantly greater than .50" does not mean it is very much above .50; it only means we're quite sure it's not *exactly* .50 or less. In the case of an election or referendum, this is important. But in most research cases, knowing that P is above .50 means little unless we also have an estimate of how much above .50 it is. Obviously, confidence intervals are more useful than significance tests in cases like this. Unfortunately, confidence intervals are rarely used.

Notice that rejecting the null hypothesis depends entirely on the probability of error we select as the cutoff point (the significance level, .01 in our example). If we set the significance level at .01, we can't reject the assumption that $P = .50$; if we set the level at .06, we can reject the null hypothesis. It's all a matter of judgment, and where you set that level makes the difference between rejecting and not rejecting. Here lies one of the major drawbacks of hypothesis tests; the selection of a significance level is somewhat arbitrary (although conventional levels of .05, .01, and .001 are normally used), but the decisions are black and white: you either reject the null hypothesis or you don't. The advantage we have over your deliberations about George is that we have a representative sample and we can calculate exact probabilities. The decision itself, however, depends ultimately on human judgment.

There is one possible result that we should mention before moving on. What if our sample result had been $p = .45$ instead of $p = .54$? What then? Well, since our substantive hypothesis is that P is greater than .50, our sample result of .45 is in direct contradiction. There's no way a sample result of .45 can support the hypothesis that P is greater than .50. So, there's no need to calculate probabilities and bother with rejecting or failing to reject a null hypothesis. If p had been .45, Jock would have told you to get busy politically.

The kind of statistical test we've just done is called a *one-tailed test* because we used only one tail of the sampling distribution to calculate probabilities. If our substantive hypothesis had been "P is greater than or less than but not equal to .50," then the null hypothesis would still have been "$P = .50$," but we would have used both tails to calculate probabilities (since our sample result could have been above or below .50 and could still support the substantive hypothesis). Since substantive hypotheses almost always predict the direction of the outcome, two-tailed tests are rarely appropriate and you don't really need to worry about them.

An Example of Two-Sample Tests

The most common use of hypothesis tests is to decide whether two groups are different on some variable. For example, suppose we're interested in the opinions of blacks and whites on the question: "In general, do you think your children will be better off than you are?" The substantive hypothesis might be that whites will be more hopeful than blacks (the white proportion will be larger than the black); the null hypothesis is that there's no difference (i.e., the white proportion minus the black proportion equals zero). Suppose we draw representative samples of blacks and whites and get the results shown in Table 12-1. As with confidence intervals, we're now dealing with the sampling distribution of *differences* between two sample proportions. As with single-sample hypothesis tests, we have to (1) be able to assume the sampling distribution is normal, (2) assume a value for the mean of the sampling distribution (the average difference between black and white samples),

Table 12-1 Proportion
Who Feel Their Children
Will Be Better Off than
They Were, by Race
(Hypothetical)

Race	Proportion	N
Whites	.65	900
Blacks	.55	100
Total	.64	1,000

and (3) calculate the standard error for the sampling distribution of differences between sample proportions.

We have a sample of 1,000 respondents, certainly large enough to make the normal-shape assumption.

We've assumed in the null hypothesis that the difference between the populations is zero. Since the mean of the sampling distribution equals the difference between the two populations, we're assuming that the mean of the sampling distribution is zero.

The final step is the standard-error calculation. The formula for the standard error of the sampling distribution of differences between sample proportions is

$$\sigma_{P_{s_1} - P_{s_2}} = \sqrt{\frac{P_1 Q_1}{N_1} + \frac{P_2 Q_2}{N_2}} = \sqrt{\frac{(.5)(.5)}{900} + \frac{(.5)(.5)}{100}} = \sqrt{\frac{250}{90,000}} = .05$$

We could have estimated P in this formula with a weighted average of the two sample proportions (i.e., with .64), but we really don't need to do this here because the answers won't be that different and using .50 is more conservative.

Again, a picture may help summarize what we have (see Fig. 12-2).

Figure 12-2 Sampling distribution for differences between
sample proportions.

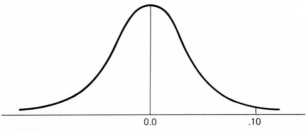

0.0   .10

Shown on the sampling distribution are the assumed population difference (0) and the difference observed between our two samples (.65 − .55 = .10). Before going into the normal table we have to decide on our cutoff point: how rare must our observations be (given the assumption about the populations) in order for us to conclude that our assumption is false? Let's assume that a 5-percent chance of error is acceptable.

The question now is: "If we assume that we're drawing samples from two *populations* that are identical on this variable, what's the probability of drawing two *samples* that differ by .10 or more?" To find this, we have to convert the proportional difference into standard errors:

$$\frac{.10 - 0}{.05} = 2.0 = Z$$

Our observed difference of .10 is two standard errors above the assumed difference of zero. How likely are we to observe a difference this large or larger, given an assumption of no difference? We look in the normal table under 2.00 and find an area of .4773. Subtracting from .5000, we get .0227. Our observed difference is very inconsistent with the assumed difference of zero. In fact, if the difference between the populations were actually zero, we would expect to draw samples that differed as much as ours only 2 percent of the time. If we reject the null hypothesis and conclude that whites are in fact more optimistic than blacks, the probability of error is only 2 percent, somewhat below our cutoff point. We're 97.73-percent sure (or, 1 − .0227) that whites are more hopeful than blacks.

Note that we can accomplish just as much and more by constructing a confidence interval. If we constructed a confidence interval in which the probability of error in *each direction* was 5 percent, we'd have

$$.10 \pm (1.645 \times .05) = .10 \pm .08 = .02 \text{ to } .18$$

We would be 90-percent sure that the actual difference was between .02 and .18, and 95-percent sure that the difference was above .02. Using confidence intervals, we get not only a test of all possible null hypotheses, but an estimate of the actual difference to boot.

About "Significant Differences"

You'll often read statements like "The two groups were significantly different at the .05 level." (Remember the old "Those who used brand X toothpaste had significantly fewer cavities"?) If you don't understand the statistical meaning of the word *significant*, you're likely to read "important" or "large" for the word *significant*, a common and gross error. "The two groups were significantly different (at the .05 level)" means *only* that there's a 5-percent chance we'd make a mistake in concluding that the two groups were not *exactly equal*. Two groups can be "significantly different" even when the actual difference, although real, is very, very small. For example, suppose we had taken samples of 9,000 whites and 1,000 blacks instead of 900 and 100, respectively. The standard error would be reduced from .050 to .017, and a difference of as little as .03 would be statistically significant. While 3 percent is a difference, it certainly isn't a very notable one.

The significance level only expresses our degree of *confidence* in our conclusion. Especially when we're dealing with large samples, being confident that there's a difference does *not* mean the difference is very large. It only tells us that we're confident the two groups aren't exactly identical.

As a rule, when you see the word *significant* being used, search for the actual size of the group difference to find out if it's large enough to get excited about. You can't tell from "statistical significance" alone.

Significant Relationships in Cross Tabulations: Chi-Square

We don't always confine ourselves to differences between two groups. As we described in Chap. 6, we often approach questions by relating variables in cross tabulations. We gather data from a sample, and note the relationship between two variables. Our ultimate interest, however, is in the relationship in the population we drew the sample from. Does a relationship observed in a sample indicate a relationship in the population, or is it a product of random sampling fluctuations? As we've seen, differences between groups can occur in samples even when there are no differences between the parent populations. The same is true for relationships between variables.

Suppose we interview people in central city, suburban, and rural areas and ask them the following question: "In general, are you optimistic about the future of the United States?" Suppose we find the results shown in Table 12-2. If we percentage the table across the rows, we get the results shown in Table 12-3. There is certainly a relationship in the sample between type of residence and optimism, although not a strong one. Gamma is −.27 in this table, indicating that the less urban the environment is, the more prevalent optimism is. (Remember that measures of association range from −1.0 to +1.0; the sign indicates the direction of the relationship and the number indicates the strength.)

We've observed a relationship in our sample; but can we use this result to infer a relationship in the population? We approach this question as we have others: If we assume that the correlation in the popula-

Table 12-2 Optimism by Place of Residence (Hypothetical)

Degree urban	OPTIMISTIC		
	Yes	No	Total
Central city	7	13	20
Suburban	9	11	20
Rural	11	9	20
Total	27	33	$60 = N$

tion is zero, what's the probability of observing a relationship this strong or stronger in a sample? The null hypothesis is "There is no relationship"; the variables are independent of each other in the population. The substantive hypothesis is that there is a relationship in the population (i.e., the variables are not independent).

If we find that the probability of finding a relationship as strong or stronger than ours is small enough, given an assumption of no relationship, then we can reject the null hypothesis and support the substantive hypothesis with a small, known chance of error.

In previous kinds of problems, we proceeded by comparing our sample results with our assumption about the population (e.g., comparing an observed difference between two means to an assumed difference of zero). We do the same thing here. In the null hypothesis, we assumed the variables were independent of each other in the population. If we kept the marginals in Table 12-2 the same, what would the table look like if the variables were independent? Remember that independence exists if all the percentage distributions are the same. To do this (and not change the marginals), the percentage distributions across the rows would all have to be identical to the "total" row in Table 12-3. (See Table 12-4.) In this table, there is no relationship between place of residence and optimism, but the marginal totals are identical to those in

Table 12-3 Optimism by Place of Residence

Degree urban	OPTIMISTIC		
	Yes	No	Total (N)
Central city	35%	65	100% (20)
Suburban	45%	55	100% (20)
Rural	55%	45	100% (20)
Total	45%	55	100% (60)

Table 12-4 Optimism by Place of
Residence, Assuming Independence

Degree urban	OPTIMISM		
	Yes	No	Total (N)
Central city	45%	55	100% (20)
Suburban	45%	55	100% (20)
Rural	45%	55	100% (20)
Total	45%	55	100% (60)

our sample results (Table 12-2). In frequencies, our "independence" table looks like Table 12-5. The frequencies in our original table (12-3) are called *observed frequencies;* those in the "independence" table (12-5) are called *expected frequencies.*

We now have two tables (12-2 and 12-5) with identical marginals, the first from our sample, and the second representing a condition of independence. In previous problems we measured the difference between our sample result and our assumption, and used that measure (the number of standard errors, for example) in a sampling distribution to calculate probabilities. In the case of cross tabulations, we measure the difference between our sample results and independence by comparing frequencies in each pair of corresponding cells across tables (i.e., a seven in Table 12-2 versus a nine in Table 12-5; a thirteen in Table 12-2 versus an eleven in Table 12-5, etc.). We take the difference between each pair of scores (7 − 9, 13 − 11, etc.) and square it $[(-2)^2, (+2)^2,$ etc.] since they would add to zero otherwise (as in the case of variances). Finally, since we're interested in our results *relative* to what we'd expect in an independence situation, we divide each squared difference by the frequency we'd expect to get if the variables were independent $[(-2)^2/9;$ $(2)^2/11,$ etc.]. A 3×2 table has six cells, so we'll have six comparisons

Table 12-5 Optimism by Place of
Residence, Assuming Independence

Degree urban	OPTIMISM		
	Yes	No	Total
Central city	9	11	20
Suburban	9	11	20
Rural	9	11	20
Total	27	33	60 = N

(refer to Tables 12-2 and 12-5 and be sure you see where these numbers come from):

$$\frac{(7-9)^2}{9} + \frac{(13-11)^2}{11} + \frac{(9-9)^2}{9} + \frac{(11-11)^2}{11} + \frac{(11-9)^2}{9} + \frac{(9-11)^2}{11}$$

$$= \frac{4}{9} + \frac{4}{11} + 0 + 0 + \frac{4}{9} + \frac{4}{11} = 1.6162$$

The sum (1.6162) is called *chi-square*, and is usually represented by the symbol χ^2.

Let's review what we've done before going on to what it means. We had two tables, one based on sample data, one based on the null-hypothesis assumption that the variables were independent. To see how inconsistent our table was with the independence assumption, we compared the two tables cell by cell, squaring each difference between expected and observed frequencies to avoid having them all add to zero. We then divided each difference by the frequency expected in an independence situation in order to get the difference *relative* to the independence condition. By adding up these six deviations from independence, we got a summary measure (chi-square) of how much our sample results deviate from independence.

So, we have our measure of how inconsistent our sample result is with the null-hypothesis assumption. Our question now is: "What's the probability of observing a sample relationship this strong, or stronger, given our assumption of no relationship in the population?" Or "What's the probability of getting a value of chi-square this large or larger, given the null hypothesis of no relationship?"

It just so happens that mathematicians have worked out a sampling distribution of chi-square. The distribution tells us the probability of getting values of chi-square when no relationship exists in the population.

The chi-square table has to compensate for the fact that large tables will tend to have large values of chi-square, regardless of the nature of the relationship in the table. Think of it this way: if you have a 2×2 table, you're going to add up four fractions; if you have a 50×50 table, you're going to add up 2,500. Even with equal sample sizes, it's going to be a lot easier to get a large chi-square with 2,500 fractions than with four. We compensate by requiring that chi-square be much larger in a 50×50 table than in a 2×2 table to achieve a given level of statistical significance. This means we have a separate distribution of chi-square for each table size.

Table size is measured by a quantity called *degrees of freedom*. This is found by multiplying the number of rows in the table minus one, times the number of columns minus one. In our case, there are $(3-1) \times (2-1) = 2$ degrees of freedom.

To use the chi-square table (Table 12-6), we go down the left-hand column to the proper degrees of freedom (two in our case). The numbers in the body of the table are values of chi-square. The probabilities are found in the top row (.99, .98, etc.). As an example, note the first number in the second row (.0201), which appears under the .99. This tells us that with two degrees of freedom, there is a 99-percent chance of getting a chi-square of .0201 or *larger, given that there is no relationship in the population*. Our chi-square was 1.6162. Going across the table, we find chi-squares of 1.386 and 2.408. Given independence, there's a 50-percent chance of getting a chi-square of 1.306 or larger and a 30-percent chance of getting one of 2.408 or larger (note that the larger chi-square is, the lower the probabilities are). This is an abbreviated table, so we have to interpolate. The probability of getting a chi-square of 1.6162 or larger, with two degrees of freedom, is between .50 and .30, roughly .45.

Table 12-6 Distribution of χ^2 Probability

df*	.99	.98	.95	.90	.80	.70	.50	.30	.20	.10	.05	.02	.01	.001
1	.0³157	.0²628	.00393	.0158	.0612	.148	.455	1.074	1.642	2.706	3.841	5.412	6.635	10.827
2	.0201	.0404	.103	.211	.446	.713	1.386	2.408	3.219	4.605	5.991	7.824	9.210	13.815
3	.115	.185	.352	.584	1.005	1.424	2.366	3.665	4.642	6.251	7.815	0.837	11.341	16.268
4	.297	.429	.711	1.064	1.649	2.195	3.357	4.878	5.089	7.779	9.488	11.668	13.277	18.465
5	.554	.752	1.145	1.610	2.343	3.000	4.351	6.064	7.289	9.236	11.070	13.388	15.086	20.517
6	.872	1.134	1.635	2.204	3.070	3.828	5.348	7.231	8.558	10.645	12.592	15.033	16.812	22.457
7	1.239	1.564	2.167	2.833	3.822	4.671	6.346	8.383	9.803	12.017	14.067	16.622	18.475	24.322
8	1.646	2.032	2.733	3.490	4.594	5.527	7.344	9.524	11.030	13.352	15.507	18.168	20.090	26.125
9	2.088	2.532	3.325	4.168	5.380	6.393	8.343	10.656	12.242	14.684	16.919	19.679	21.666	27.877
10	2.558	3.059	3.940	4.865	6.179	7.267	9.342	11.781	13.442	15.987	18.307	21.161	23.209	29.588
11	3.053	3.609	4.575	5.578	6.989	8.148	10.341	12.899	14.631	17.275	19.675	22.618	24.725	31.264
12	3.571	4.178	5.226	6.304	7.807	9.034	11.340	14.011	15.812	18.549	21.026	24.054	26.217	32.909
13	4.107	4.765	5.892	7.042	8.634	9.926	12.340	15.119	16.985	19.812	22.362	25.472	27.688	34.528
14	4.060	5.368	6.571	7.790	9.467	10.821	13.339	16.222	18.151	21.064	23.685	26.873	29.141	36.123
15	5.229	5.985	7.261	8.547	10.307	11.721	14.339	17.322	19.311	22.307	24.996	28.259	30.578	37.697
16	5.812	6.614	7.962	9.312	11.152	12.624	15.338	18.418	20.465	23.542	26.296	29.633	32.000	39.252
17	6.408	7.255	8.672	10.085	12.002	13.531	16.338	19.511	21.615	24.769	27.587	30.995	33.409	40.790
18	7.015	7.906	9.390	10.865	12.857	14.440	17.338	20.601	22.760	25.989	28.860	32.346	34.805	42.312
19	7.633	8.567	10.117	11.651	13.716	15.352	18.338	21.689	23.900	27.204	30.144	33.687	36.191	43.820
20	8.260	9.237	10.851	12.443	14.578	16.266	19.337	22.775	25.038	28.412	31.410	35.020	37.566	45.315
21	8.897	9.915	11.591	13.240	15.445	17.182	20.337	23.858	26.171	29.615	32.671	36.343	38.932	46.797
22	9.542	10.600	12.338	14.041	16.314	18.101	21.337	24.939	27.301	30.813	33.924	37.650	40.289	48.268
23	10.196	11.293	13.091	14.848	17.187	19.021	22.337	26.018	28.429	32.007	35.172	38.968	41.638	40.728
24	10.856	11.992	13.818	15.659	18.062	19.943	23.337	27.006	29.553	33.196	36.415	40.270	42.980	51.179
25	11.524	12.697	14.611	16.473	18.940	20.867	24.337	28.172	30.675	34.382	37.652	41.566	44.314	52.620
26	12.198	13.409	15.379	17.292	19.820	21.792	25.336	29.246	31.795	35.563	38.885	42.856	45.642	54.052
27	12.879	14.125	16.151	18.114	20.703	22.719	26.336	30.319	32.912	36.741	40.113	44.140	46.963	55.476
28	13.565	14.847	16.928	18.939	21.588	23.647	27.336	31.391	34.027	37.916	41.337	45.419	48.278	56.893
29	14.256	15.574	17.708	19.768	22.475	24.577	28.336	32.461	35.139	39.087	42.557	46.693	49.588	58.302
30	14.953	16.306	18.493	20.599	23.364	25.508	29.336	33.530	36.250	40.256	43.773	47.962	50.892	59.703

* For larger values of df, the expression $\sqrt{2\chi^2} - \sqrt{2\,df - 1}$ may be used as a normal deviate with unit variance, remembering that the probability of χ^2 corresponds with that of a single tail of the normal curve.

SOURCE Table I is taken from table IV of R. A. Fisher and F. Yates, *Statistical Tables for Biological, Agricultural and Medical Research*, published by Longman Group Ltd., London (previously published by Oliver & Boyd, Edinburgh), by permission of the authors and publishers.

There's a 45-percent chance of getting a result like ours even when there's no relationship in the population. In other words, tables like ours are quite likely to be drawn from populations with no relationship between the two variables. Therefore, we cannot reject the null hypothesis of no relationship without a large risk of error (45 percent).

Suppose .01 is the maximum probability of error we would tolerate. In this case we go to the chi-square table, two degrees of freedom, and follow the row until we're under the .01 column. The corresponding value of chi-square is 9.210. This tells us that in order for the probability of type 1 error to be .01 or less, we must get a value of chi-square of 9.210 or more. For the relationship to be significant at the .05 level, chi-square must be 5.991 or larger.

Notice that for any given level of significance, the required value of chi-square varies directly with table size. With two degrees of freedom (a 2 × 3 table) we need a chi-square of 13.815 for significance at the .001 level; with six degrees of freedom (a 4 × 3 table), we need a chi-square of at least 22.457 for the same level of significance.

We haven't talked about the effects of sample size on chi-square, only that of the number of cells in the table. Sample size has a direct effect on the size of chi-square: if you double the sample size, you double chi-square (go through our example and double all the expected and observed frequencies and you'll see very readily that chi-square is doubled also).[1] This is an important fact, because given a large enough sample, *any* relationship, no matter how weak, will show up as "significant." If we had 600 cases in our earlier example instead of 60, chi-square would have been 10 times as large, or $1.6162 \times 10 = 16.162$. With two degrees of freedom, our result would be significant at the .001 level (since it's greater than 13.815).

This can get us into trouble only if we misinterpret the meaning of the word *significant*, a problem we've already described in some detail. In general, cross tabulations will appear in the literature as shown in Table 12-7. The value of chi-square only leads us to a certain level of confidence that a relationship does exist in the population. Since there's a 1-percent chance that we'd make an error if we rejected the null hypothesis and concluded that there was a relationship in the population, there's a 99-percent chance that there is a relationship. This does *not* indicate how strong the relationship is. When you see a value of chi-square for a cross tabulation, always look for a measure of association to see how strong the relationship is. The significance level is only half the story.

---

[1] This is also why you must use *frequencies*, not proportions or percentages, in calculating chi-square.

Table 12-7 Optimism by Place of
Residence, with Larger Sample

Degree urban	OPTIMISM		
	Yes	No	Total
Central city	70	130	200
Suburban	90	110	200
Rural	110	90	200
Total	270	330	600 = N
$\chi^2 = 16.162$		$p < .01$	

Chi-Square and Goodness-of-Fit Tests

From 1959 to 1961, the U.S. Department of Health, Education, and Welfare conducted the Health Examination Survey (HES) of American adults. The survey gathered detailed clinical evaluations of the respondents' health as well as an abundance of psychological and sociological information. Before using such a body of data, the researcher wants to see if the sample is representative of the population of American adults.

The best way to do this is to compare the sample distribution of key variables with distributions generated by the decennial census. For example, we could compare the sample's age distribution with the known population distribution (since a census was taken in 1960, midway through the survey). Table 12-8 shows the frequency distribution for age in the HES data and the percentage distribution for the American adult population (columns 1 and 2).

We want to compare the entire HES distribution with the known pop-

Table 12-8 Comparison of HES and 1960 Census Age Structures, with the Computation of Chi-Square

Age	(1) HES f	(2) 1960 census (percent)	(3) Expected frequency	(4) $(O - E)^2$	(5) $(O - E)^2/E$
18–24	945	13.8%	921	576	.625
25–34	1,421	19.9	1,328	8,649	6.513
35–44	1,487	20.9	1,394	8,649	6.204
45–54	1,252	17.7	1,181	5,041	4.268
55–64	861	13.4	894	1,089	1.218
65+	706	14.3	954	61,504	64.470
Total	6,672	100.0%	6,672		$83.298 = \chi^2$

ulation distribution to see if there's any bias in the sample. There are 6,672 respondents in the HES data. If we converted the *population* distribution into frequencies based on the 6,672 HES respondents, we'd have the number of people that we'd *expect* to find in each age category *assuming the HES data accurately represent the parent population*. The expected frequencies are shown in column 3.

This should be looking familiar to you at this point. We have a set of observed frequencies and a set of expected frequencies that depend on a null hypothesis: the HES data and the census data come from the same population, or the observed *differences* between the HES and census data are no more than we'd expect to find by *chance* and there's no bias in the HES sample.

We can use chi-square to test the null hypothesis of "no difference." We calculate it as we did with cross tabulations. In column 4 of Table 12-8 we take the difference between the expected and observed frequencies for each age group and square those differences. In column 5 we divide each squared difference by the expected frequency. The sum of these ratios is chi-square (83.298).

In this case, the number of degrees of freedom is equal to the number of *categories* minus one, or $(6 - 1) = 5$. We look in the chi-square table, down the left-hand column to 5, and across the row until we find a value close to 83.298. In this case, the highest value in the table is 20.517, much smaller than our value. If we'd found a value of, say, 21, in our data, we'd conclude that rejecting the null hypothesis of *no* difference would carry with it a probability of error less than .001. Our actual value (83) is so large that we can reject the null hypothesis at a level approaching zero.

What does this tell us about the representativeness of the HES data? We've rejected the null hypothesis that there's no difference between the survey and the census, with a probability of error that's very close to zero. We're thus sure there's some bias in the HES data. What direction is the bias in? If we compare columns 1 and 3 in Table 12-8, we see there are too many young people (column 1 is larger than column 3 for the age groups 18 to 24, 25 to 34, 35 to 44, and 45 to 54) and there are too few older people (column 1 is smaller than column 3 for the age groups 55 to 64 and 65 and over). Thus, the HES sample is biased in favor of younger respondents.

How serious is the bias? The answer to this is a matter of judgment. There are no statistical rules that classify bias as "serious" or "not so serious." In comparing entire distributions (as we are here), there's a useful measure that tells us how dissimilar two distributions are (somewhat analogous to a measure of association). If we convert column 1 of Table 12-8 into percentages and compare it with column 2, we get the results shown in Table 12-9.

Table 12-9 Comparison of HES and 1960 Census Age Structures with Computation of Index of Dissimilarity

Age	(1) HES	(2) Census	(3) (1) − (2)
18–24	14.2%	13.8%	+0.4%
25–34	21.3	19.9	+1.4
35–44	22.2	20.9	+1.3
45–54	18.8	17.7	+1.1
55–64	12.9	13.4	−0.5
65+	10.6	14.3	−3.7
Total	100.0%	100.0%	0.0%

In column 1 we have the HES percentage distribution for age; in column 2 we have the comparable distribution for the 1960 census. In column 3 we subtracted the census percentage for each age group from the comparable HES percentage. Notice that the sum of these differences is zero, which will always be the case. (Remember the similar problem we ran into with the computation of variances and standard deviations?) Also, notice, however, that the absolute sum of the minus differences equals the absolute sum of the plus differences (4.2 percent in each case). If we add up either the negative or the positive differences, and take the absolute value (i.e., ignore the minus sign if we add up the minus differences), the resulting number is called the *index of dissimilarity* and has a precise interpretation. If we rearranged 4.2 percent of the HES respondents and put them in different age categories, the two age distributions would be identical. We could accomplish the same result by recategorizing 4.2 percent of the 1960 census respondents, or by recategorizing 2.1 percent of the HES respondents and 2.1 percent of the census respondents, etc. In general, the index of dissimilarity tells us what percentage of cases must be recategorized to make two distributions identical.

Given this interpretation, this index is a quantitative measure of how dissimilar the two distributions are. It hasn't enjoyed extensive use in the social sciences, but some of its applications have been dramatic. For example, if we examine the residential patterns of whites and nonwhites in United States cities, we can compare the way in which nonwhites are distributed across census tracts[1] with the way we'd expect them to be distributed if the only factor governing their proportional representation in any area of the city was their relative numbers in the city as a whole

---

[1] The small subdivisions of a city that the Census Bureau defines for statistical purposes.

(i.e., if there were no tendency for housing to be concentrated along racial lines). In this case, the index of dissimilarity is a measure of residential segregation, and in many United States cities the value of the index exceeds 90 percent. In other words, in order to do away with residential segregation among whites and nonwhites, almost all of one group or the other would have to be redistributed. This has served as an effective and dramatic documentation of the extensiveness and pervasiveness of racial segregation in housing throughout cities in the United States.[1]

Returning to our previous example, we now have a three-part result. First, we're confident that the HES data do not represent the United States adult population as far as the age structure is concerned (the probability that we're wrong is almost zero). Second, the direction of the bias is downward; i.e., the overall structure is too young. Third, bias is not very great, since the redistribution of only 4.2 percent of the cases would make the two distributions identical. This is an exhaustive way of comparing two distributions, and tells us just about everything we'd want to know.

Notice that, as before, the value of chi-square is dependent on the number of cases. If the HES sample had only 1,000 cases instead of 6,672, chi-square would have been reduced proportionally to 12.48. The degrees of freedom would still be five, and the null hypothesis could be rejected at just under the .05 level. The huge HES sample size explains why the difference is significant statistically (p almost zero) even though the actual difference is quite small (index of dissimilarity = 4.2 percent).

Significance Tests and the Strength of Relationships between Variables

In Chaps. 6, 7, and 8, we discussed relationships between and among variables. Earlier in the present chapter we discussed the use of chi-square to test the null hypothesis of independence between two variables in a cross tabulation. In this section we'll briefly describe the methods for testing the significance of the measures of association introduced earlier.

For the most part, the sampling distributions of nominal-scale measures of association are either quite complex or unknown.[2] For this

---

[1] See, for example, Karl Taeuber, "Negro Residential Segregation: Trends and Measurement," *Social Problems*, vol. 12, no. 1, Summer 1964 (also Bobbs-Merrill Reprint S-638); and Karl E. Taeuber, "Residential Segregation," in *Scientific American*, vol. 213, no. 2, August 1965, pp. 12–19. For an application to residence and occupation, see Otis Dudley Duncan and Beverly Duncan, "Residential Distribution and Occupational Stratification," *American Journal of Sociology*, vol. LX, March 1955 (also Bobbs-Merrill Reprint S-380).

[2] See parts II and III of "Measures of Association for Cross-Classifications" by Goodman and Kruskal in the *Journal of the American Statistical Association*, 49 (1954): 723–764.

reason, the usual practice is to test for independence with chi-square and, if the relationship is statistically significant, to report the measure of association (for example, Q, tau, or phi).[1]

When we have data suitable for rank-order measures of association, there are a series of significance tests that can be employed to test the null hypothesis of no relationship between ranks. These are generally known as *nonparametric statistics* because no assumptions about the normality of sampling distributions are required.

The most popular of these tests are the Wald-Wolfowitz runs test, the Mann-Whitney (or Wilcoxon) test, the Kolmogorov-Smirnov test, and the Wilcoxon matched-pairs signed-ranks test.[2] Keep in mind that these are simply hypothesis tests used to establish the significance of relationships between ordinal variables. They are used in situations where rank-order measures of association are typically employed. The results are reported in terms of the probability of type I error, just as before.

Finally, we can test for the significance of correlation coefficients, regression coefficients, both standardized and unstandardized partial-regression coefficients, and partial-correlation coefficients. Correlation coefficients and slopes are rarely estimated with confidence intervals; this, as we've mentioned previously, is unfortunate. The usual procedure is to test the null hypothesis that the correlation or slope is zero. If that hypothesis is rejected (with a known probability of error), then the hypothesis that the slope or correlation is greater or less than zero is supported.

The typical form of such results is: "There is a significant correlation $(r = .15, p < .05)$ between X and Y"; or "The slope is significantly different from zero $(p < .01)$." I can't stress too strongly that you must look beyond the significance level to the actual value of the coefficients involved. "Significant relationship" only tells us that we're confident that r is not exactly zero. With a large sample, a small correlation (such as .08) can be statistically significant.

Also keep in mind, however, that if the sample is small, a substantial, important relationship may *not* be statistically significant. Thus, with large samples we're in danger of overrating trivial relationships by overreacting to the word *significant*; with small samples, we're in danger of dismissing substantial relationships because they don't achieve statistical significance.

---

[1] For confidence intervals for Yule's Q, see James A. Davis, *Elementary Survey Analysis* (Englewood Cliffs, N.J.: Prentice-Hall, 1971), pp. 51–58.

[2] For discussions of the use of nonparametric statistics and the computations involved, see Sidney Siegel, *Nonparametric Statistics* (New York: McGraw-Hill Book Company, 1956); Herman J. Loether and Donald G. McTavish, *Inferential Statistics for Sociologists* (Boston: Allyn and Bacon, 1974), chap. 9.4; and Hubert M. Blalock, Jr., *Social Statistics*, 2d ed. (New York: McGraw-Hill Book Company, 1972), chap. 14.

Conclusion: What Are
Hypothesis Tests Good For?

Hypothesis tests serve several useful functions. First, if we find there are no significant differences between groups, this can be important in two ways. It can indicate that we've reached a dead end and need to push research in other directions. It can also be an important substantive finding; imagine what the impact would be if researchers started finding *no* significant differences between black and white IQ scores.

Second, if we do find significant differences between groups, it at least indicates there's something going on that should be pursued further. Significance tests, however, are only the first step, never the last. For example, when researchers found significant differences in blood-clot deaths of users and nonusers of birth-control pills, they should have been quick to publicize the fact that the actual differences in death rates, although probably real, were extremely small. By stopping with the statement that "there were significant differences . . . ," they stopped short of the most important question: "How *much* of a difference does pill use make?"

The most unfortunate aspect of hypothesis testing is that it phrases research questions in terms of decision making, when the advancement of knowledge is rarely in such black-and-white terms.[1] Research leads us to give greater cognitive support to one idea than to another, not to decisively reject one and accept another. If a researcher says, "I'll reject the null hypothesis of no difference between the groups only if the probability is .05 or less," he's forcing a decision-making framework on the problem. For example, if he observed a sample difference that would occur only 10 percent of the time given no differences between the populations, he would *not* reject the null hypothesis of no difference even though there is a 90-percent chance that there is in fact a difference. As currently used, statistical significance is an either/or situation, which is in sharp contrast to the perspective of confidence intervals, especially open-ended confidence intervals. The difference is most sharply seen in the contrast between two ways of stating the above hypothetical findings: "The difference was not significant at the .05 level" and "We're 90-percent sure there's a difference." Each approach is statistically correct. The choice of one rather than the other depends on the investigator's views of the nature of scientific research and its application to the advancement of knowledge and real-life decision making.

Like all statistical tools, hypothesis tests can help us learn about

---

[1] For a thorough treatment of this point of view, see William W. Rozeboom, "The Fallacy of the Null-Hypothesis Significance Test," in Bernhardt Lieberman, *Contemporary Problems in Statistics* (New York: Oxford University Press, 1971).

things important to us; but we have to use them intelligently, always keeping in mind what they mean. All the technical competence in the world can't make up for poor judgment and hasty or arbitrary decisions.

We've introduced a number of new ideas and terms in this chapter, and before going on, you should convince yourself that you understand them in your own terms. You should know the difference between *substantive* and *null hypotheses*; for any given substantive hypothesis you should be able to formulate the appropriate null hypothesis. You should understand the logic of hypothesis testing and the meaning of the *significance level* of a result (not to be confused with a confidence level; be sure you understand the difference). You should understand what *chi-square* measures mean and what the results mean. Finally, you should be aware of the theoretical and practical shortcomings of using hypothesis tests to approach substantive research problems.

Problems

12-1 "We drew representative samples of 200 executives and 200 white-collar workers in Chicago and used sophisticated measures of alienation from one's job. For a variety of theoretical reasons we expected white-collar workers to report higher levels of alienation as a group than executives. We found that the proportions reporting alienation were .48 for executives and .56 for white-collar workers. This clearly confirms our hypothesis; there is a significant difference between the two groups in the predicted direction." Assume the samples are properly drawn and large enough to warrant the assumption that the sampling distribution of differences is "normally" shaped. Also assume that the measures used are valid.

  a. Are the researchers drawing a conclusion that is justified by the data? Answer this question in two ways: (1) using a one-tailed hypothesis test with a .01 chance of error; (2) using a 98-percent confidence interval. How do the two approaches differ in terms of their usefulness? Do they lead you to the same conclusion? In calculating the standard error, assume that P and Q equal .50.

12-2 "We found a significant difference between the two groups $(p < .01)$. Clearly such differences indicate an important direction for future research."

  a. Is this a valid conclusion to draw from such data? Why or why not?

12-3 "The relationship between the two variables was highly significant $(\chi^2 = 20.4$ with three degrees of freedom, $p < .001)$, a finding that is very exciting. (Based on a representative sample of 1,600 cases.)"

a. Do these data alone provide grounds for excitement? Why or why not?

12-4 The data indicate a significant relationship between social class and voting behavior.

Voting Behavior

Social class	Voted	Didn't vote	Total
Upper	32	8	40
Middle	70	30	100
Lower	24	36	60
Total	126	74	200 = N

a. Use chi-square to verify (or refute) the researcher's assertion.

b. What do your results *mean?*

12-5 "We drew representative samples of 50 men and 50 women. We found that 40 percent of the women agree that a woman's place is in the home and 60 percent of the men agreed." If we want to test for significant differences:

a. What is the substantive hypothesis?

b. What is the null hypothesis?

c. With these data, at what level of significance can we reject the null hypothesis?

d. What would a rejection of the null hypothesis mean (one or two sentences)?

e. What would a failure to reject the null hypothesis mean?

12-6 Consider the following research report: "We tested the academic achievement of children who went through our Special Education Program. Their scores were significantly higher ($p < .05$) than those of students who didn't go through the program. These data suggest that the pilot program be expanded and that necessary funds be appropriated to send all our children who need help through the program."

a. Do the results justify the recommendation? (Explain briefly.)

12-7 "While the relationship between social class and racial prejudice is negative and significant in our data ($\chi^2 = 17.2$, 6 df, $p < .01$), it is not particularly strong ($\gamma = -.12$). While the relationship does seem to exist, social class doesn't seem to make much of a difference in this racial attitude."

    a. Is the above a proper presentation and interpretation of the results?

    b. If we observed the same value of gamma in this relationship but had a sample only half as large, what would happen to the value of chi-square?

    c. In part *b*, what would the new significance level be?

12-8 "In 1970, we drew a national sample of American adults and were concerned about possible bias. As one check, we compared our sample's educational distribution with that obtained in the 1970 census. For our goodness-of-fit test, we obtained a chi-square of 15.1 with 7 df."

    a. Is this finding evidence of bias in the sample? Explain *briefly*.

12-9 Critically interpret the following statements:

    a. "None of the correlations we examined were statistically significant at the .05 level."

    b. "The relationship is highly significant ($p < .001$)."

    c. "Clearly, the independent variable has an important effect on the dependent variable ($r = +.67$)."

    d. "The slope is not significantly different from zero."

    e. "The correlation between school expenditures and student achievement is significant, providing support for the argument that what we need is a larger school budget."

Suggested Readings

1 Blalock, Hubert M., Jr.: *Social Statistics*, 2d ed., chaps. 10, 11, 13–15 and secs. 18.1 and 19.7. New York: McGraw-Hill Book Company, 1972.

2 Davis, James A.: *Elementary Survey Analysis*, pp. 51–58. Englewood Cliffs,N.J.: Prentice-Hall, 1971.

3 Hays, William L.: *Statistics for the Social Sciences*, 2d ed., chaps. 9–11, 15, 17, 18. New York: Holt, Rinehart and Winston, 1973.

4 See the excellent collection of articles on hypothesis tests and the use of chi-square in Lieberman, Bernhardt: *Contemporary Problems in Statistics*. New York: Oxford University Press, 1971.

5 Loether, Herman J., and Donald G. McTavish: *Inferential Statistics for Sociologists*, chaps. 6, 7, 8, and 9. Boston: Allyn and Bacon, 1974.

6 Mueller, John H., Karl F. Schuessler, and Herbert L. Costner: *Statistical Reasoning in Sociology*, 2d ed., chap. 14. Boston: Houghton Mifflin Company, 1970.

7 Runyon, Richard P., and Audrey Haber: *Fundamentals of Behavioral Statistics*, 2d ed., chaps. 11–14, 17, and 18. Reading, Mass.: Addison-Wesley Publishing Company, 1971.

8 Siegel, Sidney: *Nonparametric Statistics*. New York: McGraw-Hill Book Company, 1956.

9 See the collection of substantive examples of hypothesis testing in action in Tanur, Judith M., et al. (eds.): *Statistics: A Guide to the Unknown*. San Francisco: Holden-Day, 1972.

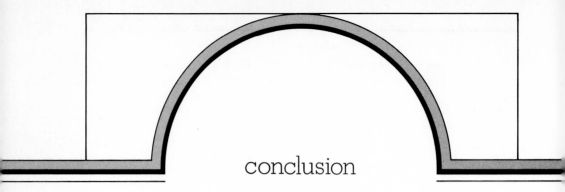

conclusion

Some Topics Not Covered

Although we've come a long way, there are several techniques that we've neglected because they're complicated and/or infrequently used. It might help you to be familiar with at least the names of such techniques and the situations in which they're used.

One technique applies to situations in which we have an interval- or ratio-scale dependent variable and an ordinal or nominal independent variable. Its purpose is to explain variance in the dependent variable (in the sense that r^2 represents explained variance) and is called *analysis of variance*. It's possible to use analysis of variance with several independent variables. In both cases we can make probabilistic inferences from sample data to populations. If you're interested in exploring this in some detail (and you feel confident of your understanding of elementary algebra), there are several good treatments of the technique.[1]

The most sophisticated techniques apply to the multivariate case in which we have several independent variables and wish to identify the independent effects of each on a dependent variable. In the case of ordinal- or nominal-scale independent variables and interval- or ratio-scale dependent variables, *multiple-classification analysis* is a useful technique. It allows us to determine explained variance (comparable to

---

[1] See Hubert M. Blalock, Jr., *Social Statistics*, 2d ed. (New York: McGraw-Hill, 1972), chap. 16; and William L. Hays: *Statistics for the Social Sciences*, 2d ed. (New York: Holt, Rinehart and Winston, 1973), chaps. 12 and 13. The latter is quite mathematical, although no calculus is involved.

the partial and multiple-correlation coefficients in Chap. 8) and to make inferential statements about population relationships. At this time there's only one source that describes this technique in detail.[1]

You should also be aware of a new development in analysis techniques. Goodman's loglinear models give us another way to analyze multiple relationships among qualitative variables.[2]

There are other techniques that we won't mention even here; but I think this will serve you in the majority of situations.

Some Parting Thoughts on Statistics

A great deal of what you stand to gain by understanding the uses of data and statistics depends on the perspective from which you approach them. Many people are either cynical or gullible about statistics: neither of these orientations is useful or fair.

As individuals, we all have ideas about our physical and social environments. We often say, "People are this way or that way" and too often we accept such generalizations as fact when the only support comes from our experience as individuals. While our experience is real and valuable, it's a poor and biased sample of the endless populations that we want to understand.

Systematic data gathering helps us to extend our knowledge beyond our individual realities. In spite of its limitations, statistics helps us test our ideas in a broader and more representative framework.

We need to keep in mind the fact that the numbers have no meaning in themselves. We must always put data in the context of ideas and human experience. The information must be interpreted and used by *people*, and in this most important sense data and statistics are like all information. They have no life of their own.

While I hope you'll be increasingly less in awe of statistical applications, I also hope you won't be hypercritical, either. All empirical research is flawed in one way or another (especially research in the social sciences) because it's impossible to do research on human behavior and control all sources of error and bias. So the reader is always in the position of being able to tear a piece of research apart, if he wants to. It

---

[1] See Frank Andrews, James Morgan, and John Sonquist, *Multiple Classification Analysis* (Ann Arbor, Mich.: Institute for Social Research, University of Michigan, 1969), especially chaps. 1, 2, and 6.

[2] See, for example, Leo Goodman, "How to Ransack Social Mobility Tables and Other Kinds of Cross-Classification Tables," *American Journal of Sociology*, 75: 1–39; Leo Goodman, "The Multivariate Analysis of Qualitative Data: Interactions among Multiple Classifications," *Journal of the American Statistical Association*, 65: 225–256; Leo Goodman, "A General Model for the Analysis of Surveys," *American Journal of Sociology*, 77: 1036–1086; and James A. Davis, "Hierarchical Models for Significance Tests in Multivariate Contingency Tables: An Exegesis of Goodman's Recent Papers," in H. L. Costner (ed.), *Sociological Methodology 1973–1974* (San Francisco: Jossey-Bass, 1975).

would be unfortunate if you became so enamored of criticism that you overlooked the valuable information that is often there to be used.

There's a recurring debate about the scientific nature of social research. A substantial portion of this book has focused on the problems associated with studying human behavior: error creeps into the research process at many points and often makes it difficult to draw definitive conclusions. This has formed the basis of many attacks on claims that social research is scientific.

The nature of science lies less in its results than in its methodology. Social science aspires to formulate logically interrelated propositions about human behavior: the tasks are both descriptive and explanatory. In testing both propositions and theory, the social scientist tries to select methods that are replicable and yield unambiguous results. Because the causes of human behavior are so complex and often hidden from direct observation, the verification of social theory is particularly difficult.

One might imagine a chemist trying to conduct an experiment. A window is open, allowing the temperature in the room to fluctuate unpredictably. The chemicals contain impurities that are impossible to remove and difficult to identify. The chemist still approaches his research task from a scientific point of view, but under conditions which make it difficult to draw definitive conclusions from his experiments.

The social scientist is in much the same position. The "impurities" and uncontrollable conditions surrounding human behavior make social research particularly challenging. Descriptive, explanatory, and inferential statistics are tools that help social scientists describe and explain human behavior, tools without which we could not even begin to test theoretical propositions empirically. They are of enormous value when properly used.

There is also a recurring debate between the empiricist and theoretical schools of social science. The empiricists criticize the theoreticians for neglecting the task of verifying theoretical propositions. The theoreticians respond that the survey researchers, for example, are applying sophisticated techniques to trivial theories. Such a division is most unfortunate, for the future of social science rests with those who can both think creatively on the causes of human behavior *and* apply sound empirical techniques in the search for verification of theoretical formulations. We need well-rounded social scientists more than we need methodological or theoretical specialists.

Should you be considering a career in social science, I would urge you to resist the temptation to neglect either methodological or substantive training in the social science you pursue. It is especially tempting to become expert at things statistical because there's something comfortable about the precision of numbers and curves. Don't be misled: alone, neither statistics nor theory is sufficient to advance our understanding of human behavior.

In parting, I hope I've managed to make the gullible less gullible, the cynical less cynical, and those who want to learn from quantitative data more capable of doing so.

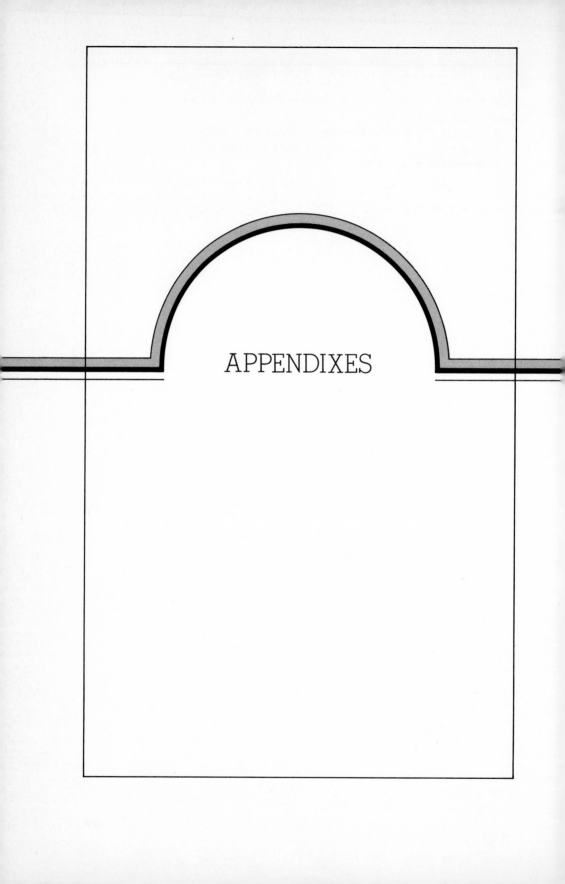

APPENDIXES

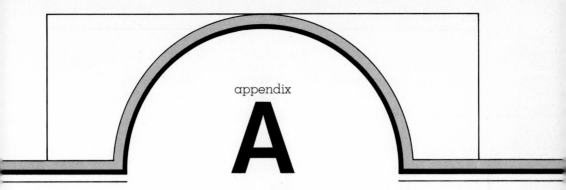

appendix

A

a glossary
of terms and symbols

Antecedent Variable
If we have a two-variable relationship, a variable that causes the independent variable is called an antecedent variable (pp. 129–131).

Beta Weight β
See "Standardized Regression Coefficient."

Bias
If there is a tendency for error to go in one direction more than others, we have bias (pp. 14–15).

Categorical Variable
See "Nominal-Scale Variable."

Census
A gathering of information from all members of a population (p. 4).

Central-Limit Theorem
Regardless of the shape of the parent population, the larger our sample is, the closer the corresponding sampling distribution will be to a normal shape (pp. 186–190).

Chi-square χ^2
A measure used to determine the statistical significance of the difference between two frequency distributions or the lack of independence in a cross tabulation (pp. 228–237).

Cluster Sample
A complex sample in which observations are concentrated in small geographic areas (usually city blocks) in order to save time and money (pp. 171–173).

Codes
The symbols (usually numbers) assigned to the categories of a variable for the purpose of processing data (p. 5).

Coefficient of Alienation
A measure of the degree to which points in a regression analysis *don't* hug the line; it is thus the opposite of the product-moment correlation coefficient and is equal to $\sqrt{1 - r^2}$ (pp. 109, 152).

Coefficient of Determination r^2
This is the proportion of variation in the dependent variable that is statistically explained by the independent variable in a regression analysis (p. 109).

Complex Sample
A sample which must be drawn in stages (e.g., a sample of states, then a sample of counties within the selected states, etc.) (pp. 170–171).

Component Variable
A component variable is one which forms a part of another variable. For example, making a moderate amount of money is part of being in the middle class, as is a belief in upward mobility. When we control for component variables, we clarify the meaning of the more general variable (in this case, social class) (pp. 128–129).

Confidence Interval
An estimate of a population value (e.g., the population mean) that consists of a range of scores (for example, 424 to 468) with a sample result at its center. Attached to the interval is a level of confidence in our estimation procedures, expressed as a percentage (e.g., a 95-percent confidence interval) (pp. 200–216).

Constant
A characteristic that is the same for all observations (p. 10).

Continuous Variable
A variable that can take on any value within its range (e.g., age, height, distance) (pp. 59–60).

Data
Facts or information gathered by empirical observation. Plural of *datum* (p. 4).

Descriptive Statistics SYMBOL
Statistical quantities and techniques used to portray a population or sample on one or more variables (Part One).

Discrete Variable
A variable that can take on only certain values within its range (e.g., number of children ever born to a person) (pp. 59–60).

Error, Random
If errors in each direction are equally likely, then error is random (pp. 14, 165–166).

Estimation, Interval
See "Statistical Inference."
See "Confidence Interval"

Estimation, Point
The use of sample characteristics (e.g., the sample mean) as the estimate of the population characteristic (e.g., the population mean) (pp. 198–200).

Expected Value $p*(N)$
Technically, the expected value is the probability of success multiplied by the number of trials. If the probability of winning a game is .40 and I play 90 games, I can expect to win $(.40)(90) = 36$ games (p. 78).

Extraneous Variable
See "Spuriousness."

Frequency Distribution
The display of the number of people or things falling into each category of a variable (e.g., the number of men and women in a group) (pp. 21–24).

Gamma (Goodman and Kruskal's) γ
A measure of association used only with ordinal-scale variables in tables that are 2×3 or larger (Yule's Q is gamma in the 2×2 case) (pp. 97–99).

Hypothesis
An untested proposition (Chap. 12).

Independence
Between events: If two events are independent, then the occurrence of one in no way affects the likelihood that the other will occur (the conditional probabilities are the same) (pp. 74–76).

Between variables: If two variables are independent of each other, then the distribution of one variable will look the same

within all categories of the second. In other words, the likeli-   SYMBOL
hood of holding a characteristic isn't in any way affected by
one's score on the second variable (pp. 83–84, 107–109).

Index of Dissimilarity   δ
A measure which gauges the difference between two per-
centage distributions. Its value is the percentage of cases that
must be redistributed in order for the two distributions to be
identical (pp. 235–237).

Inductive Statistics
See "Inferential Statistics."

Inferential Statistics
The set of quantitative techniques employed to use sample information to make empirical generalizations about populations (Part Two).

Interval-Scale Variable
The second highest scale of measurement. Scores of interval
variables can be compared in terms of similarity, order, and
relative distance between scores, but *not* in terms of the relative magnitudes of the scores themselves (pp. 16–17).

Intervening Variable
If we have two variables that are related in a causal way
(e.g., education and income), an intervening variable is one
that comes between the two and is part of the causal chain
(e.g., occupation). Controlling for an intervening variable
should make the partial-correlation coefficients lower than the
zero-order coefficients (pp. 124–127).

Kendall's Tau   τ
A measure of association designed to measure the degree to
which two sets of ranks agree with each other (pp. 101–102).

Kurtosis
The degree of "peakedness" in a distribution relative to a
normal curve (p. 191).

Least-Squares Regression Line
Given a scattergram showing the relationship between two
interval- or ratio-scale variables (see pp. 103–105), the least-
squares regression line is that line which best fits the set of
points. "Best fits" means that the average squared vertical distance between the points and the line is the smallest possible
for any line (pp. 103–112). See "Regression Analysis."

Leptokurtic
A curve that is symmetrical and more peaked than a normal
curve is leptokurtic. See "Kurtosis" (p. 191).

Mean   SYMBOL
The balancing point of a distribution of interval- or ratio-scale
variables, found by adding up the individual scores and then
dividing by the number of scores (pp. 47–52, 57–61).

In a sample: $\bar{X}$
In a population: μ

Measurement Instrument
A set of procedures that detail how to observe and classify
empirical observations. See "Operationalization," "Validity,"
and "Reliability" (p. 9 ff).

Median Md
The center of a numerical distribution that has been ordered
from high to low: the score of the middle case (pp. 52–54, 57–61).

Mode
The most frequent score in a distribution (pp. 54, 58).

Multiple-Correlation Coefficient R
A measure of association used with interval- and ratio-scale
variables when there are two or more independent variables.
It's comparable to the product-moment correlation coefficient,
but is used in multiple-regression analysis (p. 141).

Multiple-Regression Analysis
A regression analysis in which we use a best-fitting line to
describe the relationship between a dependent variable and
two or more independent variables (pp. 140–150).

Multistage Sample
See "Complex Sample."

Nominal-Scale Variable
The lowest scale of measurement. Nominal-scale variable
scores can be compared in terms of similarity only (e.g., sex,
religion, race, etc.) (pp. 16–17).

Normal Curve
A shape taken on by many theoretical distributions used in
statistical inference. We use it to make probability statements
about population estimates based on sample data (pp.
186–190).

Operationalization
The process of constructing a measurement instrument that
measures a particular concept (pp. 9–10 ff).

Ordinal-Scale Variable
The third highest scale of measurement. Scores of ordinal
variables can be compared in terms of similarity and order
only (pp. 16–17).

Oversampling   SYMBOL
The practice of selecting a disproportionately large number of
people from a subgroup of a population. This is normally
done to ensure a large enough number of cases. See "Sampling Weights" (pp. 167–168).

Partial Correlation $r_{12.3}$
This represents the strength of the relationship between two
variables (1 and 2) after controlling for one or more other independent variables (for example, 3). See "Spuriousness," "Intervening Variable," "Partial Slopes" (p. 123).

Partial-Regression Coefficient
See "Partial Slopes."

Partial Slopes $b_1, b_2,$
In a multiple-regression analysis (i.e., when we have more than $b_3,$ etc.
one independent variable), the partial slopes measure the *im-
pact* that each independent variable has over and above the
effects of the remaining independent variables (pp. 141–143).

Path Analysis
When we have a causal model with two or more independent
variables, we often want to spell out the interrelationships
among the independent variables and the various causal
paths through which each independent variable affects the
dependent variable. This is done through the use of path
analysis, which consists of several multiple-regression analyses (pp. 150–153).

Percentage   %
A percentage is the number of people or things who have a
certain characteristic, *relative to* the total number of people or
things under study, all multiplied by 100. Thus, the percentage
of men in a group of people is the number of men divided by
the number of people, all times 100 (pp. 24–34, 179 ff).

Percentile
The Xth percentile is that score below which lie X percent of
all the cases in a distribution. Thus, the 70th percentile is the
score below which lie 70 percent of the cases (pp. 61–62).

Phi Coefficient (Pearson's) ϕ
A measure of association used with nominal- and ordinal-
scale variables, each with two categories. In the 2×2 case,
phi is equal to the product-moment correlation coefficient (r),
and phi squared (ϕ^2) is the proportion of the variance in the
dependent variable explained by its relationship with the independent variable (pp. 93–94).

Platykurtic
A curve that is symmetrical but flatter than a normal curve is platykurtic. See "Kurtosis" (p. 191).

Point Estimates
See "Estimation, Point."

Population
Any precisely defined group of people or things. The group must be defined in such a way as to allow an unambiguous determination of what is in the population and what is not (p. 4).

Probability, Conditional
The likelihood that something will occur given that something else also occurs or has already occurred (pp. 71–76).

Probability, Joint
The likelihood that two events will both occur (pp. 68, 72–76).

Product-Moment Correlation Coefficient (Pearson's) r
A measure of association used with interval- and ratio-scale variables. It measures the degree to which points in a regression analysis "hug" the regression line. The square of this coefficient represents the proportion of the variation in Y that is statistically explained by its relationship with X (pp. 106–107, 110–112, 141). See "Phi Coefficient."

Proportion p
The number of people or things with a certain characteristic, relative to (i.e., divided by) the total number of people or things being studied (pp. 24–34).

Qualitative Variable
A variable that can be expressed only in terms of similarity or dissimilarity between characteristics. See "Quantitative Variable" and "Nominal-Scale Variable" (p. 15 ff).

Quantitative Variable
A variable that can be expressed in terms of "more than," "less than," "high," "low," or in exact numerical terms. See "Ordinal-Scale Variable," "Interval-Scale Variable," and "Ratio-Scale Variable" (p. 15 ff).

Quota Sample
Sample in which an interviewer gets interviews with a group of people with certain specified characteristics. The sample is thus representative on those characteristics, but may not be on characteristics for which there was no quota (p. 174).

Random Error
See "Error, Random."

Range
The difference between the highest and the lowest score in a numerical distribution (p. 61).

Ratio
The ratio of one number to another is the first divided by the second. It measures the magnitude of the first *relative* to the second (pp. 34–37, 51).

Ratio-Scale Variable
The highest scale of measurement. Scores of ratio-scale variables can be compared in terms of similarity, order, relative distance between scores, and the relative magnitudes of scores (pp. 16–17).

Regression Analysis
A set of techniques used to describe relationships between two interval- or ratio-scale variables. It treats the relationship as if it were a straight line (linear regression) and allows us to make the most sophisticated description of a relationship possible in statistics (pp. 103–112). See "Product-Moment Correlation Coefficient," Regression Constant," "Least-Squares Regression Line," and "Regression Coefficient."

Regression Coefficient b
In a regression equation, the regression coefficient for an independent variable is the number of units the dependent variable changes for every change of one unit in the independent variable. It measures the steepness of the regression line or the impact of the independent variable on the dependent variable. See "Partial Slope" (pp. 104–106, 110–112).

Regression Constant α
When the values for all independent variables in a regression equation (either linear or multiple) are set to zero, the dependent variable will have the value of the regression constant. In a linear equation, the regression constant (α) appears as $Y = a + bX$. In a multiple-regression equation, the regression constant appears as $Y = a + b_1X_1 + b_2X_2 + \cdots$ (p. 105).

Reliability
A characteristic of measurement instruments. If a measurement instrument is "reliable," then measurements taken at two points in time, or by more than one observer, should yield the same results, assuming there is no change in the characteristic being measured (p. 11).

Response Rate
When we set out to gather information on a population or
sample of people or things, the percentage on whom we actually get information is called the response rate (pp.
168–170).

Sample
The gathering of data from only a part of a population (pp.
4, 161 ff).

Sampling Distribution
A theoretical probability distribution of sample results (means,
proportions, etc.) for all possible samples of a given size that
can be drawn from a given population (pp. 182–191, 212).

Sampling Error
See "Error, Random" and "Bias."

Sampling Frame
The exhaustive listing or precise definition of all members
of a population (p. 162).

Sampling Weights
Sampling weights are correction factors which are applied to
data in which the probabilities of selection were not equal for
all members of the population. See "Oversampling" (pp.
168, 173).

Significance (Statistical)
When a finding is statistically significant, we are very sure
that the null hypothesis is false. If the null hypothesis is that
two groups are identical on an attitude, and we find that there
is a "significant difference" between them, then we are quite
confident (at some stated probability of error) that the two
groups aren't *identical* (pp. 224–225, 227–228).

Simple Random Sample
A sample in which (1) all members of the population are
equally likely to be selected, (2) all combinations of individuals are equally likely to occur, and (3) all selections are independent of each other (pp. 162–165).

Skewness
The degree to which scores tend to be concentrated at one
end of a distribution (p. 58).

Spearman's r_s r_s
A measure of association used to measure the degree to
which two sets of ranks agree with each other (pp. 100–101).

Specification
When we examine a relationship between two or more vari-

ables within subgroups, then we're specifying. For example, if   SYMBOL
we examine the relationship between occupation and income
for both blacks and whites, then we're "specifying for race"
(pp. 133–135).

Spuriousness
A relationship between two variables is spurious whenever it
is not causal in nature and is due entirely to common relationships with a third (extraneous) variable. For example, the
more firemen there are at a fire, the greater the damage. If we
control for the seriousness of the fire, the original relationship
disappears (pp. 119–124).

Standard Deviation
The square root of the variance (pp. 54–61).

Sample: s

Population: σ

Standard Error
The standard deviation in a sampling distribution. It measures
the degree to which the results from samples of a given size
will cluster about the population value we're trying to estimate. Thus, the smaller the standard error, the more likely it
is that any given sample will be accurate (pp. 184, 186, 208,
212, 214).

For the mean: $\sigma_{\bar{X}}$

For proportions: σ_{P_s}

For differences: $\sigma_{\bar{X}_1 - \bar{X}_2}$

$\sigma_{P_{s1} - P_{s2}}$

Standardized Regression Coefficient B

In a regression equation, either multiple or linear, the standardized regression coefficient is the number of standard
deviations the dependent variable changes for every change
of one standard deviation in the independent variable. It
measures the steepness of the regression line, or the impact of
an independent variable on a dependent variable, in standard deviation units (pp. 142–143).

Statistical Inference
Statistical inference is the set of techniques used to make estimates of population values using data from samples. It consists of two parts: first, an estimate (a mean, proportion, correlation coefficient, difference between two groups, etc.); second,
a degree of confidence (as in a confidence interval or null
hypothesis test).

Stratification
This is a technique used to avoid samples that are unrepre-

sentative on selected characteristics. If we wanted to be sure
of drawing a sample with the proper proportions of men and
women, for example, we would draw separate samples of
men and women, thereby forcing the sample to be representative of the population as far as sex is concerned (pp.
166–167).

Suppressor Variable
If we find that a relationship between two variables is weaker
than we expected it to be, this might be due to the uncontrolled influence of a suppressor variable. If this is true, then
when we control for the suppressor variable, the partial relationships should be stronger than the zero-order relationships
(pp. 131–132).

Systematic Sample
A sample drawn by "skipping" through a well-shuffled list
of all members of a population. All members are equally
likely to be selected, but all combinations are not (pp.
164–165).

Tau (Goodman and Kruskal's)
A measure of association used only with nominal-scale variables of more than two categories. If we try to predict the
dependent variable, tau measures the proportional reduction τ_a, τ_b
in prediction error that results from knowing the scores of the
independent variable (pp. 94–97).

Validity
In general, validity refers to the appropriateness of measures
or study techniques to the questions we're asking (pp.
11–14).

Validity, Construct
A measurement instrument has construct validity if it is appropriate to the group of whom observations are being made
(p. 12).

Validity, Internal
A study design has internal validity if appropriate control
groups are used to allow the researcher to draw conclusions
about the effects of the independent variables on the dependent variable (p. 13).

Validity, Measurement
A measurement instrument is valid if it reflects the concept it
is designed to measure for all observations (p. 11 ff).

Variable
A characteristic that is not the same for all observations (p.
10 ff).

Variance   SYMBOL
A measure of heterogeneity in the distributions of ratio- and interval-scale variables. It is the average squared deviation of the individual scores about the mean. It tells us how spread out about the mean the scores are (pp. 54–61).

Sample: s^2
Population: σ^2

Yule's Q Q
A measure of association used only with nominal- and ordinal-scale variables, each with two categories (pp. 90–93).

Z Score Z
The distance between a score and the mean of a distribution, measured in standard deviations (pp. 192–193).

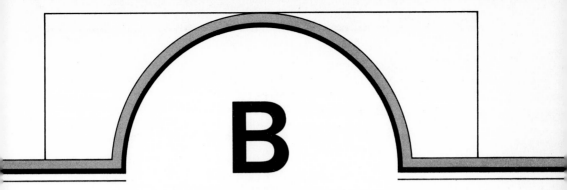

B

answers to
selected problems

Chapter 3

3-4a Yes, whites

3-4b No, must percentage in opposite direction

3-4c No, because there's no "total" distribution

3-4d No, must percentage in opposite direction

3-4e Yes, up at all educational levels, largest jumps at the lowest levels; no nonwhite data for 1955

3-4f Yes, elementary, 7 percent

3-4g 83 percent (Or if you include "At least some college" among those with a high school diploma, the question cannot be answered with this table.)

Chapter 4

4-1 2.0

4-2 2.0

4-3 1.128

Chapter 5

5-1 $p(A) = .5546$ $p(C) = .1849$
$p(B) = .4454$ $p(D) = .8151$

5-2 $p(A,C) = .1092$ $p(B,C) = .0756$
$p(A,D) = .4454$ $p(B,D) = .3697$

5-3 With replacement:

With replacement:

First draw	Second draw	Probability
Female	Female	.3076
Female	Male	.2470
Male	Female	.2470
Male	Male	.1984
		1.0000

Without replacement:

First draw	Second draw	Probability
Female	Female	.3055
Female	Male	.2491
Male	Female	.2491
Male	Male	.1963
		1.0000

5-4 $p(B$ or $C) = .5546$

5-7 No; the conditional probabilities and the unconditional probabilities aren't equal.

5-8 510

Chapter 6

6-1b Yule's $Q = .95$
Goodman and Kruskal's tau $= .49$
Phi $= .70$

6-2b Gamma $= -.16$

6-3 Spearman's $r = .60$
Kendall's tau $= .40$
There's a moderate tendency for the judges to agree more than they disagree.

6-5a Each year brings with it an average of $500 in additional income.

6-5b The relationship is quite strong.

6-5c 40 percent

Chapter 8

8-2a X_3

8-4d The indirect effect is -0.11.

8-4e The total indirect effects are $-.0658$.

8-4f 17 percent

Chapter 10
 10-1a(1) 0.2266
 10-1a(2) 0.2922
 10-1a(3) 0.2029
 10-1a(4) 0.7642
 10-1a(5) 0.6826
 10-1b 0.7422, or 74th percentile
 10-2a 0.6826
 10-2b 0.0244
 10-2c 0.9546
 10-2d 0.0124

Chapter 11
 11-1a No. Interval runs from .45 to .53.
 11-1b 0.274
 11-2a The interval runs from .51 to .59.
 11-2b 0.9986
 11-3a Yes. The 98-percent confidence interval runs from .01 to .17.

Chapter 12
 12-1a Not significant at the .01 level; 98-percent confidence interval runs from -0.04 to $+0.20$.
 12-4a Chi-square $= 20.7$ with two degrees of freedom. The relationship is significant at the .001 level.
 12-5c We can reject H_0 at the .02 level.

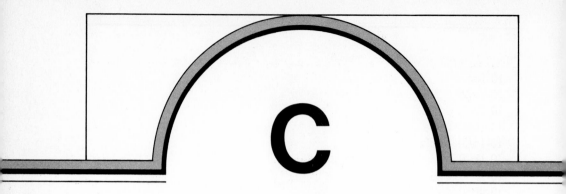

C

tables

Table C-1 Distribution of χ^2 Probability

df*	.99	.98	.95	.90	.80	.70	.50	.30	.20	.10	.05	.02	.01	.001
1	.0²157	.0²628	.00393	.0158	.0642	.148	.455	1.074	1.642	2.706	3.841	5.412	6.635	10.827
2	.0201	.0404	.103	.211	.446	.713	1.386	2.408	3.219	4.605	5.991	7.824	9.210	13.815
3	.115	.185	.352	.584	1.005	1.424	2.366	3.665	4.642	6.251	7.815	0.837	11.341	16.268
4	.297	.429	.711	1.064	1.649	2.195	3.357	4.878	5.089	7.779	9.488	11.668	13.277	18.465
5	.554	.752	1.145	1.610	2.343	3.000	4.351	6.064	7.289	9.236	11.070	13.388	15.086	20.517
6	.872	1.134	1.635	2.204	3.070	3.828	5.348	7.231	8.558	10.645	12.592	15.033	16.812	22.457
7	1.239	1.564	2.167	2.833	3.822	4.671	6.346	8.383	9.803	12.017	14.067	16.622	18.475	24.322
8	1.646	2.032	2.733	3.490	4.594	5.527	7.344	9.524	11.030	13.362	15.507	18.168	20.090	26.125
9	2.088	2.532	3.325	4.168	5.380	6.393	8.343	10.656	12.242	14.684	16.919	19.679	21.666	27.877
10	2.558	3.059	3.940	4.865	6.179	7.267	9.342	11.781	13.442	15.987	18.307	21.161	23.209	29.588
11	3.053	3.609	4.575	5.578	6.989	8.148	10.341	12.899	14.631	17.275	19.675	22.618	24.725	31.264
12	3.571	4.178	5.226	6.304	7.807	9.034	11.340	14.011	15.812	18.549	21.026	24.054	26.217	32.909
13	4.107	4.765	5.892	7.042	8.634	9.926	12.340	15.119	16.985	19.812	22.362	25.472	27.688	34.528
14	4.660	5.368	6.571	7.790	9.467	10.821	13.339	16.222	18.151	21.064	23.685	26.873	29.141	36.123
15	5.229	5.985	7.261	8.547	10.307	11.721	14.339	17.322	19.311	22.307	24.996	28.259	30.578	37.697
16	5.812	6.614	7.962	9.312	11.152	12.624	15.338	18.418	20.465	23.542	26.296	29.633	32.000	39.252
17	6.408	7.255	8.672	10.085	12.002	13.531	16.338	19.511	21.615	24.769	27.587	30.995	33.409	40.790
18	7.015	7.906	9.390	10.865	12.857	14.440	17.338	20.601	22.760	25.989	28.869	32.346	34.805	42.312
19	7.633	8.567	10.117	11.651	13.716	15.352	18.338	21.689	23.900	27.204	30.144	33.687	36.191	43.820
20	8.260	9.237	10.851	12.443	14.578	16.266	19.337	22.775	25.038	28.412	31.410	35.020	37.566	45.315
21	8.897	9.915	11.591	13.240	15.445	17.182	20.337	23.858	26.171	29.615	32.671	36.343	38.932	46.797
22	9.542	10.600	12.338	14.041	16.314	18.101	21.337	24.939	27.301	30.813	33.924	37.659	40.289	48.268
23	10.196	11.293	13.091	14.848	17.187	19.021	22.337	26.018	28.429	32.007	35.172	38.968	41.638	49.728
24	10.856	11.992	13.848	15.659	18.062	19.943	23.337	27.096	29.553	33.196	36.415	40.270	42.980	51.179
25	11.524	12.697	14.611	16.473	18.940	20.867	24.337	28.172	30.675	34.382	37.652	41.566	44.314	52.620
26	12.198	13.409	15.379	17.292	19.820	21.792	25.336	29.246	31.795	35.563	38.885	42.856	45.642	54.052
27	12.879	14.125	16.151	18.114	20.703	22.719	26.336	30.319	32.912	36.741	40.113	44.140	46.963	55.476
28	13.565	14.847	16.928	18.939	21.588	23.647	27.336	31.391	34.027	37.916	41.337	45.419	48.278	56.893
29	14.256	15.574	17.708	19.768	22.475	24.577	28.336	32.461	35.139	39.087	42.557	46.693	49.588	58.302
30	14.953	16.306	18.493	20.599	23.364	25.508	29.336	33.530	36.250	40.256	43.773	47.962	50.892	59.703

SOURCE Table 1 is taken from table IV of R. A. Fisher and F. Yates, *Statistical Tables for Biological, Agricultural and Medical Research,* published by Longman Group Ltd., London (previously published by Oliver & Boyd, Edinburgh), by permission of the authors and publishers.

Table C-2 Areas under the Normal Curve

Fractional parts of the total area (10,000) under the normal curve, corresponding to distances between the mean and ordinates which are Z standard-deviation units from the mean.

Z	.00	.01	.02	.03	.04	.05	.06	.07	.08	.09
0.0	0000	0040	0080	0120	0159	0199	0239	0279	0319	0359
0.1	0398	0438	0478	0517	0557	0596	0636	0675	0714	0753
0.2	0793	0832	0871	0910	0948	0987	1026	1064	1103	1141
0.3	1179	1217	1255	1293	1331	1368	1406	1443	1480	1517
0.4	1554	1591	1628	1664	1700	1736	1772	1808	1844	1879
0.5	1915	1950	1985	2019	2054	2088	2123	2157	2190	2224
0.6	2257	2291	2324	2357	2389	2422	2454	2486	2518	2549
0.7	2580	2612	2642	2673	2704	2734	2764	2794	2823	2852
0.8	2881	2910	2939	2967	2995	3023	3051	3078	3106	3133
0.9	3159	3186	3212	3238	3264	3289	3315	3340	3365	3389
1.0	3413	3438	3461	3485	3508	3531	3554	3577	3599	3621
1.1	3643	3665	3686	3718	3729	3749	3770	3790	3810	3830
1.2	3849	3869	3888	3907	3925	3944	3962	3980	3997	4015
1.3	4032	4049	4066	4083	4099	4115	4131	4147	4162	4177
1.4	4192	4207	4222	4236	4251	4265	4279	4292	4306	4319
1.5	4332	4345	4357	4370	4382	4394	4406	4418	4430	4441
1.6	4452	4463	4474	4485	4495	4505	4515	4525	4535	4545
1.7	4554	4564	4573	4582	4591	4599	4608	4616	4625	4633
1.8	4641	4649	4656	4664	4671	4678	4686	4693	4699	4706
1.9	4713	4719	4726	4732	4738	4744	4750	4758	4762	4767
2.0	4773	4778	4783	4788	4793	4798	4803	4808	4812	4817
2.1	4821	4826	4830	4834	4838	4842	4846	4850	4854	4857
2.2	4861	4865	4868	4871	4875	4878	4881	4884	4887	4890
2.3	4893	4896	4898	4901	4904	4906	4909	4911	4913	4916
2.4	4918	4920	4922	4925	4927	4929	4931	4932	4934	4936
2.5	4938	4940	4941	4943	4945	4946	4948	4949	4951	4952
2.6	4953	4955	4956	4957	4959	4960	4961	4962	4963	4964
2.7	4965	4966	4967	4968	4969	4970	4971	4972	4973	4974
2.8	4974	4975	4976	4977	4977	4978	4979	4980	4980	4981
2.9	4981	4982	4983	4984	4984	4984	4985	4985	4986	4986
3.0	4986.5	4987	4987	4988	4988	4988	4989	4989	4989	4990
3.1	4990.0	4991	4991	4991	4992	4992	4992	4992	4993	4993
3.2	4993.129									
3.3	4995.166									
3.4	4996.631									
3.5	4997.674									
3.6	4998.409									
3.7	4998.922									
3.8	4999.277									
3.9	4999.519									
4.0	4999.683									
4.5	4999.966									
5.0	4999.997133									

SOURCE Harold O. Rugg, *Statistical Methods Applied to Education* (Boston: Houghton Mifflin Company, 1917), appendix table III, pp. 389–390, reprinted by permission of the publisher.

Table C-3 Distribution of *t*

	LEVEL OF SIGNIFICANCE FOR ONE-TAILED TEST					
	.10	.05	.025	.01	.005	.0005
	LEVEL OF SIGNIFICANCE FOR TWO-TAILED TEST					
df	.20	.10	.05	.02	.01	.001
1	3.078	6.314	12.706	31.821	63.657	636.619
2	1.886	2.920	4.303	6.965	9.925	31.598
3	1.638	2.353	3.182	4.541	5.841	12.941
4	1.533	2.132	2.776	3.747	4.604	8.610
5	1.476	2.015	2.571	3.365	4.032	6.859
6	1.440	1.943	2.447	3.143	3.707	5.959
7	1.415	1.895	2.365	2.998	3.499	5.405
8	1.397	1.860	2.306	2.896	3.355	5.041
9	1.383	1.833	2.262	2.821	3.250	4.781
10	1.372	1.812	2.228	2.764	3.169	4.587
11	1.363	1.796	2.201	2.718	3.106	4.437
12	1.356	1.782	2.179	2.681	3.055	4.318
13	1.350	1.771	2.160	2.650	3.012	4.221
14	1.345	1.761	2.145	2.624	2.977	4.140
15	1.341	1.753	2.131	2.602	2.947	4.073
16	1.337	1.746	2.120	2.583	2.921	4.015
17	1.333	1.740	2.110	2.567	2.898	3.965
18	1.330	1.734	2.101	2.552	2.878	3.922
19	1.328	1.729	2.093	2.539	2.861	3.883
20	1.325	1.725	2.086	2.528	2.845	3.850
21	1.323	1.721	2.080	2.518	2.831	3.819
22	1.321	1.717	2.074	2.508	2.819	3.792
23	1.319	1.714	2.069	2.500	2.807	3.767
24	1.318	1.711	2.064	2.492	2.797	3.745
25	1.316	1.708	2.060	2.485	2.787	3.725
26	1.315	1.706	2.056	2.479	2.779	3.707
27	1.314	1.703	2.052	2.473	2.771	3.690
28	1.313	1.701	2.048	2.467	2.763	3.674
29	1.311	1.699	2.045	2.462	2.756	3.659
30	1.310	1.697	2.042	2.457	2.750	3.646
40	1.303	1.684	2.021	2.423	2.704	3.551
60	1.296	1.671	2.000	2.390	2.660	3.460
120	1.289	1.658	1.980	2.358	2.617	3.373
∞	1.282	1.645	1.960	2.326	2.576	3.291

SOURCE Table 3 is taken from table III of R. A. Fisher and F. Yates, *Statistical Tables for Biological, Agricultural and Medical Research*, published by Longman Group Ltd., London (previously published by Oliver & Boyd, Edinburgh), by permission of the authors and publishers.

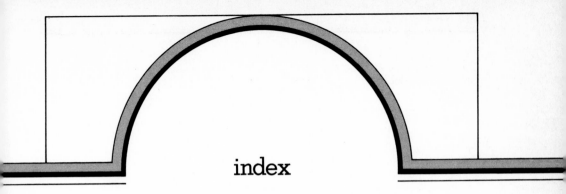

index